Guide to
Genealogy
Software

Guide to Genealogy Software

By
Donna Przecha
Joan Lowrey

GENEALOGICAL PUBLISHING Co., Inc.

Copyright © 1993
Donna Przecha and Joan Lowrey
All Rights Reserved.
No part of this publication may be
reproduced, in any form or by any means,
including electronic, without permission
of the authors.
Published by Genealogical Publishing Co., Inc.
1001 N. Calvert St., Baltimore, Md. 21202
Second printing 1994
Library of Congress Catalogue Card Number 93-77635
International Standard Book Number 0-8063-1382-X
Made in the United States of America

Table of Contents

Preface

Basics	3
What to Expect from a Genealogy Program	3
Decisions	3
Types of Programs	7
Where to Obtain Programs	7
Bulletin Board System (BBS)	8
How Programs Work	10
Printed Reports	13
GEDCOM Compatible Programs	33
Brother's Keeper	37
Cumberland Tree	44
Everyone's Family Tree	47
Family Connections	51
Family History Program (for Windows)	53
Family History System	54
Family Origins	59
Family Reunion	65
Family Roots	66
Family Scrapbook	68
Family Ties	75
Family Treasures	77
Family Tree Journal	80
Family Tree Maker	85
GENE-GENEX-GEDCOMG	91
Genealogical Data Base Systems	92
Genealogical Information Manager	93
HeartWood	95
It's All Relative	97
Lineages	98
MacRoots II	99
Origen	101
Pedigree	103
Pedigree Pursuit	105
Personal Ancestral File	106

    Relativity   110
    Reunion   114
    Roots III   115
    The Family Edge   120
    The Master Genealogist   124
    Tree Easy   126
    Your Family Tree   127

Non-GEDCOM Genealogy Programs   129

Utilities   137

Other Programs   169

Omitted Programs   183

Glossary   189

Index   191

Preface

Our original intention in writing our first book was to provide a complete list and evaluation of all currently available genealogy software. It very quickly became obvious that for several reasons such an ambitious undertaking would be impossible.

Genealogy software is not a product that is readily available to the casual shopper. First time buyers might think that a catalog covering the whole range could be contained in one slim pamphlet. In fact there is a wide variety of programs available for genealogists using computers. Some are fairly simple programs developed by programmers originally for their own use. Others are specialized programs designed to handle one specific function — create box charts or organize census records, for example. Others are large, complex programs designed to serve many functions. Some of the programs may no longer be available. The majority are produced and distributed by individuals or small companies which sometime disappear without a trace.

To try to do an in-depth analysis of so many programs would be presumptuous. Both authors have written manuals on using specific programs, but they spent many months learning all the possibilities of the respective programs. To judge other programs based on a few hours use, or just reading promotional material, would not be fair.

Computer programs are probably one of the fastest changing items on the market. Programmers are constantly changing their software to suit the needs of their users and frequently come out with new, improved versions. In trying to review one utility program for a newsletter, there were two updates in a two-month period requiring rewriting of the article. Frequently updates are not widely publicized so a reviewer may not even be aware that a later version is available.

We decided to do a sampling of the more popular programs plus a variety of other programs available. Rather than trying to describe all the details of each program, we want to present concepts and guidelines. We have tried to avoid judging programs. What one person will find difficult, another may find easy. One person may use one chart constantly while another will never use it. We have tried to point out characteristics of a program that are markedly different from other programs.

Source

We tried to solicit information on a wide variety of software. However, it is impossible to cover every program in this rapidly changing area and we regret if the program in which you might have a particular interest is omitted. We solicited information from many different producers. We asked them to complete a questionnaire and, if possible, send us demo disks or copies of the programs for evaluation. Every effort has been made to make sure these are current, supported programs. For the most part, if the letter was returned because of an address change or if the author did not respond, we did not include the program, especially if it was a commercial program rather than shareware. In the case of shareware, we included the program if it was available on a national board (CompuServe or GEnie) and we were able to obtain a copy to evaluate. Since these bulletin boards with their files are available nationwide, we did not always contact the producers, especially for small utility programs. We also included some commercial programs where the producers did not respond, but we had information on the program or a copy of it and knew it was still current and available. Needless to say, our information was always more complete if the author also completed our questionnaire.

Non-DOS

The majority of genealogy software is for DOS. We have made every attempt to include non-DOS software in the book but it is extremely limited. Unfortunately, many of the producers of non-DOS software did not respond to our questionnaire and, even if it were shareware, we had no way to test non-DOS programs. In the listings for GEDCOM compatible programs we have indicated the operating system for each program. In other sections, where the information included is briefer, we have noted the operating system only if it is non-DOS.

The Basics

The Basics

What to Expect from a Genealogy Program

Some people, usually non-genealogists, think that genealogy by computer means you push a few keys and your whole family tree is revealed. Although more and more information is being computer indexed, genealogy still consists largely of looking through old records and documents searching for your ancestors and families.

A computer program will help you organize the information you have found. You have to decide which people are related and how; a computer program will not decide for you. If you enter a father and son as unrelated, they will remain that way until you link them. It will not automatically combine duplicates. If you put a name in three times and later find that all three are the same person, you will have to combine the records and information and delete the duplicates.

Many programs will sort your data on several different fields which will help you decide who might be related. Many programs will check for names that might be duplicates, then you can review the list and see if an individual was inadvertently entered twice.

With most computer programs data is entered one person at a time. You fill in a standard form on the screen giving date and place of birth, christening, death, burial and other events. Once the data has been entered correctly, you can print different charts without having to enter the information again. This means that the information is consistent and accurate on each printout. (How many times have you found that you have shown a person on one handwritten chart as being born in 1838, for example, and on another 1836, or six children in the family on one chart and seven on another?)

As more and more information is being entered into computer programs, it is becoming more likely that you may find several generations of one of your lines already researched. The Ancestral File produced by the Church of Jesus Christ of Latter-day Saints (LDS) consists of millions of records submitted by people who have researched their families. The Ancestral File is available on computer at most LDS Family History Centers throughout the country. You can search this database and if you find information on any of your families, you can download the information onto a floppy disk. If your program accepts GEDCOM, you can then transfer the data directly to your program without having to type it all in. However, you should keep in mind that this information represents research by other genealogists and may not necessarily be accurate. While it can be used as a guide, you should verify the data before accepting it yourself.

Decisions

Deciding on a genealogy program is difficult, even for experienced computer users. If you want an accounting or word processing program, you can go to your local software store. If you are lucky, a knowledgeable clerk will recommend and demonstrate a program. Selecting a genealogy program is a little more complex. A software store will most likely have a very limited selection if any at all.

In order to see a full range of genealogy programs, in addition to visiting a software store, you may need to contact a local dealer for one program, order by mail for another, visit a shareware store to study the catalog and even buy a modem to download from bulletin boards.

You can also ask a computer genealogist which program to buy. If that person immediately replies: "You should buy XX program, it is absolutely the best," you should ignore the advice. He or she is naming the best program for his or her needs, not necessarily yours.

In order to decide what program is best for you, you have to ask yourself a few questions. What type equipment do you have? If you have an IBM compatible computer and your friend has a Macintosh, chances are his program won't work on your machine. Does your computer have a hard drive? If not, be aware that complex programs may require one or entail much disk swapping for dual floppy users. Does your machine have enough memory to accommodate the program? What do you want to accomplish with a program — organize all your research notes or link related people or sort data? What type of printouts do you want — family group sheets, pedigree charts or something else? Are you going to write a book? Do you want to be able to exchange data with other users? Are you going to need lots of help getting started?

All of these questions — and more — need to be considered. One of the most discouraging things that can happen is for you to enter lots of data in an unsatisfactory program and find you have to enter it all over again in a new program. This does not mean you only have one chance at making the right selection. You can move between many programs without having to enter any of the data again if both programs are GEDCOM compatible.

- **Equipment**: Are you thinking of buying a new computer? If the equipment you have now is not adequate for the program you want, consider very carefully before compromising. If there is a chance that you will be upgrading your equipment in the not too distant future, you might want to move up that timetable. Over a period of time you will spend a tremendous number of hours entering, editing and perfecting your information. If you cannot transfer it to your new equipment, you may decide to stay with outdated hardware later on or just give up on computer genealogy rather than having to reenter so much information. Even if you cannot afford the equipment and/or program you want now, you should be sure that what you start on is compatible with what you eventually want to be using.

- **Data Management**: What type of data management are you looking for? Do you just want families linked so you can print reports or do you want a research tool? Programs serve at least two different and important functions: managing data and producing reports. The sophisticated sort routines on some programs allow them to be used as database programs. You can enter information and sort, organize and group by names, places, dates and relationships. You can produce a list of all the John Browns born in Kentucky between 1820 and 1840. This sorting capability helps you match old and new information. Some programs will even search names using a Soundex code. Many genealogy programs seem to be weak in the sorting, analyzing and data management functions.

- **Reports**: What type of printouts do you want? Do you want to be able to add interesting biographical information in a book format? Or do you need a specialized form? See the section on printed reports for more information, p. 13.

- **Documentation**: How important is it for you to be able to record exactly where you got the information? Some programs do not permit any additional notes, some put all extra notes in one place or limit the amount of notes, while others will create separate footnotes for different events.

- **GEDCOM**: Can this program create and receive GEDCOM files? You will not want to do without this important feature. (For further information on GEDCOM, see p. 6.)

- **Learning**: Are you experienced with computers? Is learning a program something that you can do by yourself? Is this program easy to use or does it have a reputation for being difficult? Good support lines, users groups and classes might be essential for all but the most experienced. If you start with an easy program with GEDCOM capabilities, you can later transfer the data to a more complex program if you choose.

- **Manual**: Does the program have a manual, either printed or on disk? Is it complete, easy to read and indexed? Is there on-line help? All but the simplest programs need some explanation.

- **Support**: Even if you have absolute confidence in your ability to learn and operate a program on your own, you should consider the type of support that is available to you. Additional information, creative ideas and update information are often available through the following sources:

    Help Line: Is there a phone number that you can call for help? Is it toll-free or long distance? What hours is it open?
    BBS: Do you use a modem? Does the program producer answer questions via modem? Do you have access to a genealogy bulletin board that carries software questions?
    Mail: Will the developer answer questions by mail?
    Classes: Are any classes on that program offered in your area?
    Users Groups: Are there other users in your area that you could contact to share information? Is there a group that you could join?
    Local Dealer: Is the local dealer a company representative who can provide help?

Keep in mind that most producers of genealogy programs are either small companies or individuals. Most producers of shareware programs are individuals who are otherwise employed and do this as a hobby. Providing support for these programs can take up a lot of their leisure time so keep your requests reasonable and, if contacting them by phone, keep time zones in mind. Those who have indicated identification codes for various bulletin boards would probably prefer to be contacted through this medium. They can read messages and reply at their convenience. It does not interrupt their meal as does a phone call and does not require a letter, envelope, stamp and trip to the mail box.

- **Cost**: Is cost a factor? Genealogy programs range from free public domain to commercial offerings for upwards of $200. (Some of the more expensive ones are available at discounted prices.) While most public domain programs are not adequate as a primary genealogy program, there are some inexpensive commercial or shareware offerings ($35-40) that are excellent. If your needs change, you can move your data between any two programs utilizing GEDCOM. Decide on a program based on your needs, not just price alone.

- **Other Differences**: The following are probably not factors for deciding on a program for most first time buyers, but are ways in which programs can differ.

Storage Methods and Memory Use: Many programs will store a name, such as George, only once. Each time the name is reused it will be retrieved from the "master file". This saves a great deal of space and is more efficient than a program that saves the entire name every time it is used. Some programs save the data as it is entered thus keeping memory free to handle only the immediate function. Other programs require all the data to be in memory at one time and it is only saved when exiting the program. This type will require more random access memory (RAM) as the database grows. Use of disk space will vary depending on whether text files are saved in one large file or separate files. Each file has a minimum size, even if it consists of only two or three words, so many tiny separate files will use up disk space. However, the loss of some space may be worthwhile if it gives you more flexibility in printing the files.

Data Control Checks: Does the program allow you to enter dates in many different styles — 3 MAR 1990; March 3, 1990; 3/3/1990? Does it standardize the entry automatically? Does it check to see if the date makes sense — will it accept 3 March 139 as a valid date? Does it have a repeat or ditto function key so that you do not have to retype each surname or location? Not only does such a feature make data entry easier, but also makes it more accurate.

GEDCOM

GEDCOM (GEnealogical Data COMmunication) takes data from one program and puts it into a standard format that another program can read and accept. Although not all information will be transferred, most names, dates, places and notes can be transferred with a high degree of accuracy. To create and read these files, a program either has to have this capability built in or have an associated utility.

GEDCOM is not a requirement in a genealogy program and does not affect the performance of the program itself. Beginners may think that they have no reason to use GEDCOM. They intend to use one program and don't know any other genealogists using a computer with whom they might exchange information.

Computer software changes with lightning rapidity. Something new may come along that you just have to have. With GEDCOM you will probably be able to move your data into the new program.

The use of multiple programs is becoming more and more frequent among computer genealogists. They enter their data in one program but "gedcom" it into another program simply because they like some feature — either data management or printed forms — that is unique to another program.

The Ancestral File with its millions of linked names is available on computers at most LDS Family History Centers. If you find several generations of a family in those files, you can transfer the information in GEDCOM format to a floppy disk. You can take that information home and transfer it directly to your own database.

We would not say that you shouldn't use a program that doesn't have GEDCOM. A program might have some very attractive features and not be GEDCOM compatible. It might be worthwhile to use this as a secondary program to enter names to make use of these features. However, you should be very aware of the limitations that the lack of GEDCOM places on what you can do with a program. For someone looking for a primary program — the program where the majority of the data is entered and updated — GEDCOM compatibility is almost a requirement. More and more programs now include GEDCOM and the producers of many of those that do not are developing a GEDCOM utility.

Each program stores its information in a slightly different manner. In order to transfer material, both the originating (exporting) program and the destination (importing) program must have a GEDCOM program or utility. You must first use the GEDCOM portion of the program in which the data was originally entered to transfer (export) it to a GEDCOM format which can be read by other GEDCOM programs. Then you must use the GEDCOM portion of the new program into which you wish to transfer (import) the data. This will read the standard format and place it in the destination program in the format it needs.

The Family History Department of the LDS Church held a conference with other developers to set a standard for GEDCOM. A program that conforms to these specifications will create a GEDCOM file that can be submitted for inclusion into the Ancestral File. As of January 1993, the following programs create GEDCOM files that are approved by the LDS Church:

Brother's Keeper (John Steed)
DISGEN (Foreningen DIS, Sweden)
Everyone's Family Tree (The Dollarhide Systems, Inc.)
Family Origins (Parsons Technology)
Family Reunion (FAMware)
Family Roots (Quinsept, Inc.)
Family Ties (Computer Services)
Family Tree Maker Exchange Utility (Banner Blue Software, Inc.)
Family Tree Print Utility (Common Sense Software)

GAOPERSO (Perret, France)
Geneascope 2.2 (Geneascope, France)
Genealogical Information Manager (Blaine Wasden)
Generation Gap Plus (Flying Pigs Software)
Griot Alternative (Thierry Pertuy, France)
Pedigree Pursuit
Personae Dorot (Dorot Genealogy, Israel)
Personal Ancestral File
Reunion 3.0 (Leister Prod.)
ROOTS III (Commsoft, Inc.)
Sesame (Commsoft, Inc.)
The Family Edge Plus (Carl York; not yet released.)

Types of Programs

• **Commercial**: These must be purchased outright before they can be used. These programs may not be copied. Demonstration disks are frequently available; some simply show you the features of a program while others actually allow you to enter a limited amount of data and even print charts. If there is a charge for the demonstration disk, a credit is sometimes allowed towards the purchase of the complete program. Even though these are commercial programs, very few are sold through software stores. The program developer may use local dealers who are often computer consultants, genealogists or owners of genealogy bookstores. (Personal Ancestral File is a somewhat unique offering in that it is available only through the LDS Church. This program is subsidized by the church which is the sole distributor. The non-profit status of the church is a factor in its low price.)

• **Shareware**: Shareware programs can be tried out before you "buy". Copying the program is permitted and encouraged. After you have tried the program, if you find you like it and want to use it, you are obligated to send a registration fee to the developer. There are often several benefits to being a registered user — you might be advised of program updates, frequently at a reduced cost or receive a printed manual; the developer may offer help to registered owners. The most important reason for registering is that by doing so the author and other developers will be motivated to develop more programs. Without compensation, they will not have the means or incentive to continue working in this field. There are some very fine shareware programs and it helps all of us if everyone supports the developers.

• **Public Domain**: These are similar to shareware and can be obtained in the same way except there is no registration fee. Needless to say, these are usually simpler programs that perform limited functions.

• **Freeware**: Freeware is similar to public domain in that the programs are free. However, the author retains the copyright to the program.

Where to Obtain Programs

• **Directly from the Author or Producer**: Addresses are located in the second section of this book.

• **Private Dealers**: Many programs are sold through dealers who represent the software company. These may be small businesses or individuals who specialize in genealogy. The software company or computer or genealogy groups may be able to provide information on dealers.

• **Bulletin Boards**: Shareware and public domain programs are often available in the files area of bulletin boards that specialize in genealogy. These programs can be downloaded.

• **Software Stores**: Very few genealogy programs are available at commercial software stores. If you make your selection from what is available in a retail store, you will automatically eliminate several of the better programs. The programs that are distributed through the large retail computer stores are often available at a discounted price.

• **Shareware Stores**: Shareware can be obtained from shareware and public domain stores which sell copies of the program for nominal cost — $3-5 per disk. They are usually available at computer shows. These stores often advertise in computer magazines and will send you a catalog of the programs they have for sale. Most shareware stores have a limited selection of genealogy related programs and often those in stock are very old versions. Mail order shareware companies that specialize in genealogy software include Archival Vision, L. C., P. O. Box 211085, Salt Lake City, Utah 84121-8085 ($3.95 per 5.25" disk and $4.95 per 3.5" disk + shipping) or Italy & Avalon, 3500 Gentry, Irving, TX 75062 (214-650-9026), $2.00 per disk (5.25" size only) + shipping.

• **Genealogy Libraries or Bookstores**: Libraries or bookstores that specialize in genealogy or are associated with genealogy collections or organizations may sell a small selection of genealogy software.

• **Conventions or Shows**: Many software producers often participate in conventions, shows and seminars that have exhibits. This provides a good opportunity to see the programs in action and ask questions as well as make your purchase.

Bulletin Board System (BBS)

Detailed instructions on using bulletin boards is a topic outside the scope of this book. Bulletin boards are an excellent source of shareware programs. There are four different types of bulletin boards which will be mentioned briefly. Bulletin boards also are very useful for help in using the programs. Many knowledgeable people regularly read the boards and will respond to questions. Many fellow users are very helpful and will often respond with more personalized help than you can get from the producer of the program. While it can be terribly time consuming to monitor four different boards, it is worthwhile becoming acquainted with at least one of them. This method of contact with other program users should be especially helpful for people who do not live in areas where there are users groups. FidoNet is free while the three commercial boards average between $7 and $15 per month basic charges. There may be additional charges for connect time, messages or accessing certain areas.

• FidoNet: Individuals and organizations throughout the country have set up their own bulletin boards which pass messages across the country and around the world. FidoNet is a system of bulletin boards that have genealogy related topics. There are many different topics — genealogy in general, software, adoptees, Jewish genealogy, family reunions, Australian, European, German, French, etc. One board may not carry all these "echos". If you have a board in your area and your phone call is free, there is no charge to use the board. A list of bulletin boards can be downloaded from the National Genealogical Society BBS at 703 528 2612. Local boards usually have a files area where people post shareware programs which can be downloaded. The files available on a board vary according to what the system operator (sysop) has made available. The Genealogical Software Distribution System (GSDS), which some sysops may carry, is an attempt to have one central distribution point where producers can post their latest works.

• Prodigy: A commercial board with a genealogy bulletin board. You can post public messages or send private messages (up to 30 per month without additional charge). Easy to operate, in color, but slow, with a commercial always on part of the screen. Monthly fee for downloading. Few, if any, programs of genealogical interest. Prodigy, 445 Hamilton Ave., White Plains, NY 10601 (800 PRODIGY).

• GEnie: A commercial board with a genealogy area for public messages, files area with large selection of genealogy related files (both text and programs), private messages plus other areas of more general interest. Surcharges for some areas. GEnie Information Services, 401 N. Washington St., Rockville, MD 20850 (800 638 9636).

• CompuServe: A commercial board with a genealogy area for public messages, files area with large selection of genealogy programs, private messages where many program producers can be contacted plus many other areas for other subjects. Fees depend on connect time and areas accessed. CompuServe, P.O. Box 20212, Columbus, OH 43220 (800 848 8199).

Downloading Shareware

Downloading is a procedure available to bulletin board users through the communications software program they use to connect to the board. It transfers the file (program) on the board to your own computer. Usually the program is in a compressed form to take up less space and to make a smaller file which will transfer quicker.

If the file ends with the extension .ARC, it means it has been compressed by a program called ARC (File Archive Utility). If it ends in .ZIP, a program called PKZIP has been used. Both of these programs are shareware that are also posted on bulletin boards. Some programs are "self-extracting"; these end in .EXE.

When you type the program name, it will uncompress. When a file is uncompressed, it usually splits into many different files. Some of these files will very likely be instructions. You should read any file called README or READ.ME. To read on the screen, type **type <filename.ext>** (substitute the actual file name for <filename.ext>. The command to see the READ.ME file would be **type read.me**. If it is longer than one screen, it will scroll by very quickly. To see one screen at a time type **read.me ¦ more**. Press any key to move from one screen to the next. The README file may be short instructions or a description. A more complex program usually has one or more files ending in .DOC. You might first want to retrieve these in your word processor to see what information they contain and how long they are. You can print the file through your word processor or, at the DOS prompt, print the entire file by typing the command **copy <filename.ext> prn**. If a file ends in .TXT, it means it is a text file and can be retrieved in a word processor and read.

Any file that ends in .EXE, .COM or .BAT is an executable file, meaning it will run a program. If you don't have any instructions on how to run a program and you see a file ending in .EXE, type the file name (the .EXE extension doesn't have to be typed) and the program should run. If there is a file ending in .BAT, it means it is a batch file. Several commands may be needed to get the program going and these have all been combined into a batch file. Typing the name of the batch file (without the extension), will start the program.

Versions

Software programs change constantly as the authors either discover and fix problems or add more features. It is very difficult for bulletin boards and software stores to keep up with the latest version so the shareware copy you obtain may very well be an older version. One of the benefits of registering the program is that you will usually be sent a copy of the latest version. Version 1 or 1.0 indicates the original program. Any number after the decimal, 1.1, 1.3, etc. indicates a minor change to the program. When the version number before the decimal changes, it indicates a more significant change to the program. In addition, many producers are constantly fine-tuning their product with very minor changes that are not important enough to warrant a version change. Usually these are to make minor improvements or to correct very unique problems that the majority of users will not encounter. If you are having a persistent problem, you should get in touch with the developer as that may be a known bug that can only be corrected by a new copy of the program.

We have listed the bulletin board file names for the shareware programs on CompuServe and GEnie. Local boards may carry programs under different names. We may have a name like ANCES11. On the board you may find a file called ANCES2. This probably is the same program. Version 1.1 was available to us but in the meantime version 2 has been released and been posted.

Installing

Some programs require no installation. Type the name of the executable file (ending in .EXE, .COM or .BAT as above) and the program will run. You may want to create a directory on your hard drive and copy the program into it. If the program has a readme or read.me file, it will usually tell you how to get started. If there is a file called INSTALL, you may have to run this before you can use the program. Install is a set of instructions that usually creates a directory and copies files into it. It may also decompress or make other changes in the files. In some cases the install program is simply a convenience to help you create the directory and copy the files but the program can actually be installed by simply copying it. In other cases the install program may make other changes and you will not be able to run the program without using the install program. A good install program will give you the option of naming the file and subdirectory where you want your program to go. Many install programs rather rudely create their own directory in your root directory where you may not want it.

There are other problems you can run into when installing. Some programmers assume you have obtained the program on a disk that goes into drive "A" when it may actually be in your "B" drive. Sometimes you can work around this problem but you may have to copy the program to another disk. You can also use the DOS command "Assign" to temporarily change a B drive to an A drive. Another irritation is that some install programs automatically modify your config.sys or autoexec.bat file. A good programmer will not write an install program that will modify your files without telling you that it will and asking you to confirm that you want this done. If you install a program and then decide you do not like it and remove it, you might want to check these two files for changes and remove them.

How Programs Work

Menu vs. Command Line

Programs that perform a limited number of functions may be run from a command line rather than a menu. With a very simple program, such as one that will tell you the day of the week for any date, there is not a great deal of difference. With a menu, you would type the program name (PROGNAME) and a message similar to the following would appear on the screen: "Type date, such as Jan. 11, 1932" or "Type date using 1-11-1932 format". With a program that runs from a command line, you have to know the format such as "PROGNAME 1-11-1932." You usually need to read the documentation first although some programs will prompt you for the correct entry form if you just type the name of the program EXE file.

With programs that perform more functions and have more options, the command can get more complicated, especially if it involves locating an existing file and creating another one. You may find yourself having to understand and type things like "PROGNAME -n -m -s c:\directory\filename.ext a:newfile.ext". If you get any of these parameters wrong you will not get the results you want or, more likely, it will not work at all. Programs that have several functions almost have to include a menu, but somewhere between simple and complex is a middle ground where a menu is much preferred to the command line.

A stand-alone lineage-linked genealogy program will always be complex enough to begin with a menu. You will have an option of adding data which usually brings up some type of form (edit screen) in which you enter data for an individual by filling in blanks (fields). Individuals are usually entered separately and then linked with a marriage record or sometimes entered as couples. They are then cross referenced to their parents and children.

Edit Screen

An edit screen consists of fields where you enter specific pieces of information including names, dates and places. Some programs have different fields for surname, given name, middle name and titles. Other programs have one field for entering the entire name with some sort of key to distinguish the surname.

An event is a happening in the person's life, such as birth, death, burial or marriage, to be recorded by a date and a place. While some programs give you the option of recording dates numerically, this should be avoided, especially if you have any European ancestors or relatives. Americans record September 5 as 9/5 but Europeans reverse the numbers and would read this as May 9. Thus the first 12 days of every month could be read as two different dates, either month and day or day and month.

Places may also be recorded in separate fields or in one long field. If there are four fields it may be necessary for you to be consistent and always put the city, county, state and country in the same fields. If you are searching for a county, the program may only search one field.

After entering the data, you should be able to view it, make changes and deletions, search your database for information and print reports.

Verification of Data

An important part of a genealogy program is verification of data. Unfortunately, many programs have no means of verifying if the data entered is reasonable. Items that can be checked are names and dates: Are dates within the realm of possibility? Did this individual live to be 183 years old? Did the mother die three years before her child was born? Was the father eight years old when his child was born? Is the spelling of the name consistent with other names in the database? Is this a duplicate name? (You may actually have two or more individuals of the same name but this should alert you if you start entering the same person twice.) Any of the above errors, which could be simple typos, could cast serious doubts on your ability as a genealogist. Some programs do certain tests as the data is entered and question irregular information or have an option that will run certain tests.

The following are entry or edit screens from three popular genealogy programs: Brother's Keeper, PAF and ROOTS III.

```
       Record: __233              Last edited on: [new record]
         Name: _____
          Sex: M  Ref: _____   Parent Code: N   Ancestor Interest: 0            *: N
          Occ: _____   Birth Code:  L   Descendant Interest: 0    ArlCem: N
                                (Interest and sure flags: 0 = lowest, 3 = highest)   HlyCem: N
         Born: __ __ __  2 _____  ActPol: N
         Died: __ __ __  2 _____  HarUni: N
          Chr: __ __ __  2 _____  GraLaw: N
       Buried: __ __ __  2 _____  PbBook: N
         Prob: __ __ __  2 _____  HCrCem: N
       Immigr: __ __ __  2 _____  MrInfo: N
               DATE    SURE              PLACE                      FLAGS
       Father: _____
       Mother: _____
       RecFnt: _____
       Double Dating: From 1 Jan to 24 Mar, enter later year from 1583 to 1752

       |   |  |  |  |  |  |  |  |   |        |KENNEDY|    | 6 Jan 1993|
       f6
       f7
       f8
       f9
       10
```

Edit screen: ROOTS III.

```
                    INDIVIDUAL DATA
----------------------------------------------------------------
   Sex:     SURNAME:            Given1:                 RIN:3493
            Given2:              Given3:        Title:
----------------------------------------------------------------
   BIRTH      Date:
      PLACE Level 1:             Level 2:
            Level 3:             Level 4:
   CHRISTENING Date:
      PLACE   L 1:                L 2:
              L 3:                L 4:
   DEATH      Date:
      PLACE   L 1:                L 2:
              L 3:                L 4:
   BURIAL     Date:
      PLACE   L 1:                L 2:
              L 3:                L 4:
----------------------------------------------------------------
   BAPTISM       Date:          Temple Code:
   ENDOWMENT     Date:          Temple Code:
   SEAL to PAR   Date:          Temple Code:    ID NO.:
----------------------------------------------------------------

   F1 SAVE CHANGES AND EXIT    F2 QUIT WITHOUT SAVING CHANGES
```

Edit Screen: Personal Ancestral File.

```
                         ── Husband ── ADD ──
  Husband:                                               Sex: M
      Born:           in
  Baptized:           in
      Died:           in
    Buried:           in
     Other:           in
       Ref:        Occupation:
                          ── Wife ──
     Wife:                                               Sex: F
      Born:           in
  Baptized:           in
      Died:           in
    Buried:           in
     Other:           in
       Ref:        Occupation:
                        ── Marriage ──
   Married:           in
     Other:           in
   Marr. Ceremony? Y/N:    Divorced/Annulled/Separated:   End Year:

 Add one family at a time. If a person has multiple spouses, finish each family
 by pressing F1  until form is cleared again and then enter the next spouse and
 family. You may use *UNKNOWN for the "spouse" of an unmarried person with kids
 Type existing name + F8, or number, or new name, or just Enter if finished.
```

Edit screen: Brother's Keeper.

Printed Reports

Different genealogy programs will print many different types of reports. However, there are at least four types that almost every program produces: family group sheet, ancestry or pedigree chart, descendant chart and ahnentafel. A fifth format, the report or register style printout, which actually is a form used for printed books, is becoming more popular.

Following are examples of charts from some of the programs. The exact format varies with all programs, but unless one program prints a form that is very different, we will not reproduce these forms under the individual program listings which follow.

Some programs have options on the various charts. Are names or surnames highlighted in some way — bold print, upper case letters — and can the type of highlighting be changed? Can the information included in a chart be varied? Are spouses always included or can they be omitted? Are children's spouses included? What happens if there is more than one spouse? Can notes or text files be included or suppressed? Can different type fonts be used? Will numbers which are assigned to each person and each marriage always print out? Are dates included? We have not included all these details in our summaries, but if any of these items are important to you, verify these details before committing to the program.

Most of the examples have been printed directly from the programs. However, some have been reduced to fit the page size and some have been written to disk and printed through a word processor.

Family Group Sheet

This is probably the workhorse form for genealogists. It is the most commonly used by individuals and organizations to arrange and exchange information.

Traditionally, this form has been 8.5" high and 11" or 14" wide. Since this size is not easily reproduced by most computer printers, it has been redesigned to fit a sheet 11" high and 8.5" wide. The information it contains can vary widely, but basically it lists the father at the top of the form, the mother below and then all of their children. It usually will give a date and place for birth, christening, death and burial for each person along with marriage date and place for the parents. The names of the parents of the husband and wife are also listed so that you can link them to previous generations. It also lists names of other spouses of the husband or wife. The children's spouse or spouses may be listed as well as other information which might be optional or standard depending on the program: record numbers, printing or editing date, LDS ordinances, other events, notes or footnotes, biographical information, name of person preparing the chart, relationship of preparer to ancestor on the chart, sources of information, etc. Charts may be printed in standard type size (10 or 12 characters per inch) or condensed (17 cpi).

We have included some typical family group sheets. Examples will not be shown with individual program listings as the format is similar with all programs.

FAMILY GROUP RECORD-6

4 Feb 1993   Page 1   of 2

HUSBAND William Otis BULLOCK-18   LDS ORDINANCE DATA

BORN:	22 Sep 1805	PLACE: ,Franklin,GA
CHR.:		PLACE:
DIED:	19 Oct 1890	PLACE: Lisbon,Claiborne,LA
BUR.:		PLACE:
MARR:	1829	PLACE: ,Pike,MS

FATHER: William BULLOCK-20
MOTHER: Spicey BOWMAN-21

B:
E:
SP:
SS:

PARENTS' MRIN: 7

WIFE Sarah AKIN-19

BORN:	1812	PLACE: ,,MS
CHR.:		PLACE:
DIED:	1862	PLACE: Lisbon,Claiborne,LA
BUR.:		PLACE:

FATHER: Samuel AKIN-22
MOTHER:

B:
E:
SP:

PARENTS' MRIN: 8

CHILDREN

1. NAME: Mary Angelina BULLOCK-254
   F   BORN: 23 Jul 1831   PLACE: ,Pike,MS
       CHR.:   PLACE:
       DIED: 25 Jan 1872   PLACE: Weldon,Union,LA
       BUR.:   PLACE: Weldon,Union,LA
       SPOUSE: George W. LOWREY-253
       MARR: 23 Jan 1850   PLACE: ,Claiborne,LA

   B:
   E:
   SP:
   MRIN: 114
   SS:

2. NAME: Sicily BULLOCK-255
   F   BORN: 16 Mar 1837   PLACE: Lisbon,Claiborne,LA
       CHR.:   PLACE:
       DIED: 8 Apr 1874   PLACE: Weldon,Union,LA
       BUR.:   PLACE: Weldon,Union,LA
       SPOUSE: George W. LOWREY-253
       MARR: Abt   1872   PLACE: ,,LA

   B:
   E:
   SP:
   MRIN: 115
   SS:

3. NAME: Ezimila Unice BULLOCK-15
   F   BORN: 12 Jun 1839   PLACE: Lisbon,Claiborne,LA
       CHR.:   PLACE:
       DIED: 23 Jul 1906   PLACE: Lisbon,Claiborne,LA
       BUR.:   PLACE: Lisbon,Claiborne,LA
       SPOUSE: Francis Marion LOWREY-14
       MARR: 29 Nov 1855   PLACE: Lisbon,Claiborne,LA

   B:
   E:
   SP:
   has other marriages
   MRIN: 4
   SS:

4. NAME: Miranda Fletcher BULLOCK-1974
   F   BORN: 22 Aug 1841   PLACE: ,Claiborne,LA
       CHR.:   PLACE:
       DIED: Aft   Sep 1914 PLACE:
       BUR.:   PLACE:
       SPOUSE: Robert Francis COOK-1975
       MARR: 27 Oct 1860   PLACE:

   B: 1 Jun 1983   OGDEN
   E: 30 Nov 1983   OGDEN
   SP: 13 Dec 1983 OGDEN
   has other marriages
   MRIN: 645
   SS:

Check one option for all individuals on this form: Joan Neumann Lowrey   Relationship to
[ ] 1. I will provide proxies for []Bap []End []Seal   7371 Rue Michael   Husband_____
       at the _____ temple.   La Jolla, CA 92037   Wife_____
[ ] 2. Please provide all proxies at any temple.
[ ] 3. Send all names to the Ancestral File.   Phone:619-454-7046

Family Group Record: Personal Ancestral File.

HUSBAND: Peter David **Neister**[1]		10	Edited: 19 Nov 1988
Born: 29 Dec 1846	West Unity, Williams, OH		Mar Ed: 1 Nov 1988
Marr: 14 Aug 1876	Leeds, Ont, Canada[2]	4	
Div: 6 Dec 1901			
Died: 26 Mar 1914	Flandreau, Moody, SD		
Buried:	Union Cem, Flandreau, SD		
Father: Joseph **Nichter**		210	
Mother: Salamina (Salome) **Ruch**		293	
Other w:			
1902: Mary **Maxton**		24	

WIFE: Elizabeth **Shipman**		11	Edited: 27 Oct 1988
Born: 10 Jan 1849	Leeds, Ont, Canada		
Died: **31 Mar 1932**	Pomona, Los Angeles, CA		
Buried:			
Census: 11 Feb 1852	Escott, Leeds, Ont., Can.[3]		
Father: Charles **Shipman**		445	
Mother: Ann **Truesdell**		446	

CHILDREN

1 M	Name: Perley Irwin **Neister**[4]		22	Edited: 21 Jan 1993
	Born: 19 Feb 1878	Guthrie, IA		
	Marr: 5 Jun 1907	Sioux Falls, Minnehaha, SD	48	
	To: Ethel **Riley**		156	
	Died: 5 Apr 1939	Los Angeles, Los Angeles, CA		

2 M	Name: Charles Blaine **Neister**		6	Edited: 27 Oct 1988
	Born: **1 May 1884**	Richland Twp, Guthrie, IA[5]		
	Marr: 9 Sep 1914	Flandreau, Moody, SD	3	
	To: Florence **Rice**		18	
	Marr: 13 Jul 1937		2	
	To: Susan Mumford **Wavell**		7	
	Died: **29 Apr 1960**	Sioux Falls, Minnehaha, SD		
	Buried: **3 May 1960**	Union Cem, Flandreau, SD		

3 F	Name: Mary Abigail **Neister**		23	Edited: 21 Jan 1993
	Born: 1 Jun 1890	Guthrie, IA		
	Marr: 23 Mar 1923	Pomona, Los Angeles, CA	44	
	To: Perry F **Hormell**		146	
	Died: 3 Oct 1980	Los Angeles, Los Angeles, CA		

REFERENCES

[1] History of Guthrie and Adair Counties, Iowa Continental Historical Company, Springfield, Ill., 1884

[2] Marriage certificate.

[3] 1851 census, Leeds Co., Escott Twp., ED 1.

Family Group Sheet: ROOTS, Commsoft format with footnotes, choice of included information.

```
14-Jan-1993                     Family group sheet
========================================================================
   Husband: Thomas McKenna    #37
   ------------------------------------------------------------------------
      Born: 4 Apr. 1876       in: Felling-on-Tyne, Northumberland, Eng.
  Baptized:                   in:
      Died: 14 Oct. 1939      in: Middlesbrough, Yorkshire, Eng.
    Buried:                   in: No. Ormesby, Middlesbrough, Eng.
     Other:                   in:
       Ref:                   Occupation:
    Father: Thomas McKenna    #44
    Mother: Rose Anne Callighan   #45
           In 1930 he was elected SEcretary of the British Section of the International
           Metalworkers Federation and received the O.B.E. in 1934

           He was a member of the Middlesbrough town Council for 11 years and served on
           the Saltburn and Marske Urban Council for nine years.
           According to a biographical sketch from an unidentified book Thomas commenced
           work at the West Stockton Iron Works in 1892. He was president of the
           Cleveland and Durham Blastfurnacemen's Association in 1905 and secretary in
           1912. He was elected president of the National Federation in 1914 and
           secretary in 1917. When the five unions amalgamated in 1921, he became the
           first General Secretary of the National Union.
========================================================================
      Wife: Theresa Harrington    #35
   Married:                   in:
Marr. Ceremony? Y/N:          Divorced/Annulled/Separated:    End Year:
   ------------------------------------------------------------------------
      Born:                   in:
  Baptized:                   in:
      Died: 1 Feb. 1960       in: Middlesbrough, Yorkshire, Eng.
    Buried:                   in: No. Ormesby, Middlesbrough, Eng.
     Other:                   in:
       Ref:                   Occupation:
    Father: Jeremiah Harrington   #27
    Mother: Catherine O'Kane    #28
========================================================================
  1  Mary Theresa McKenna    #38
  F  Born: 1904               in:
     Died: 1925               in:
        She was killed in a motor accident.
   ------------------------------------------------------------------------
  2  Katherine Agnes McKenna    #39
  F  Born: 17 Oct. 1905       in:
     Died:                    in:
   ------------------------------------------------------------------------
  3  Rose McKenna    #40
  F  Born: 17 Jul. 192-       in:
     Died:                    in:
        She had 2 children.
   ------------------------------------------------------------------------
  4  Norah McKenna    #41
  F  Born:                    in:
     Died:                    in:
        She had 4 children.
   ------------------------------------------------------------------------
```

Family Group Sheet: Brother's Keeper with messages in compressed font.

Ancestry or Pedigree Chart

This is probably the second most commonly used chart. It shows the ancestors of one individual. Usually the subject is listed on the left side of the page and each generation is progressively indented to the right in a graphic display. In addition to name, it may also list date and place of birth, marriage and death and ahnentafel or record number. With some programs you can select the information you wish to include. Usually the more generations you include on a page, the less information you can have with each person. Pedigree lines may be continued on other charts which are cross referenced. These are called cascading pedigree charts. A wall chart is printed on several sheets of paper which are taped together to produce one large chart.

```
            PREDECESSORS OF ESTHER JOSEPHINE MAYER (RN=3117)          01 Nov 1991


                                   GREAT
                           GRAND   GRAND
 PERSON       PARENTS      PARENTS PARENTS
                                   |JACOB MAYER (RN=3442)
                           GOTLIEB FREDRIC MAYER (RN=3109)
                           |
                                   |CATRINA DONNER (RN=3443)
              ERNEST JACOB MAYER (RN=3110)
              |
                                   |GEORGE CHRISTOPHER SCHAEFER (RN=3444)
                           MINNIE SHAEFER (RN=3111)
                           |
                                   |MARIE BREHM (RN=3445)
 ESTHER JOSEPHINE MAYER (RN=3117)
 |
                                   |JOSIAH BICE (RN=3116)
                           WILLIAM HENRY BICE (RN=3113)
                           |
                                   |HARRIET COCHRAN (RN=3115)
              LAURA BICE (RN=3114)
              |
                                   |WILLIAM YEAST (RN=3446)
                           ELIZABETH YEAST (RN=3112)
                           |
                                   |FLORISSA ENGLE (RN=3447)

            FREE-FORM PEDIGREE CHART, NAMES ONLY, LONG LINES
```

Pedigree Chart: Family Roots.

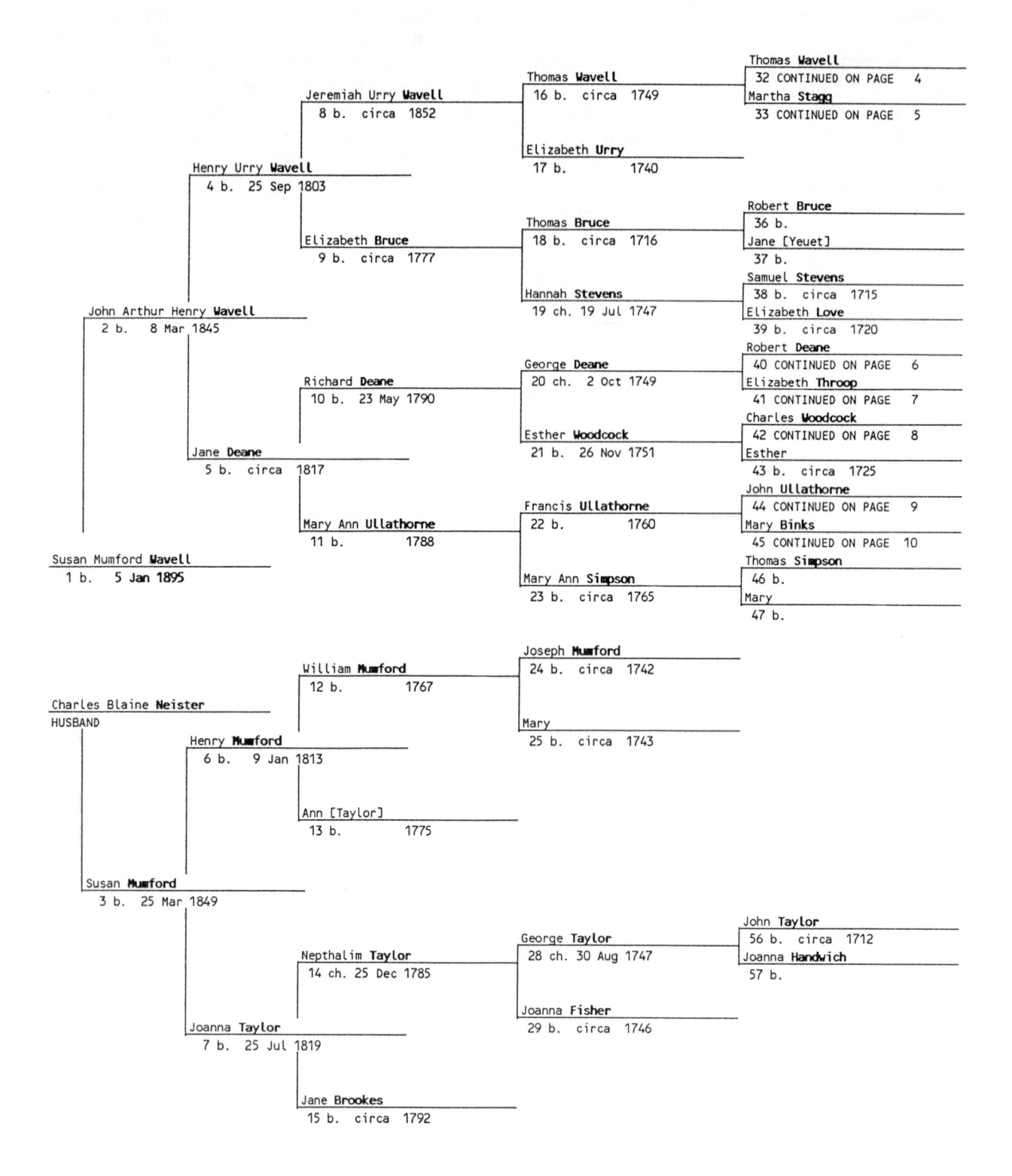

```
                                                                        Thomas Wavell
                                                Thomas Wavell           32 CONTINUED ON PAGE   4
                        Jeremiah Urry Wavell    16 b.  circa  1749      Martha Stagg
                        8 b.  circa 1852                                33 CONTINUED ON PAGE   5

                                                Elizabeth Urry
    Henry Urry Wavell                           17 b.         1740
    4 b.  25 Sep 1803
                                                                        Robert Bruce
                                                Thomas Bruce            36 b.
                        Elizabeth Bruce         18 b.  circa  1716      Jane [Yeuet]
                        9 b.  circa 1777                                37 b.
                                                                        Samuel Stevens
                                                Hannah Stevens          38 b.  circa  1715
                                                19 ch. 19 Jul 1747      Elizabeth Love
John Arthur Henry Wavell                                                39 b.  circa  1720
2 b.   8 Mar 1845                                                       Robert Deane
                                                George Deane            40 CONTINUED ON PAGE   6
                        Richard Deane           20 ch.  2 Oct 1749      Elizabeth Throop
                        10 b. 23 May 1790                               41 CONTINUED ON PAGE   7
                                                                        Charles Woodcock
                                                Esther Woodcock         42 CONTINUED ON PAGE   8
    Jane Deane                                  21 b. 26 Nov 1751       Esther
    5 b.  circa 1817                                                    43 b.  circa  1725
                                                                        John Ullathorne
                                                Francis Ullathorne      44 CONTINUED ON PAGE   9
                        Mary Ann Ullathorne     22 b.         1760      Mary Binks
                        11 b.         1788                              45 CONTINUED ON PAGE  10
                                                                        Thomas Simpson
                                                Mary Ann Simpson        46 b.
Susan Mumford Wavell                            23 b.  circa  1765      Mary
1 b.   5 Jan 1895                                                       47 b.

                                                                        Joseph Mumford
                                                William Mumford         24 b.  circa  1742
                        William Mumford         12 b.         1767
Charles Blaine Neister                                                  Mary
HUSBAND                                                                 25 b.  circa  1743
                        Henry Mumford
                        6 b.  9 Jan 1813

                        Ann [Taylor]
                        13 b.         1775

    Susan Mumford
    3 b. 25 Mar 1849
                                                                        John Taylor
                                                George Taylor           56 b.  circa  1712
                        Nepthalim Taylor        28 ch. 30 Aug 1747      Joanna Handwich
                        14 ch. 25 Dec 1785                              57 b.

                                                Joanna Fisher
    Joanna Taylor                               29 b.  circa  1746
    7 b. 25 Jul 1819

                        Jane Brookes
                        15 b.  circa 1792
```

Six Generation Pedigree Chart: ROOTS III.

PEDIGREE CHART

4 Feb 1993

Chart no. 1

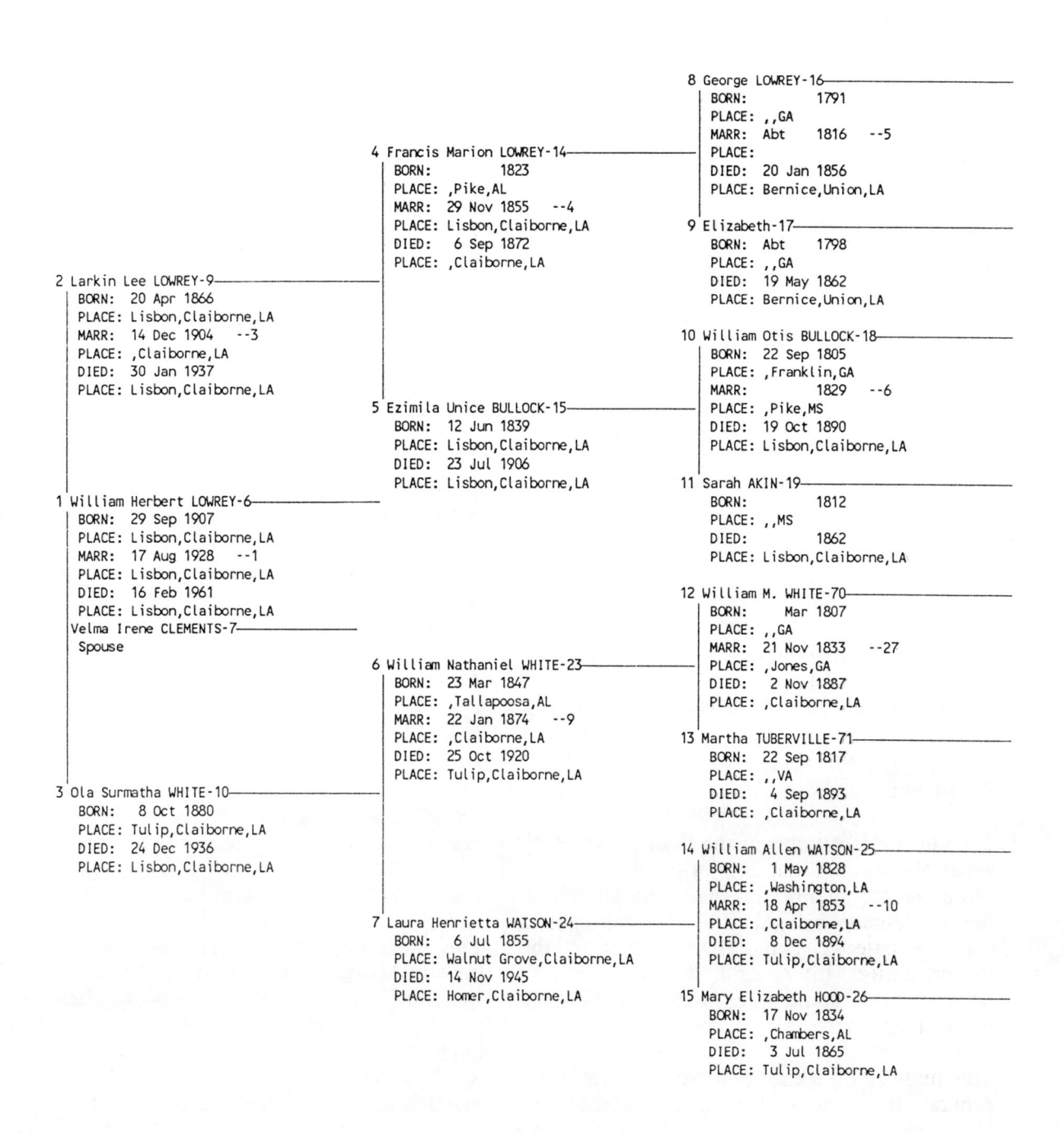

```
                                                                        8 George LOWREY-16
                                                                          BORN:            1791
                                                                          PLACE: ,,GA
                                                                          MARR: Abt        1816   --5
                                          4 Francis Marion LOWREY-14     PLACE:
                                            BORN:            1823         DIED: 20 Jan 1856
                                            PLACE: ,Pike,AL               PLACE: Bernice,Union,LA
                                            MARR: 29 Nov 1855   --4
                                            PLACE: Lisbon,Claiborne,LA  9 Elizabeth-17
                                            DIED:  6 Sep 1872             BORN: Abt        1798
                                            PLACE: ,Claiborne,LA          PLACE: ,,GA
  2 Larkin Lee LOWREY-9                                                   DIED: 19 May 1862
    BORN: 20 Apr 1866                                                     PLACE: Bernice,Union,LA
    PLACE: Lisbon,Claiborne,LA
    MARR: 14 Dec 1904   --3                                              10 William Otis BULLOCK-18
    PLACE: ,Claiborne,LA                                                   BORN: 22 Sep 1805
    DIED: 30 Jan 1937                                                      PLACE: ,Franklin,GA
    PLACE: Lisbon,Claiborne,LA                                             MARR:            1829   --6
                                          5 Ezimila Unice BULLOCK-15       PLACE: ,Pike,MS
                                            BORN: 12 Jun 1839              DIED: 19 Oct 1890
                                            PLACE: Lisbon,Claiborne,LA     PLACE: Lisbon,Claiborne,LA
                                            DIED: 23 Jul 1906
                                            PLACE: Lisbon,Claiborne,LA  11 Sarah AKIN-19
                                                                           BORN:            1812
  1 William Herbert LOWREY-6                                               PLACE: ,,MS
    BORN: 29 Sep 1907                                                      DIED:            1862
    PLACE: Lisbon,Claiborne,LA                                             PLACE: Lisbon,Claiborne,LA
    MARR: 17 Aug 1928   --1
    PLACE: Lisbon,Claiborne,LA                                          12 William M. WHITE-70
    DIED: 16 Feb 1961                                                      BORN:     Mar 1807
    PLACE: Lisbon,Claiborne,LA                                             PLACE: ,,GA
  Velma Irene CLEMENTS-7                                                   MARR: 21 Nov 1833   --27
    Spouse                                6 William Nathaniel WHITE-23     PLACE: ,Jones,GA
                                            BORN: 23 Mar 1847              DIED:  2 Nov 1887
                                            PLACE: ,Tallapoosa,AL          PLACE: ,Claiborne,LA
                                            MARR: 22 Jan 1874   --9
                                            PLACE: ,Claiborne,LA        13 Martha TUBERVILLE-71
                                            DIED: 25 Oct 1920              BORN: 22 Sep 1817
                                            PLACE: Tulip,Claiborne,LA     PLACE: ,,VA
                                                                           DIED:  4 Sep 1893
  3 Ola Surmatha WHITE-10                                                  PLACE: ,Claiborne,LA
    BORN:  8 Oct 1880
    PLACE: Tulip,Claiborne,LA                                           14 William Allen WATSON-25
    DIED: 24 Dec 1936                                                      BORN:  1 May 1828
    PLACE: Lisbon,Claiborne,LA                                             PLACE: ,Washington,LA
                                                                           MARR: 18 Apr 1853   --10
                                          7 Laura Henrietta WATSON-24      PLACE: ,Claiborne,LA
                                            BORN:  6 Jul 1855              DIED:  8 Dec 1894
                                            PLACE: Walnut Grove,Claiborne,LA PLACE: Tulip,Claiborne,LA
                                            DIED: 14 Nov 1945
                                            PLACE: Homer,Claiborne,LA  15 Mary Elizabeth HOOD-26
                                                                           BORN: 17 Nov 1834
                                                                           PLACE: ,Chambers,AL
                                                                           DIED:  3 Jul 1865
                                                                           PLACE: Tulip,Claiborne,LA
```

Pedigree Chart: Personal Ancestral File.

Ahnentafel

An ahnentafel is a type of pedigree or ancestor chart developed by German genealogists. A numbered pedigree chart in graphics form actually has ahnentafel numbers, but a traditional ahnentafel is listed in text form.

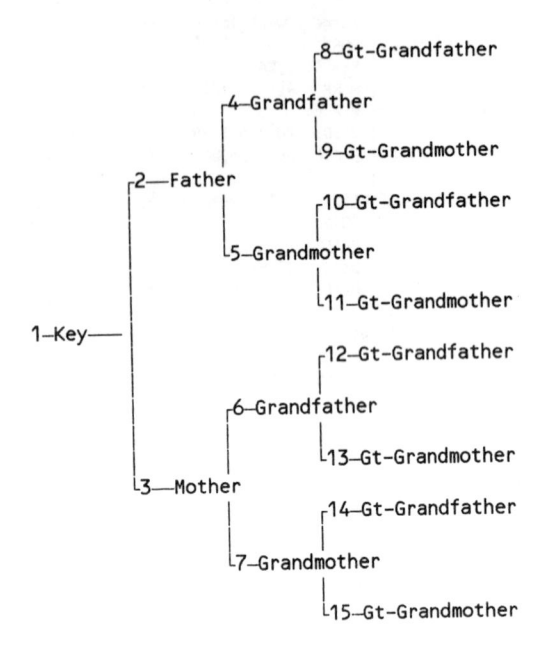

```
                            ┌─8—Gt-Grandfather
              ┌─4—Grandfather
              │             └─9—Gt-Grandmother
     ┌─2—Father
     │        │             ┌─10—Gt-Grandfather
     │        └─5—Grandmother
     │                      └─11—Gt-Grandmother
1—Key
     │                      ┌─12—Gt-Grandfather
     │        ┌─6—Grandfather
     │        │             └─13—Gt-Grandmother
     └─3—Mother
              │             ┌─14—Gt-Grandfather
              └─7—Grandmother
                            └─15—Gt-Grandmother
```

The same numbers always apply to the same relationship on the chart, i.e., the maternal grandfather is always #6. The paternal grandmother's father is always #10. Using these numbers you can make a compact genealogical list of individuals.

The ahnentafel number at the beginning of each generation is the number two raised to the power of the number of that generation with the key person being two to the zero power (1), the paternal grandfather is two to the second power (four) and the key person's paternal great grandfather is two to the third power (eight).

The number of the first person in any given generation is equal to the number of people in that generation. Thus, the great-grandparents generations begins with #8 and a person has eight great-grandparents; the great-great-grandparents generation begins with #16 and there are 16 people in that generation.

In each generation the first half of the numbers are on the father's side, the second half on the mother's. Even numbers are male and odd numbers are female.

To find a person's father, multiply his number by two. Add one to the father's number to get the mother's number.

An ahnentafel of the above chart would be:

1. Key person
2. Father
3. Mother
4. Grandfather (paternal)
5. Grandmother (paternal)
6. Grandfather (maternal)
7. Grandmother (maternal)
8. Great-grandfather (paternal)
9. Great-grandmother   "
10. Great-grandfather   "
11. Great-grandmother   "
12. Great-grandfather (maternal)
13. Great-grandmother   "
14. Great-grandfather   "
15. Great-grandmother   "

Tiny Tafels

A tiny tafel is a small version of an ahnentafel. It is a list of surnames preceded by soundex codes and dates and followed by locations. Included can be a code showing your level of interest in that line. For example:

L600 1786 1846*Lowrey\GA/PikeCo AL

Tiny tafels are shared for matching purposes on bulletin boards which participate in the Tafel Matching System (TMS). Each board maintains a database of tiny tafels which have been uploaded to it. Each new tiny tafel is checked for matches and then sent on with a list of matches to the next BBS which does the same. Soon the tiny tafel arrives back at its origination with a list of all accumulated matches. TMS matches only on soundex codes, so is most successful with uncommon surnames.

1 Susan Mumford **Wavell**, b. 5 Jan 1895 in Troy Twp, Pipestone, MN, d. 17 Jul 1983 in Fresno, Fresno, CA, ma. 13 Jul 1937.

2 John Arthur Henry **Wavell**, b. 8 Mar 1845 in Ryde, IOW, England, d. 18 May 1928 in Flandreau, Moody, SD, ma. 30 Mar 1880 in Chicago, Cook, IL.

3 Susan **Mumford**, b. 25 Mar 1849 in Rodney Stoke, Som, England, d. 17 Apr 1932 in Flandreau, Moody, SD.

4 Henry Urry **Wavell**, b. 25 Sep 1803 in Newchurch, IOW, Hants, Eng., d. 11 Oct 1873 in London, Eng., ma. 15 Apr 1844 in Brighton, Sussex, Eng.

5 Jane **Deane**, b. circa 1817, d. 2 Apr 1845 in Ryde, IOW, Hants, Eng.

6 Henry **Mumford**, b. 9 Jan 1813 in Rodney Stoke, Som, Eng., d. 17 Jul 1879 in Rodney Stoke, Som, Eng., ma. 23 May 1848 in Rodney Stoke, Som, Eng.

7 Joanna **Taylor**, b. 25 Jul 1819 in Rodney Stoke, Som, Eng., d. 31 Jul 1891 in Rodney Stoke, Som, Eng.

8 Jeremiah Urry **Wavell**, b. circa 1852, d. 8 Oct 1852 in London, Eng., ma. 24 Feb 1800.

9 Elizabeth **Bruce**, b. circa 1777, d. 10 Dec 1858 in London, Eng.

10 Richard **Deane**, b. 23 May 1790 in E. Harling, Norfolk, Eng., d. Aug 1825, ma. 16 Sep 1810 in London, Eng.

11 Mary Ann **Ullathorne**, b. 1788, d. 13 Oct 1871 in Kensington, London, Eng.

12 William **Mumford**, b. 1767, d. 7 Sep 1838 in Rodney Stoke, Som, Eng., ma. 24 Sep 1804 in Rodney Stoke, Som, England.

13 Ann [Taylor], b. 1775, bu. 12 Nov 1818 in Rodney Stoke, Som, England.

14 Nepthalim **Taylor**, ch. 25 Dec 1785 in Rodney Stoke, Som, Eng., d. 30 Sep 1844 in Rodney Stoke, Som, Eng., ma. 12 Jul 1814 in Rodney Stoke, Som, Eng.

15 Jane **Brookes**, b. circa 1792 in Weare, Som, Eng., d. 26 Mar 1867 in Rodney Stoke, Som, Eng.

16 Thomas **Wavell**, b. circa 1749, d. 1 Sep 1798 in Newchurch, IOW, Hants, Eng., ma. 13 Aug 1769 in Newchurch, IOW, Hants, Eng.

17 Elizabeth **Urry**, b. 1740, d. 31 Mar 1816.

18 Thomas **Bruce**, b. circa 1716, d. 20 Oct 1797, ma. 15 May 1777 in Newchurch, IOW, Hants, Eng.

19 Hannah **Stevens**, ch. 19 Jul 1747 in Ryde, IOW, England, d. 6 May 1825.

20 George **Deane**, ch. 2 Oct 1749 in Linton, York., Eng., d. 6 Mar 1816 in E. Harling, Norfolk, Eng., ma. 29 Sep 1774 in E. Harling, Norfolk, Eng.

21 Esther **Woodcock**, b. 26 Nov 1751 in E. Harling, Norfolk, Eng., d. 11 Jun 1826.

Ahnentafel: ROOTS III with birth, death and marriage dates.

A.num	Name	Birt	Birth place	Died	Place of death	Ch
1	Susan Mumford Wavell	1895	Troy Twp, Pipestone, MN	1983	Fresno, Fresno, CA	1

Parents

2	John Arthur Henry Wavell	1845	Ryde, IOW, England	1928	Flandreau, Moody, SD	8
3	Susan Mumford	1849	Rodney Stoke, Som, England	1932	Flandreau, Moody, SD	8

Grand Parents

4	Henry Urry Wavell	1803	Newchurch, IOW, Hants, Eng.	1873	London, Eng.	2
5	Jane Deane	1817		1845	Ryde, IOW, Hants, Eng.	1
6	Henry Mumford	1813	Rodney Stoke, Som, Eng.	1879	Rodney Stoke, Som, Eng.	7
7	Joanna Taylor	1819	Rodney Stoke, Som, Eng.	1891	Rodney Stoke, Som, Eng.	7

Great Grand Parents

8	Jeremiah Urry Wavell	1852		1852	London, Eng.	3
9	Elizabeth Bruce	1777		1858	London, Eng.	3
10	Richard Deane	1790	E. Harling, Norfolk, Eng.	1825		3
11	Mary Ann Ullathorne	1788		1871	Kensington, London, Eng.	3
12	William Mumford	1767		1838	Rodney Stoke, Som, Eng.	7
13	Ann Taylor	1775				5
14	Nepthalim Taylor			1844	Rodney Stoke, Som, Eng.	12
15	Jane Brookes	1792	Weare, Som, Eng.	1867	Rodney Stoke, Som, Eng.	12

Great Great Grand Parents

16	Thomas Wavell	1749		1798	Newchurch, IOW, Hants, Eng.	4
17	Elizabeth Urry	1740		1816		4
18	Thomas Bruce	1716		1797		5
19	Hannah Stevens			1825		1
20	George Deane			1816	E. Harling, Norfolk, Eng.	7
21	Esther Woodcock	1751	E. Harling, Norfolk, Eng.	1826		7
22	Francis Ullathorne	1760	Pontefract, York., Eng.	1837	Upper Holloway, Middlesex, Eng	11
23	Mary Ann Simpson	1765		1837	London, Eng., Burton Crescent,	11
24	Joseph Mumford	1742				2
25	Mary	1743		1811	Rodney Stoke, Som, Eng.	2
28	George Taylor					8
29	Joanna Fisher	1746		1812	Rodney Stoke, Som, Eng.	8

Great Great Great Grand Parents

32	Thomas Wavell	1718		1770		10
33	Martha Stagg	1729				10
36	Robert Bruce	1685		1717	I O W, Eng.	1
37	Jane Yeuet	1688				4
38	Samuel Stevens	1715		1758	Ryde, IOW, England	5

Ahnentafel: Brother's Keeper. Custom designed chart with choice of events and size of field.

THE BASICS

AHNENTAFEL CHART

4 Feb 1993   Page 1

1st GENERATION

1 Carolina (Lena) GUTH-110: b 3 Apr 1876 Zweibruecken,Pfalz,Bav, Germany; d 28 Apr 1929 Philadelphia,Philadelphia,PA

2nd GENERATION

2 Jacob GUTH-141: b 12 Dec 1848 Oberlustadt,Pfalz,Bavaria,Germany; m 22 Oct 1875 Rockenhausen,Pfalz,Germany; d 12 Feb 1909 Philadelphia, Philadelphia,PA

3 Elisabetha (Elizabeth) MICHEL-142: b 30 May 1857 Rockenhausen,Pfalz, Bavaria,Germany; d 10 Apr 1940 Philadelphia,Philadelphia,PA

3rd GENERATION

4 Philipp Heinrich GUTH-143: b 2 Nov 1819 Oberlustadt,Pfalz,Bavaria, Germany; m 15 Oct 1843 Oberlustadt,Pfalz,Germany; d Bef 1875

5 Eva Margaretha DEUBEL-144: b 2 Jul 1823 Oberlustadt,Pfalz,Bavaria, Germany; d Aft 1875

6 Friedrich MICHEL-171: b 25 Apr 1811 Contwig,Pfalz,Bavaria,Germany; m 8 Aug 1854 Rockenhausen,Pfalz,Bavaria,Germany; d 18 Oct 1882 Rockenhausen,Pfalz,Bavaria,Germany

7 Anna Maria FUNK-172: b 1817; d 3 Aug 1872 Rockenhausen,Pfalz,Bavaria, Germany

4th GENERATION

8 Johann Friedrich GUTH-145: b 19 Oct 1796 Oberlustadt,Pfalz,Bavaria, Germany; m 14 May 1816 Oberlustadt,Pfalz,Germany

9 Maria Barbara OTT-146: b 1803; d 1 Jul 1831 Oberlustadt,Pfalz, Bavaria,Germany

10 Philipp Jacob DEUBEL-147: b 24 Sep 1794 Oberlustadt,Pfalz,Bavaria, Germany; m 18 Feb 1816 Oberlustadt,Pfalz,Germany

11 Maria Barbara THEISS-148: b 30 Sep 1796 Oberlustadt,Pfalz,Bavaria, Germany

12 Friedrich MICHEL-173: b 1774/1775; m 31 Aug 1802 Contwig,Pfalz, Germany; d 18 Jul 1824 Contwig,Pfalz,Bavaria,Germany

13 Charlotta GIESSEN-174: b 1776/1778; d 28 Apr 1822 Contwig,Pfalz, Bavaria,Germany

14 Philipp Jacob FUNK-175: b Bef 1795 ,,,Germany; m 24 Apr 1814 Hambach, Pfalz,Bavaria,Germany

15 Apollonia KAUB-176

5th GENERATION

16 Johannes GUTH-149: b 28 Apr 1767 Zeiskam,Pfalz,Bavaria,Germany; m 29 Jul 1792 Oberlustadt,Pfalz,Bavaria,Germany

17 Maria Eva THEISS-150

18 Johann Barnhardt OTT-151: b 1763 Oberlustadt,Pfalz,Bavaria,Germany; d 1815

19 Apollonia SCHMITT-152

20 Sabastian DEUBEL-153: b 18 Dec 1757 Oberlustadt,Pfalz,Bavaria, Germany; m 31 Aug 1784 Oberlustadt,Pfalz,Germany; d 27 Jan 1844 Oberlustadt,Pfalz,Bavaria,Germany

21 Eva Barbara LEHR-154: b 13 Oct 1749 Oberlustadt,Pfalz,Bavaria, Germany; d 1 Feb 1815 Oberlustadt,Pfalz,Bavaria,Germany

Ahnentafel: Personal Ancestral File.

Descendant Chart

This is a listing of the descendants of one individual. The number of generations to be included can be selected. The progenitor is listed at the top. His or her spouse may be listed on the next line. On the next line will be the first child whose listing will be indented a set number of spaces. Each generation will be indented the same number of spaces. All the children, grandchildren, etc. of each person are listed below the ancestor's name with each generation being indented. All the descendants of the first child will be listed before the second child is listed. It is a concise chart and shows a family in a fairly small amount of space. The amount of data included usually is just birth and death date. The amount of indentation and how the generations are indicated can vary.

Descendents of Henry I Ledden

Henry I Ledden 96
Birth: 21 Mar 1761
Death: 1 Jan 1827
  Jane Rhodes 144
  Birth: 30 May 1772
  Death: 15 Oct 1857
|__ Moelita Ledden 145
| Birth: 5 May 1792
|__ Samuel Ledden 95
   Birth: 26 Sep 1796
   Death: 1 Jan 1854
   Hannah Dubois 94
   Birth: 9 Oct 1799
   |__ Richard D Ledden 136
   | Birth: 23 Jun 1818
   |__ Joseph M Ledden 93
   | Birth: 1 Jan 1828
   | Death: 1 Jan 1904
   | Sarah Hoffman 60
   | |__ B Elmer Ledden 125
   | | Birth: 1 Jan 1851
   | | Death: 1 Jan 1881
   | |__ John A Ledden 92
   | Birth: 12 Nov 1866
   | Married: 30 Nov 1897 in Glassboro
   | Death: 1 Feb 1942
   | Minnie Brannen 2
   | Birth: 20 Apr 1871
   | Death: 26 Aug 1956
   | |__ George Elmer Ledden 38
   | Birth: 17 Apr 1899
   | Death: 1 Jan 1986
   | Edna Frances Griffith 37
   | Birth: 16 Jul 1899
   | Death: 25 Jun 1980

Descendant Chart: Family Treasures.

Descendants of Nathaniel Bonnell

Itasca Softworks, P.O. Box 427, Bagley, MN 56621, USA

Nathaniel Bonnell
  Born 1640
  Died 1695
+ Susannah Whitehead
  Born 5 Aug 1650
  Died 12 Feb 1733 in Hunterdon Cty, NJ
  Marr 1 Jan 1665 in New Haven, CT
  | Issac Bonnell
    Born 1665 in Elizabeth, Hunterdon Cty, NJ
    Died 17 Jan 1712 in Hunterdon Cty, NJ
  + Elizabeth Unknown
    | Issac Bonnell Jr.
    | Abraham Bonnell
      Born 1700 in Elizabeth Town, NJ
      Died 1767 in Kingwood, Hunterdon Cty, NJ
    + Mary Shinn
      Born 1705 in Elizabeth Town, NJ
      Marr 23 Nov 1731
      | Abraham Bonnell Jr.
        Born 23 Nov 1731 in Hunterdon Cty, NJ
        Died 1 Nov 1797
      + Elizabeth Foster
        Born 4 Aug 1743
        Died 27 Jul 1822
        Marr 1756
        | Clement (duMont) Bonnell
          Born 4 Jan 1766 in Hunterdon Cty, NJ
          Died 24 Jan 1856
        + Rachel Wolverton
          Born 17 Apr 1766
          Died 16 Nov 1807
        | Alexander Bonnell
          Born 31 Jan 1768 in Hunterdon Cty, NJ
          Died Aug 1819 in Hunterdon Cty, NJ
          Buried 1819 in Flemington, Hunterdon Cty, NJ
        + Catherine Matteson
          Born 12 Jan 1770
          Died 25 May 1954
          Buried in Flemington, Hunterdon Cty, NJ
          Marr in Hunterdon Cty, NJ
          | Joseph Bonnell
            Born Abt 1790 in Hunterdon Cty, NJ
          | Charles Bonnell
            Born Abt 1793 in Hunterdon Cty, NJ
          | Alexander Victor Bonnell
            Born Abt 1794 in Hunterdon Cty, NJ

Descendant Chart: MacRoots II.

DESCENDANCY CHART

4 Feb 1993

```
1-- Johann Peter GUTH-3290 (1719-1794)
 sp-Maria Barbara-3291 (1692-1749)
 sp-Eva Margaretha FREY-3292 (1729-1762)
    2-- Johann Tobias GUTH-3273 (1751-1819)
     sp-Helene MEESH-3274
        3-- Eva Margaretha GUTH-3279 (1771)
        3-- Johann Jacob GUTH-3275 (1773)
        3-- Anna Maria GUTH-3280 (1775)
        3-- Johann Conrad GUTH-3276 (1776)
        3-- Anna Maria GUTH-3281 (1780-1819)
        3-- John Frederick GUTH-3278 (1782)
        3-- Johann GUTH-3277 (1786)
         sp-Katherina WEINHEIMER-3282
            4-- Johann Georg GUTH-3283 (1811)
            4-- Johann Jacob GUTH-3284 (1814-1873)
               5-- Tobias GUTH-3288
            4-- Frederick GUTH-3285 (1816)
            4-- Tobias GUTH-3286 (1820)
            4-- Johann GUTH-3287 (1832)
    2-- Eva Margaretha GUTH-3342 (1753-1756)
    2-- Maria Eva GUTH-3343 (1755-1756)
    2-- Johann Frederick GUTH-3293 (1757)
     sp-Barbara Catherina SINN-3295
        3-- George Jacob GUTH-3296 (1781)
        3-- Philip Jacob GUTH-3297 (1782)
        3-- Philip Henry GUTH-3298 (1784)
        3-- Maria Katherina GUTH-3299 (1786)
        3-- George Adam GUTH-3300 (1788)
         sp-Maria Katherina WEBER-3305 (1790-1859)
            4-- Helena GUTH-3306 (1812)
             sp-Peter GROH-3311
                5-- GROH-3312
                5-- GROH-3313
             sp-Valentine HICKEY-3314
                5-- Margaretha HICKEY-3315
                 sp-John LEINER-3316
                    6-- (female) LEINER-3317
                    6-- (male) LEINER-3318
            4-- Conrad GUTH-3307 (1814-1888)
             sp-Barbara KRUMM-3319
                5-- George Frederick GUTH-3320 (1843)
                 sp-Amalia ZINN-3327 (1845-1873)
                    6-- Rene Dyson Oscar GUTH-3328 (1869)
                    6-- Friedrich Arthur Valentine GUTH-3329 (1871)
                 sp-Katherina Rosa BEST-3330
                    6-- Arthur Edwin Edwin GUTH-3331 (1874)
                    6-- Ronald Mike GUTH-3332
                5-- Katherina GUTH-3321 (1845)
                 sp-Melchior GEHRIG-3324
                    6-- Frederick GEHRIG-3325
                5-- Jacob GUTH-3322 (1848)
                    6-- Oscar GUTH M.D.-3326
                5-- Barbara GUTH-3323
            4-- Jacob GUTH-3308 (1816)
            4-- Barbara GUTH-3309 (1825)
            4-- Frederick Adam GUTH-3310 (1826)
```

Descendant Chart: Personal Ancestral File.

Book Form

This is not the official name of a form, but a type of format which produces a printout for books. Most use the register system which was developed by the New England Historic Genealogical Society as the standard for published genealogies. Most journals and organizations follow this standard or a modification of this system. For clarity, this will simply be called book form in this publication as it represents a format used in published books rather than a chart or list.

ROOTS III refers to this type of report as genealogy format (register or record), Brother's Keeper calls it the report format and Everyone's Family Tree calls it a descendancy chart.

In all forms, an individual is listed along with dates and places for events such as birth, christening or death. Biographical information follows this listing. Then the individual's spouse, marriage information and details on the spouse's birth/death are followed by biographical information on the spouse. Biographical information is created in the writer's own words utilizing notes or separate text files which are automatically incorporated into the report.

Register: The first individual is number 1. His or her children will be numbered with small Roman numerals. If a child had descendants, an Arabic number will appear to the left of the Roman numeral and that child's history will be continued later in the narrative where he or she will appear as a head of household.

Modified Register: All children are given an Arabic number. Those that have descendants and are continued later in the narrative have a plus sign (+) to the left of their number.

In either format, the first child of a family will have a superscript number indicating the generation number.

Henry: The oldest ancestor is 1. His children are numbered in order starting at 1 for the oldest. This child takes his father's number (1) plus his number reflecting his position in the family so the progenitor's fifth child would be number 15. The children in each family in each generation are numbered beginning with 1 and take all the numbers from the previous generations. Thus if a person is the fifth child in her family and her father was the second child in his family and her grandmother was the fourth child with her great grandfather being the progenitor, her number would be 1425.

The Printed Report

Several programs will do a book format which can either be printed directly from the program or printed to disk and edited with a word processor. If you wish to further edit in a word processor, it is important to know whether the program will print to disk in ASCII format only or if it can print with formatting codes for a particular word processor. Most programs only print in ASCII format which would be acceptable if you only want to do minor editing.

In the book format (usually in courier type font) the information for children is often indented and printed after the parents' listing as shown in the example on the next page.

In the ASCII format example, between the words "elected" and "35th" there is actually a series of spaces. If you add or delete words, or change font size, the line length will change. However, it will not continue to wrap evenly as the spaces will still be there, although not in the right places, so the text will wrap to the margin instead of being indented and there will be gaps in the lines. If the printout was edited to include "in the presence of a large gathering of family and friends" after the marriage information, the font changed and right margin justified, it would change to the second example. You cannot easily edit the text. If you do remove all the extra spaces and indent the text, you will still have a problem with the index which was created to match the pages as they were printed.

If the report can be printed with word processing codes, both of these problems are eliminated. The child's entry would begin with an indent code which effectively temporarily resets the left margin. If you add words or omit them, the text will continue to wrap correctly. If the word processing program has an index facility and the genealogy program creates the file with these codes embedded, then you generate the final index from the word processing program which reads the new page number from the reformatted text. You can also change to more attractive fonts, justify the right margin and insert graphics if your word processing program supports these features.

He married Jacqueline Lee Bouvier, daughter of John Vernou Bouvier III and Janet Norton Lee, 12 Sep 1953, in Newport, Newport Co, RI. Born, 28 Jul 1929 (?), in Southampton, Long Island, NY. Occupation: Editor. Children:

    i.   a child, stillborn. Born, 23 Aug 1956. Died, 23 Aug 1956. Burial: Aug 1956, in Brookline, Norfolk Co, MA.

    ii. Caroline Bouvier Kennedy. Born, 27 Nov 1957, in New York City, NY. She married Edwin Schlossberg, 19 Jul 1986, in Centerville, Barnstable Co, MA. Caroline Lee Kennedy Schlossberg was only 3 years old when her father was elected 35th President of the United States.

Book style in ASCII format.

---

    ii. Caroline Bouvier Kennedy. Born, 27 Nov 1957, in New York City, NY. She married Edwin Schlossberg, 19 Jul 1986, in Centerville, Barnstable Co, Massachusetts in the presence of a large gathering of family and friends . Caroline Lee Kennedy   Schlossberg was only 3 years old when her father was elected   35th President of the United States.

ASCII file after editing.

THE BASICS

1. Joseph Mumford born ABT 1742, married BEF 1776, Mary, born ABT 1743,[1] died 1 APR 1811, Rodney Stoke, Som, Eng., buried 5 APR 1811, Rodney Stoke, Som, Eng.. Joseph buried 29 JUN 1796, Rodney Stoke, Som, Eng..[2]
   Children:
   2. i William Mumford born 1767.
   ii Mary Mumford 3 MAR 1776, Rodney Stoke, Som, Eng..[2]

Second Generation

2. William Mumford born 1767,[3] Yeoman, married (1) 24 SEP 1804, in Rodney Stoke, Som, England, Ann Taylor, born 1775,[4] buried 12 NOV 1818, Rodney Stoke, Som, England, married (2) ABT 1801, Mary, died BEF 1805, married (3) ABT 1819, Sarah. William died 7 SEP 1838, Rodney Stoke, Som, Eng..[5]

   Children by Ann Taylor:
   i William Mumford born 31 JUL 1805, Rodney Stoke, Som, Eng.,[5] 4 SEP 1805, Rodney Stoke, Som, Eng..
   ii Mary Mumford born 26 JUN 1808, Rodney Stoke, Som, England,[2] 22 JUL 1808, Rodney Stoke, Som, England.
   iii Richard Mumford born 24 SEP 1811, Rodney Stoke, Som, Eng., 24 OCT 1811, Rodney Stoke, Som, England.
   3. iv Henry Mumford born 9 JAN 1813.
   v Thomas Mumford buried 12 NOV 1818, Rodney Stoke, Som, Eng..[2]
   Children by Mary:
   vi Joseph Mumford born 1 JAN 1803, Rodney Stoke, Som, England,[2] 2 FEB 1803, Rodney Stoke, Som, England.
   Children by Sarah:
   vii Thomas Mumford born 23 MAR 1820, Rodney Stoke, Som, Eng..

Third Generation

3. Henry Mumford born 9 JAN 1813, Rodney Stoke, Som, Eng., 14 FEB 1813, Rodney Stoke, Som, Eng., Shopkeeper, married 23 MAY 1848, in Rodney Stoke, Som, Eng., Joanna Taylor, born 25 JUL 1819, Rodney Stoke, Som, Eng.,[5] (daughter of Nepthalim Taylor and Jane Brookes) died 31 JUL 1891, Rodney Stoke, Som, Eng..[5] Henry died 17 JUL 1879, Rodney Stoke, Som, Eng., buried St. Leonard's Church, Rodney Stoke, Eng..
   Children:
   i Susan Mumford born 25 MAR 1849, Rodney Stoke, Som, England, married 30 MAR 1880, in Chicago, Cook, IL, John Arthur Henry Wavell, born 8 MAR

Register Report: Brother's Keeper.

THIRD GENERATION

3. Franciszek[3] **Szul** (Blareja[2], Macieja[1])[1]. Born, 6 Feb 1832, in Nozdrza, Rzeszow, Austria. Died, 23 Feb 1884, in Niewistka, Rzeszow, Austria. Christened, 7 Feb 1832, in Nozdrza, Rzeszow, Austria.

He married Mary Ann **Niemiec**, daughter of Stanislaw [Stanley] **Niemiec** and Anestayi [Anastasia] **Dobosz**. Born in Austria. Died, 1887 (?), in Austria. According to Wojciech's daughter, Josephine, there were six children in the family, but birth records have only been found for four. Children:

    i. Jan[4] **Szul**. Born, 10 Feb 1868, in Niewistka, Rzeszow, Austria[1]. Christened, 13 Feb 1868, in Nozdrza, Rzeszow, Austria[2].
    ii. Franciszka **Szul**. Born, 1 Dec 1869, in Niewistka, Rzeszow, Austria[2]. Christened, 3 Dec 1869, in Izdebki, Rzeszow, Austria[2]. On baptism certificate the religion for Franciszka Szul is given as Greek-Catholic.
    iii. Maciej **Szul**. Born, 28 Feb 1876, in Niewistka, Rzeszow, Austria[2]. Christened, 29 Feb 1876, in Nozdrza, Rzeszow, Austria[2].
4 iv. Wojciech **Szul**.
    v. Maryanna **Szul**. Her birth record has not been located in the parish records, but on the ships' passenger list Wojciech indicated he was going to his sister, Maryanna Szul in New York.

FOURTH GENERATION

4. Wojciech[4] **Szul** (Franciszek[3], Blareja[2], Macieja[1])[3]. Born, 27 Mar 1882, in Niewistka, Rzeszow, Austria[2]. Died, 9 Dec 1970, in Trenton, Mercer, NJ[4]. Christened, 29 Mar 1882, in Nozdrza, Rzeszow, Austria[2]. Burial in Holy Cross Cem, Trenton, NJ. Census: 11 Jun 1915, in Trenton, NJ, at 10 Home Ave.[5]. Immigration: 31 Oct 1906, in New York, NY[6]. Occupation: Potter.

Wojciech Szul was born in house #16 in the village of Niewistka, a Polish town that belonged to Austria at that time. He said he was the youngest of six children, although a report on the parish records only included four children. His father died when he was two years old and his mother died when he was five. He was raised by his older brothers who were not kind to him. He is supposed to have been in the army in Europe, but it is unclear which army. He is said to have been a guard for the King of Poland, but Poland did not exist as a country at that time.

He sailed from Antwerp aboard the S.S. Zeeland on Oct. 20, 1906, arriving in New York on Oct. 31, 1906. He listed his occupation as laboror, indicated he was able to read and write, he paid for his own passage and was destined for New York. He had $17. It appears he was going to his sister, Maryanna Szul in New York.

On the same ship were 6 other people from the same area: Josefa Telega (female), age 18 from Izdebki; Safron Til, age 45 from Izdebki; Jan Bobola, age 36, from Izdebki; Reenia Owsiana (female), age 24 from Izdebki; Josef Cioban, age 24, from Niewistka (believed to be a cousin of Wojciech, indicated as going to join friend Maryanna Szul in New York City); Wojciech Szul, age 24, from Niewistka listed next; Wahuty Bobula, age 24, from Izdebki. Telega, Til and both Bobolas were going to Pennsylvania, Owsiana was going to Michigan and Cioban and Szul both were going to Maryanna Szul in New York.

On arrival in Trenton, he went to live at a boarding house at 210-216 Home Avenue, which was owned by Rozalia Wojczynski, who was also a matchmaker and the aunt of Kornelia Kuncio. Rozalia owned four houses at this address and many of the young men from Rzeszow went to live there when they arrived in Trenton.

In 1915 he was living at 210 Home Avenue, Trenton; in 1928 at 254 Jersey St. and in 1946 when he remarried, he moved to his wife's house at 57 Jersey St. He was a potter, working for Trenton Potteries. He was naturalized when his daughter Josephine was small.

He raised pigeons for a hobby.

He married, first, Kornelia **Kuncio**, daughter of Buzylego **Kuncio** and Katarzyna **Kostenskiej**, 15 Feb 1908, in Trenton, Mercer, NJ. Born, 10 Jun 1891, in Austria. Died, 29 Dec 1940, in Trenton, Mercer, NJ. Burial in Holy Cross Cem, Trenton, NJ. Census: 11 Jun 1915, in Trenton, NJ, at 10 Home Ave.[5]. Immigration: circa 1907.

Kornelia Kuncio was born near Brzozow in Austrian occupied Poland. She was not born in the same village as Wojciech Szul as her birth is not recorded in the parish church. She was the oldest in her

---

Genealogy Format Report: ROOTS III. Printed to disk file with WordPerfect codes, reformatted into columns, right margin justified, font changed and printed through WordPerfect.

The Descendants of Johann Peter Guth

Listing 33 descendants for 3 generations.

GENERATION NO. 1

1 — Johann Peter Guth was born on Jan 1719. He was the son of Johann(es) Guth and Catherine. He married Maria Barbara on 15 Oct 1743, in Zeiskam, Pfalz, Bav, Ger. She was born on 3 Nov 1692.

They had no children.

Maria died on 8 Aug 1749, in Zeiskam, Pfalz, Bav, Ger, and was buried on 10 Aug 1749, in Zeiskam, Pfalz, Bav, Ger. NOTES for Maria follow:
BIRTH: calculated from age at death. MARR #2, DEATH: Zeiskam Parish Records; FHL #193,247.
"The Palatine Immigrant", V. VIII, No. 4, p. 213 Johann next married Eva Margaretha Frey on 9 Feb 1750, in Zeiskam, Pfalz, Bav, Ger. She was born on 16 Oct 1729, in Zeiskam, Pfalz, Bav, Ger, the daughter of Abraham Frey and Maria Margaretha.

They had 6 children:

2- Johann Tobias Guth	b. 8 May 1751	d. 22 Feb 1819
3- Eva Margaretha Guth	b. 5 Jan 1753	d. 27 Feb 1756
4- Maria Eva Guth	b. 12 Mar 1755	d. 17 Aug 1756
5- Johann Frederick Guth	b. 10 Sep 1757	d. 23 Sep
6- George Adam Guth	b. 14 Jan 1760	d.
7- Anna Catherina Guth	b. 3 Apr 1762	d. 3 Apr 1762

Eva died on 16 Jul 1762, in Zeiskam, Pfalz, Bav, Ger. NOTES for Eva follow: Was 20 when she married, 32 years 8 months when she died. "The Palatine Immigrant", V. VIII, No. 4, p.213. Sources: CHR, MARR, DEATH: Zeiskam Parish Records; FHL #193,247.

Johann next married Anna Apollonia von Gerichten on 1 Nov 1762, in Zeiskam, Pfalz, Bavaria. She was born on 1723, in Zeiskam, Pfalz, Bavaria, the daughter of Johann Michael von Gerichten and Anna Catherina.

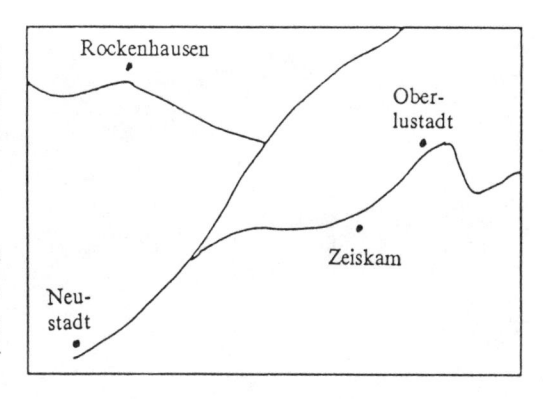

They had 2 children:

8- Eva Catherina Guth	b. 13 Feb 1764	d.
9- Johannes Guth	b. 28 Apr 1767	d.

Book format: GEN-BOOK, a Personal Ancestral File utility.

GEDCOM Compatible Genealogy Programs

GEDCOM Compatible Genealogy Programs

The following programs all have GEDCOM support. In some cases GEDCOM is included with the basic program and in others it is a separate purchase. In a few cases the GEDCOM utility has been written by someone other than the developer and you will have to refer to the utility section for more details. In a few cases, the program can only import (bring data in from other programs) or only export (take the information in the program and create the GEDCOM file), but cannot do both.

In ordering programs from the developer, if you live in the same state and it has a sales tax, please be sure to include tax. In this section we have indicated the type of computer or operating system for each program. In other sections it is noted only if non-DOS.

If you find a shareware program you like and use, please remember to send in your registration fee!

Brother's Keeper
Version 5.1

Producer

John Steed
6907 Childsdale Rd.
Rockford, MI 49341
616 866 9422

Basics

DOS
$45. Shareware
GEDCOM included
Printed manual with registration
Support by phone 616 866 9422 (8-10PM Eastern); Own BBS 616 364 1127; CompuServe 75745,1371; GEnie J.STEED1
Purchase from producer, shareware store or download from bulletin boards

Data Entry

Data usually entered on a screen that has husband and wife (name, born, baptized, died, buried and "other" date and place plus reference and occupation) and marriage (married and "other" date and location, whether or not there was a marriage ceremony, if divorced, annulled or separated and ending year). Separate edit screen for an individual. Database will accommodate one million people, eight marriages per individual, 24 children per marriage. Five events per individual (three set, two choice) and two events per marriage (one set, one choice). Foreign characters are supported (select from pop-up list); hot keys and macros for repeat information. Names and locations up to 40 characters. Dates automatically converted to standard format (choice of nine types). Supports abt, cir, bef and aft modifiers. Three lines for source on each event (prints as footnote) and seven lines for text which can be expanded to 120 lines with built-in text editor (no word wrap or other formatting capabilities) or unlimited with other word processor. Message lines print on the report printout (book form) and family group sheet. Can enter a child under two sets of parents (for adopted or foster children). An alternate name can be entered for an individual (this name prints on the birthday lists). Field for addresses from which you can print labels.

Data Management

Search by record number or name (first five letters of first name and first five letters of last name). Records that match are displayed one at a time and you can either accept or move to next one. Does not display a list and you cannot move backwards. Most sorting is done as part of the print routine which can be viewed on the screen. Can sort on names, places, record numbers and birthday month. When you retrieve the record, it is for the individual and shows the person's data as described in data entry plus father, mother and spouse's name, marriage date and location and a list of children in the lower portion of the screen. From the menu at the bottom of the screen you can rearrange children or spouses, delete spouse or children, display the record for the person's father, mother, spouse, any child, the next older or younger sibling of the person. Utility to change date format, check for quality of data, compute relationships, universal change for a particular location or source.

Printed Charts

Good printer support for dot matrix, laser and inkjet. Many choices for each chart, most of which can be sent to the printer, to the screen or to disk with or without formatting codes.

Pedigree charts (four, five and six generations per page), cascading charts and wall chart, up to seven generations on four pages. Can search for any word or name in any field, then print a custom designed report with a choice of 38 items. Once form has been designed it can be saved for future use. Alpha list for all names or descendants of one person, numerical list can start at a specific number, birthday list (choice to eliminate people without known birth dates and people who have died; select all or descendants of one person). Descendant chart with options to print notes (message lines) and relationship to a specific person. Ancestor list will display each generation and information you select from custom design form. Ahnentafel report including name, birth, christening, died and burial dates and places. Tree of descendants will display all the descendants of a person in chart form. Option to include spouses, dates; select number of characters for each name and select number of generations. Includes a great deal of information in a small amount of space. Family group sheet with 17 options including printing source/reference footnotes and message lines. Can also print group sheets for a range of record numbers, descendants or ancestors of a person. When viewing many charts on the screen, pressing enter will move down to the next screenful but you cannot go back. Register style with choice of register or modified register numbering and indented report in outline style. 3"x5" index cards. Also creates Tiny Tafels.

Box charts for descendants of a person with choice of box type (amount of information contained), width of box in characters and number of generations. Maximum 12 generations and 500 boxes horizontally. Four family box chart which shows all of the descendents of the four sets of grandparents of a husband and wife including the couple's children. Option for six generations will show all descendants of the grandparents for six generations if within limit of 200 boxes horizontally. (You cannot select which descendants. It automatically includes all.) Ancestor box chart five and a half pages long and two pages wide. The first set of pages will contain the first six generations and the second set will have the last three generations with letters printed in half height size letters and line space twice as many lines per inch; choice of shadow boxes. This is similar to a pedigree chart with the subject on the left and ancestors on the right, all enclosed in boxes. Bar charts showing distribution in database of month of birth, marriage or death (choice of all in database or descendants or ancestors of one person); number of children per marriage (choice of marriages with at least one child or all marriages including those with no children); lifespan (age at death with choice of male, female or both, everyone in database or only ancestors or descendants of one person). Bar chart can be full page, 3/4 page or half page size. Timeline shows timeline of ancestors of person from 1580 to 1970. Option to include timeline of famous people from BKEVENT file.

Other Features

Available in French, Danish, German, Norwegian, Polish and Dutch. One help screen which can be displayed at the main menu. Since all charts can be printed to disk, they can be retrieved in a word processor and further edited before printing.

Comments

Selected as "also in the running" and "editor's selection" in *Genealogical Computing*'s "Software to Beat" in 1991. The wide variety of reports is Brother's Keeper's biggest selling point. Since it will accept GEDCOM many people use it as a secondary program just for the unique charts. Its weakest area seems to be sorting records to the screen for viewing or further work. Many routines are actually separate programs so to switch from one to another you have to wait while the program reloads the data files. If you set up a chart to print and the printer is not ready or runs out of paper, the program will terminate and give you a C prompt. Benefits of registration: printed manual; free updates for a certain period of time, after which notification of updates which are available for nominal cost; support. Widely available on bulletin boards. On CompuServe as

BK5A.EXE, BK5B.EXE, BK5C.EXE, BK5D.EXE, BK5DOC.EXE. On GEnie BK5A9209.EXE thru BK5D9209.EXE and BKDOC2.EXE. Special mention in *Genealogical Computing*'s "Software to Beat" in 1992 and "Also in the running" and "Dark Horse" editor's choice in 1991.

DESCENDANTS OF: Thomas McMurphy
AS RELATED TO: Carmela Jones   PAGE 1

1 2 3 4 5 6 7 8 9 10 11 12 13 14

* Thomas McMurphy #44 m. Rose Anne Callighan #45
  (GREAT-GRAND FATHER)
     According to a handwritten note Thomas "went to England, married and had four children. Presumably he married in England.
. * Thomas McMurphy #37 (4 Apr. 1876) - (14 Oct. 1939) m. Theresa Harrington #35
  (GRAND FATHER)   ( ) - (1 Feb. 1960)
     In 1930 he was elected Secretary of the British Section of the International Metalworkers Federation and received the O.B.E. in 1934.

     He was a member of the Middlesbrough town Council for 11 years and served on the Saltburn and Marske Urban Council for nine years.
. . * Mary Theresa McMurphy #38 (1904) - (1925)
    (AUNT)
     She was killed in a motor accident.
. . * Katherine Agnes McMurphy #39 (17 Oct. 1905) -   m. Tom Jones #69
    (MOTHER)
. . . * Carmela Jones #70
      (MYSELF)
. . * Rose McMurphy #40 (17 Jul. 192-) -
    (AUNT)
     She had 2 children.
. . * Norah McMurphy #41
    (AUNT)
     She had 4 children.
. . * Bernard McMurphy #42
    (UNCLE)
     He has a son and a daughter.
. . * Agnes McMurphy #43
    (AUNT)
     She had 4 children and lives in Barcelona, Spain.
. * Esther McMurphy #66
  (GREAT AUNT)
     She had no children.
. * Margaret McMurphy #67
  (GREAT AUNT)
     She had no children.
. * Bernard McMurphy #68
  (GREAT UNCLE)

Brother's Keeper: Descendant Chart with code numbers, message lines and relationship, printed through Word Perfect.

Brother's Keeper: Bar Charts
Lifespan, 1/2 page size
Birthdays, full page size

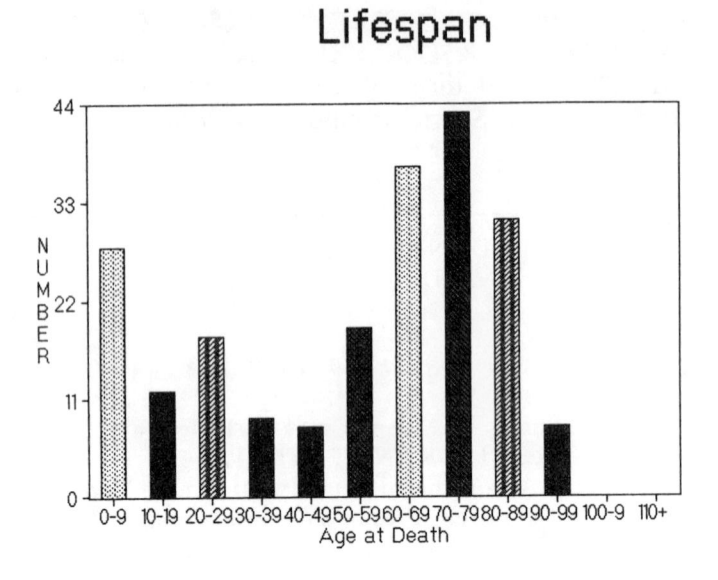

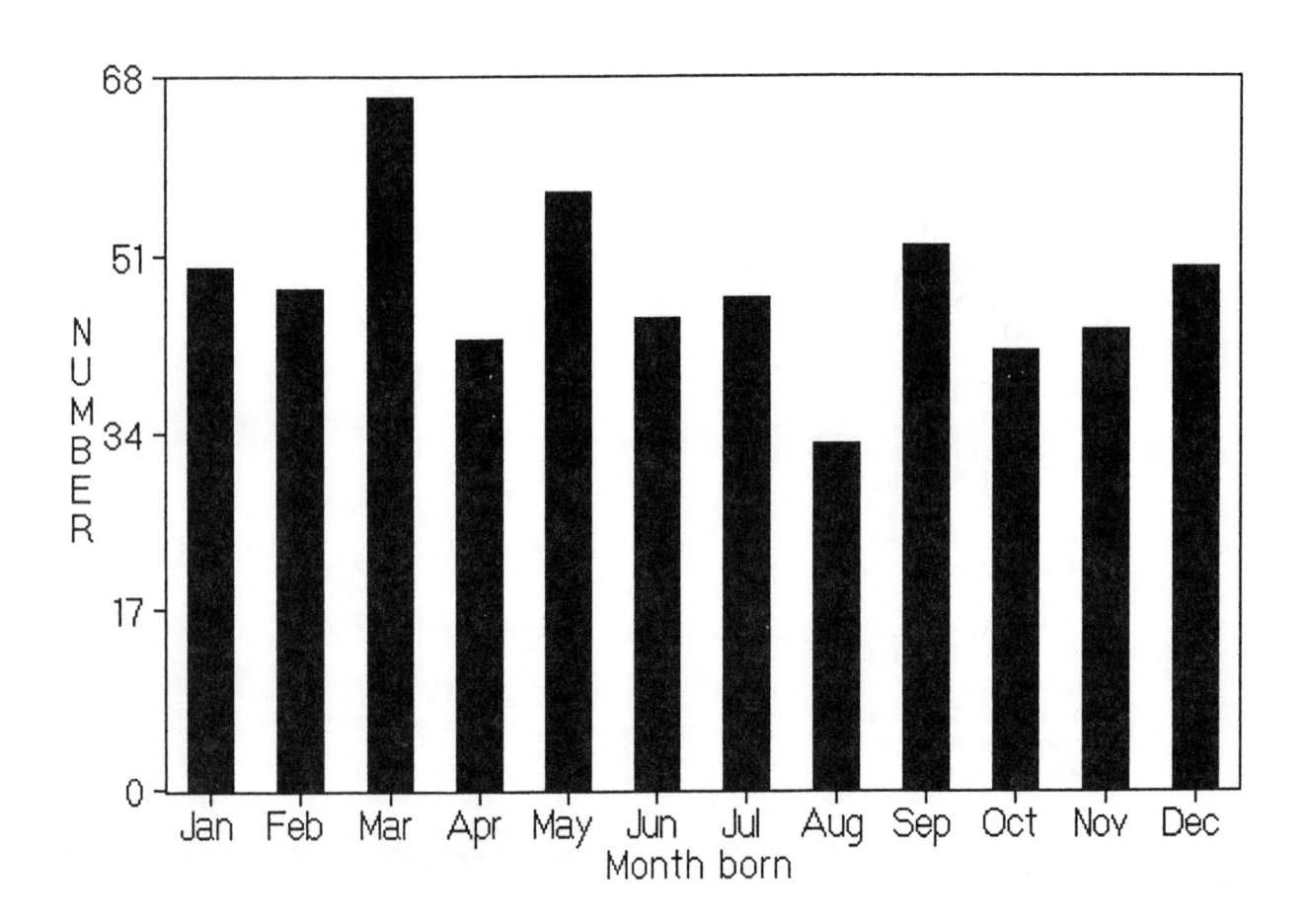

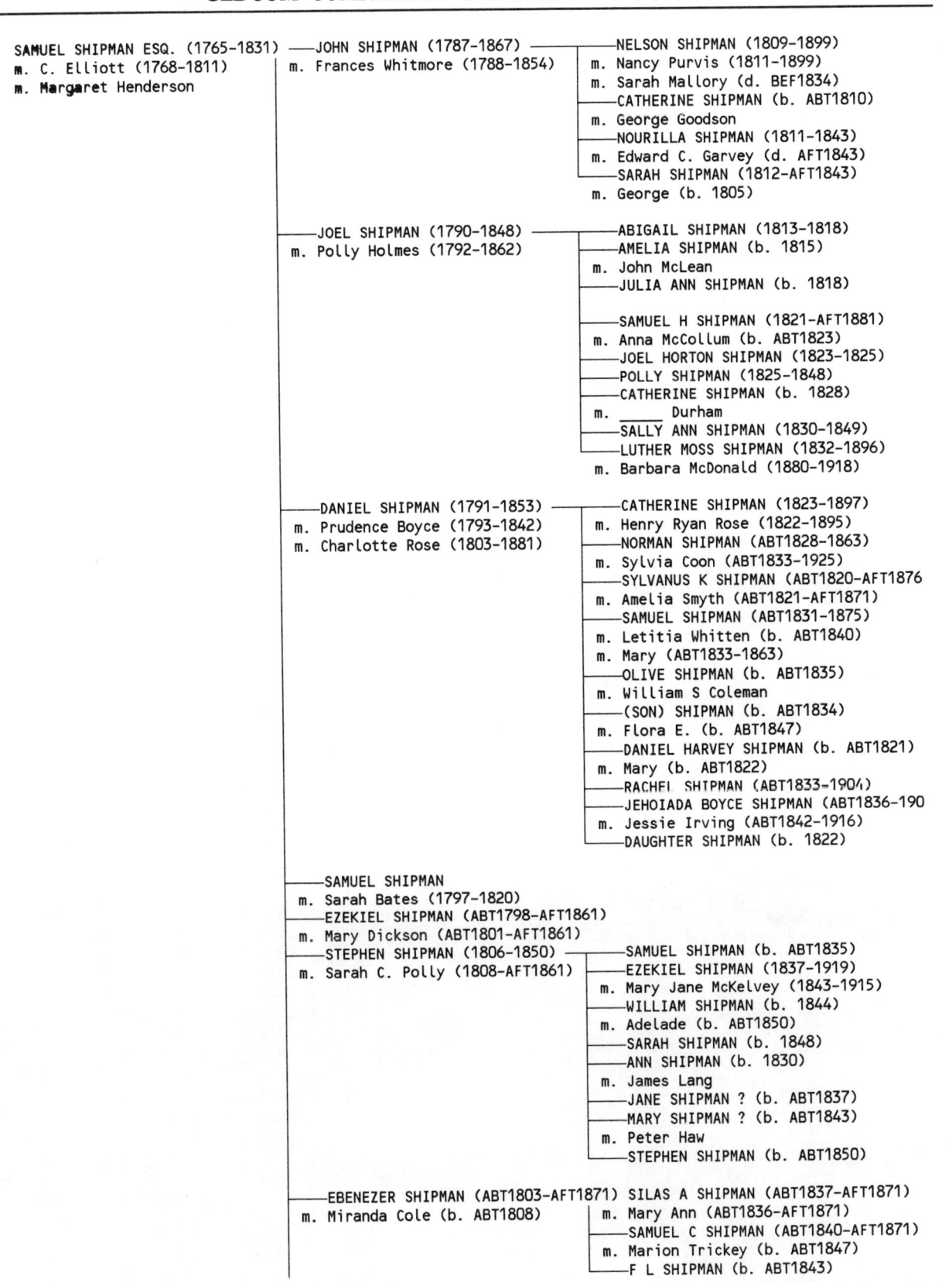

SAMUEL SHIPMAN ESQ. (1765-1831) ──── JOHN SHIPMAN (1787-1867) ──── NELSON SHIPMAN (1809-1899)
m. C. Elliott (1768-1811)   m. Frances Whitmore (1788-1854)   m. Nancy Purvis (1811-1899)
m. Margaret Henderson   m. Sarah Mallory (d. BEF1834)
                                                                          ── CATHERINE SHIPMAN (b. ABT1810)
                                                                          m. George Goodson
                                                                          ── NOURILLA SHIPMAN (1811-1843)
                                                                          m. Edward C. Garvey (d. AFT1843)
                                                                          ── SARAH SHIPMAN (1812-AFT1843)
                                                                          m. George (b. 1805)

                                       ──── JOEL SHIPMAN (1790-1848) ──── ABIGAIL SHIPMAN (1813-1818)
                                            m. Polly Holmes (1792-1862)   ── AMELIA SHIPMAN (b. 1815)
                                                                          m. John McLean
                                                                          ── JULIA ANN SHIPMAN (b. 1818)

                                                                          ── SAMUEL H SHIPMAN (1821-AFT1881)
                                                                          m. Anna McCollum (b. ABT1823)
                                                                          ── JOEL HORTON SHIPMAN (1823-1825)
                                                                          ── POLLY SHIPMAN (1825-1848)
                                                                          ── CATHERINE SHIPMAN (b. 1828)
                                                                          m. ____ Durham
                                                                          ── SALLY ANN SHIPMAN (1830-1849)
                                                                          ── LUTHER MOSS SHIPMAN (1832-1896)
                                                                          m. Barbara McDonald (1880-1918)

                                       ──── DANIEL SHIPMAN (1791-1853) ── CATHERINE SHIPMAN (1823-1897)
                                            m. Prudence Boyce (1793-1842) m. Henry Ryan Rose (1822-1895)
                                            m. Charlotte Rose (1803-1881) ── NORMAN SHIPMAN (ABT1828-1863)
                                                                          m. Sylvia Coon (ABT1833-1925)
                                                                          ── SYLVANUS K SHIPMAN (ABT1820-AFT1876
                                                                          m. Amelia Smyth (ABT1821-AFT1871)
                                                                          ── SAMUEL SHIPMAN (ABT1831-1875)
                                                                          m. Letitia Whitten (b. ABT1840)
                                                                          m. Mary (ABT1833-1863)
                                                                          ── OLIVE SHIPMAN (b. ABT1835)
                                                                          m. William S Coleman
                                                                          ── (SON) SHIPMAN (b. ABT1834)
                                                                          m. Flora E. (b. ABT1847)
                                                                          ── DANIEL HARVEY SHIPMAN (b. ABT1821)
                                                                          m. Mary (b. ABT1822)
                                                                          ── RACHEL SHIPMAN (ABT1833-1904)
                                                                          ── JEHOIADA BOYCE SHIPMAN (ABT1836-190
                                                                          m. Jessie Irving (ABT1842-1916)
                                                                          ── DAUGHTER SHIPMAN (b. 1822)

                                       ──── SAMUEL SHIPMAN
                                            m. Sarah Bates (1797-1820)
                                       ──── EZEKIEL SHIPMAN (ABT1798-AFT1861)
                                            m. Mary Dickson (ABT1801-AFT1861)
                                       ──── STEPHEN SHIPMAN (1806-1850) ── SAMUEL SHIPMAN (b. ABT1835)
                                            m. Sarah C. Polly (1808-AFT1861) ── EZEKIEL SHIPMAN (1837-1919)
                                                                          m. Mary Jane McKelvey (1843-1915)
                                                                          ── WILLIAM SHIPMAN (b. 1844)
                                                                          m. Adelade (b. ABT1850)
                                                                          ── SARAH SHIPMAN (b. 1848)
                                                                          ── ANN SHIPMAN (b. 1830)
                                                                          m. James Lang
                                                                          ── JANE SHIPMAN ? (b. ABT1837)
                                                                          ── MARY SHIPMAN ? (b. ABT1843)
                                                                          m. Peter Haw
                                                                          ── STEPHEN SHIPMAN (b. ABT1850)

                                       ──── EBENEZER SHIPMAN (ABT1803-AFT1871) SILAS A SHIPMAN (ABT1837-AFT1871)
                                            m. Miranda Cole (b. ABT1808) m. Mary Ann (ABT1836-AFT1871)
                                                                          ── SAMUEL C SHIPMAN (ABT1840-AFT1871)
                                                                          m. Marion Trickey (b. ABT1847)
                                                                          ── F L SHIPMAN (b. ABT1843)

Brother's Keeper: Tree of Descendants chart.

42 GUIDE TO GENEALOGY SOFTWARE

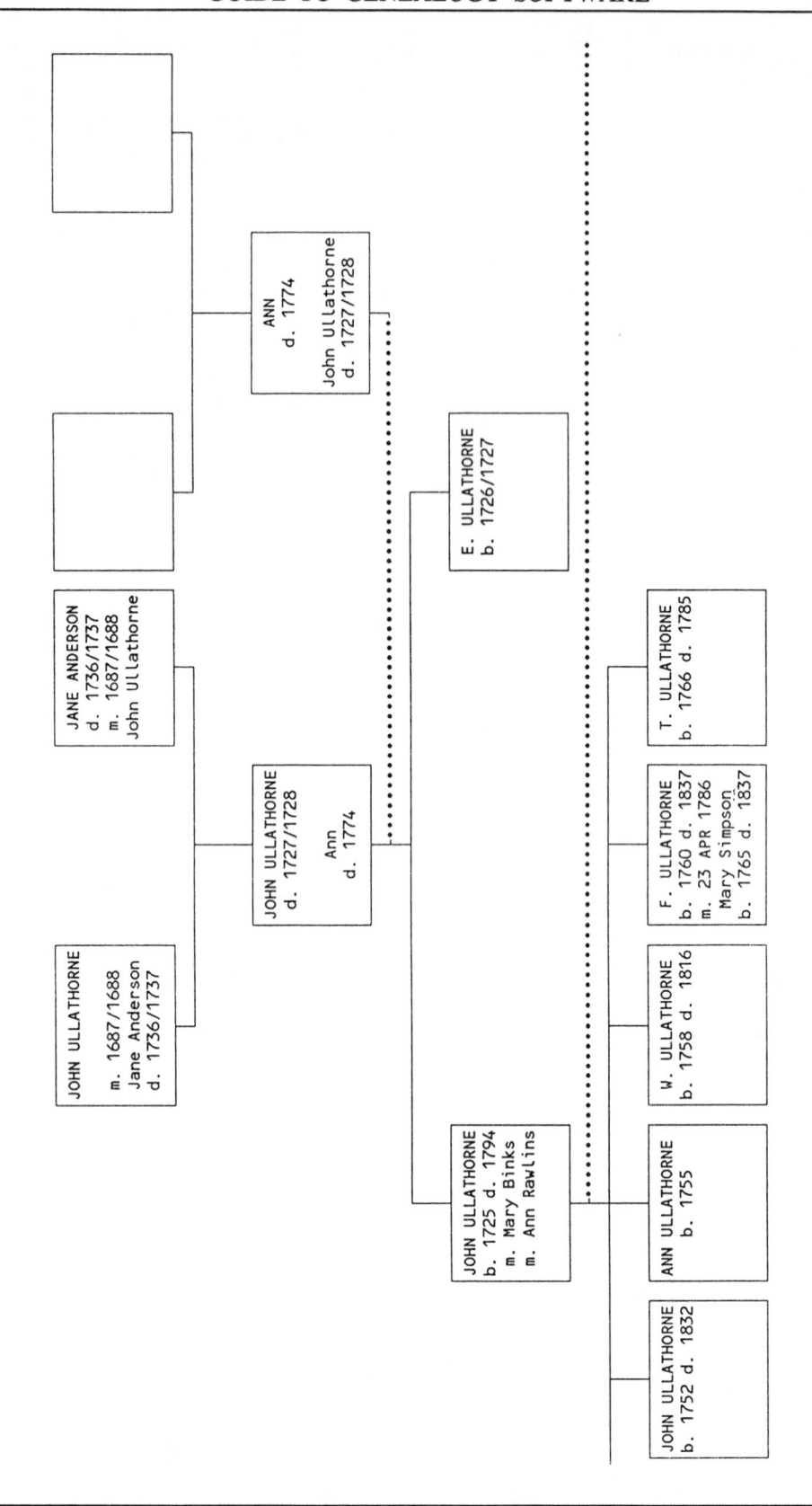

```
                    ┌──────────────┐
                    │              │
                    │              │
                    └──┐           │
                       │           │
         ┌─────────────┴─┐         │
         │ ANN           │         │
         │ d. 1774       │         │
         │ John Ullathorne│        │
         │ d. 1727/1728  │         │
         └───────────────┘         │
                    ┌──────────────┤
                    │              │
                    │              │
                    └──────────────┘

      ┌──────────────┐
      │ JANE ANDERSON│
      │ d. 1736/1737 │
      │ m. 1687/1688 │
      │ John Ullathorne│
      └──────────────┘                  ┌──────────────┐
                                        │ E. ULLATHORNE│
                                        │ b. 1726/1727 │
                                        └──────────────┘
      ┌──────────────┐
      │ JOHN ULLATHORNE│
      │ d. 1727/1728 │
      │ Ann          │
      │ d. 1774      │
      └──────────────┘
                                                              ┌──────────────┐
      ┌──────────────┐                                        │ T. ULLATHORNE│
      │ JOHN ULLATHORNE│                                      │ b. 1766 d. 1785│
      │ m. 1687/1688 │                                        └──────────────┘
      │ Jane Anderson│
      │ d. 1736/1737 │                                        ┌──────────────┐
      └──────────────┘                                        │ F. ULLATHORNE│
                                                              │ b. 1760 d. 1837│
                                                              │ m. 23 APR 1786│
                                                              │ Mary Simpson │
                                                              │ b. 1765 d. 1837│
                                                              └──────────────┘

                    ┌──────────────┐                          ┌──────────────┐
                    │ JOHN ULLATHORNE│                        │ W. ULLATHORNE│
                    │ b. 1725 d. 1794│                        │ b. 1758 d. 1816│
                    │ m. Mary Binks │                         └──────────────┘
                    │ m. Ann Rawlins│
                    └──────────────┘                          ┌──────────────┐
                                                              │ ANN ULLATHORNE│
                                                              │ b. 1755      │
                                                              └──────────────┘

                                                              ┌──────────────┐
                                                              │ JOHN ULLATHORNE│
                                                              │ b. 1752 d. 1832│
                                                              └──────────────┘
```

Brother's Keeper: Four Family Box Chart (partial) showing four generations.

GEDCOM COMPATIBLE GENEALOGY PROGRAMS

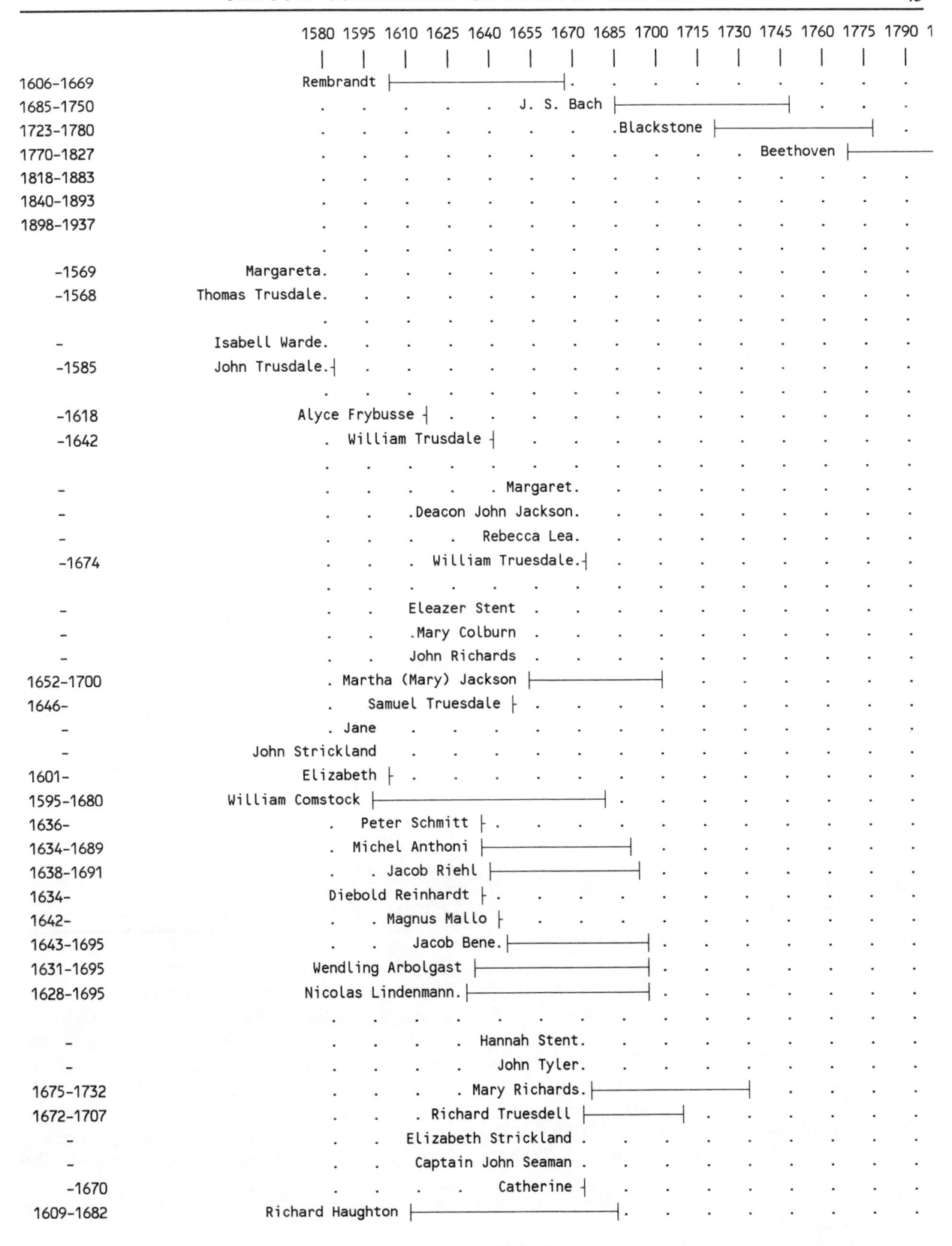

```
                1580 1595 1610 1625 1640 1655 1670 1685 1700 1715 1730 1745 1760 1775 1790
                  |    |    |    |    |    |    |    |    |    |    |    |    |    |    |
1606-1669            Rembrandt |—————————————————|.    .    .    .    .    .    .    .    .
1685-1750            .    .    .    .    .    J. S. Bach |————————————————|    .    .    .
1723-1780            .    .    .    .    .    .    .    .Blackstone |————————————|    .    .
1770-1827            .    .    .    .    .    .    .    .    .    .    . Beethoven |————————|
1818-1883            .    .    .    .    .    .    .    .    .    .    .    .    .    .    .
1840-1893            .    .    .    .    .    .    .    .    .    .    .    .    .    .    .
1898-1937            .    .    .    .    .    .    .    .    .    .    .    .    .    .    .
    -1569            Margareta. .    .    .    .    .    .    .    .    .    .    .    .    .
    -1568            Thomas Trusdale. .    .    .    .    .    .    .    .    .    .    .    .
       -             Isabell Warde.   .    .    .    .    .    .    .    .    .    .    .    .
    -1585            John Trusdale.|  .    .    .    .    .    .    .    .    .    .    .    .
    -1618                 Alyce Frybusse |  .    .    .    .    .    .    .    .    .    .    .
    -1642                 .   William Trusdale |  .    .    .    .    .    .    .    .    .    .
       -                  .    .    .    .    . Margaret.    .    .    .    .    .    .    .
       -                  .    .    .    . .Deacon John Jackson. .    .    .    .    .    .    .
       -                  .    .    .    .    . Rebecca Lea.   .    .    .    .    .    .    .
    -1674                 .    .    .    . William Truesdale.|  .    .    .    .    .    .    .
       -                  .    .    Eleazer Stent .    .    .    .    .    .    .    .    .
       -                  .    .   .Mary Colburn    .    .    .    .    .    .    .    .    .
       -                  .    .    John Richards   .    .    .    .    .    .    .    .    .
1652-1700                 .   Martha (Mary) Jackson |————————————|  .    .    .    .    .    .
1646-                     .    Samuel Truesdale |    .    .    .    .    .    .    .    .
       -                  .    Jane    .    .    .    .    .    .    .    .    .    .    .
       -             John Strickland   .    .    .    .    .    .    .    .    .    .    .
1601-                     Elizabeth |  .    .    .    .    .    .    .    .    .    .    .
1595-1680            William Comstock |————————————————————|  .    .    .    .    .    .    .
1636-                     .   Peter Schmitt |—.    .    .    .    .    .    .    .    .    .
1634-1689                 . Michel Anthoni |————————————|  .    .    .    .    .    .    .
1638-1691                 .    . Jacob Riehl |————————————|  .    .    .    .    .    .    .
1634-                     Diebold Reinhardt |—.    .    .    .    .    .    .    .    .    .
1642-                     .    . Magnus Mallo |   .    .    .    .    .    .    .    .    .
1643-1695                 .    .  Jacob Bene. |——————————|  .    .    .    .    .    .    .
1631-1695            Wendling Arbolgast |———————————————|  .    .    .    .    .    .    .
1628-1695            Nicolas Lindenmann. |———————————————|  .    .    .    .    .    .    .
       -                  .    .    .    . Hannah Stent.   .    .    .    .    .    .    .
       -                  .    .    .    . John Tyler.     .    .    .    .    .    .    .
1675-1732                 .    .    .    . Mary Richards. |————————————————|  .    .    .
1672-1707                 .    .    .    . Richard Truesdell |————————|  .    .    .    .
       -                  .    .    . Elizabeth Strickland .    .    .    .    .    .    .
       -                  .    .    . Captain John Seaman .    .    .    .    .    .    .
    -1670                 .    .    .    . Catherine |    .    .    .    .    .    .    .
1609-1682            Richard Haughton |————————————————————|.    .    .    .    .    .    .
```

Brother's Keeper: Timeline (partial).

Cumberland Tree
Version 3.3

Producer

Cumberland Software
Ira J. Lund
385 Idaho Springs Rd.
Clarksville, TN 37043
615 647 4012 (6-9PM weekdays, Central)

Basics

DOS
$40. Shareware
GEDCOM with registration
Manual on disk; printed with registration
Support by phone 615 647 4012 (6-9PM weekdays, Central) CompuServe 70713,3476 or by mail
Purchase from shareware store or download from BBS

Data Entry

Multiple databases, 10,000 names per database; eight marriages per individual, 20 children per marriage. Entry screen has place for sex, surname, record number, given name, date and place of birth, christening, death and burial, as well as LDS ordinances. Father's surname automatically inserted for child. Locations in one field limited to 32 characters separated by comma. Location will repeat if you insert its number. Pop-up list shows location numbers. Type in first few letters, then press F3 and pop-up list will begin with those letters. Supports foreign characters. Does not support single parents or illegitimacy. Parent must have spouse to enter a child. If second parent not known, create a blank spouse record. Dates can be entered in any format but only those entered day, month (in letters), year will be used for calculations for reports. One all-purpose note field limited to 10 lines. Record saved automatically when exiting. You cannot accidentally lose data but you also cannot ignore a record you decide you don't want.

Data Management

Main screen lists key individual, birth and death date, spouse, parents and children with their record numbers. "Tree" (T) will show four generation pedigree with birth dates. Continue down the tree by selecting "child" then choose name from pop-up list. Key person for main screen can be selected from pedigree. Record can be retrieved for editing by highlighting name on main screen and pressing enter. You can search by record number or name (surname with or without given name). Type a partial name and 10 names will be displayed starting with the combination you typed and continuing in alphabetical order. Can sort on names, places, birthdays, anniversaries and record numbers. Functions for rearranging children and spouses. Options for global change for all occurrences of a place name, to delete a unneeded place name or merge two place names.

Printed Charts

Supports dot matrix, laser and inkjet printers. Pedigree charts (four generations per sheet) and cascading pedigree chart, LDS and non-LDS family group sheets (maximum of 10 notes for one family group sheet), descendant charts (14 generations), timeline (editable with up to 50 people), ahnentafel (20 generations), birthday and anniversary lists, statistics, missing information, notes list, LDS submission forms and LDS ordinance check list. All reports are first printed to a file, and then can be printed or viewed on the screen. Report remains in the file until a new report is created. Up to 10 separate pedigree charts or 30 family group sheets may be printed at one time by entering marriage record numbers.

Other Features

Pull down menus. Help screens for most features. CSORT.EXE utility to fix corruption of any data in individual, marriage or place files.

Comments

Hard drive required. Well designed menus combined with help screens make the program very easy to use. Being able to view report before printing and reprinting same report without recreating is a nice feature. Benefits of registration: GEDCOM, printed enlarged manual and copies of two other shareware programs.

```
                      MISSING INFORMATION LIST

   Date: FEB  1,1993              "X" indicates Missing Information
                                  ------------------------------------
                                  Birth Birth Death Death Marr  Marr
   RIN  Name                      Date  Place Date  Place Date  Place
   =====================================================================
   0001 Joseph Brian BROWN              X     X     X
   0002 Sally Sue MARTIN                      X     X
   0003 Diane Kooi BROWN                      X     X
   0004 Joseph K BROWN                        X     X
   0005 George Robert BROWN                   X     X
   0006 Josephine SMITH                             X     X     X
   0007 Daniel John MARTIN              X           X           X
   0008 LIANG Kooi Lan                  X           X           X
   0009 Albert F SMITH                              X           X
   0010 Teresa Mary HANSEN                                      X
   0011 Hans Erik KNUDSEN                                 X     X
   0012 Magnhild Elfrida JOHANSDTR                        X     X
   0013 George Marvin SMITH                   X     X
   0014 Henrietta SMITH                       X     X
   0015 Frederick WATKINS         X     X     X     X     X     X
   0016 Elvira WATKINS            X     X     X     X
   0017 Marvin WATKINS            X     X     X     X
   0018 Emma BROWN                            X     X
   0019 Suzie BROWN                           X     X
   0020 Barbara BROWN                         X     X     X     X
   0022 Margaret ALDRIDGE         X     X     X     X
   0023 George E. DUNCAN          X     X     X     X     X     X
   0024 Sandra May CALDWELL       X     X     X     X
   0026 Jonathan CALDWELL         X     X     X     X     X     X
   0027 Eric Stuart FARNSWORTH    X     X     X     X     X     X
```

Cumberland Tree: Missing information list.

```
                       STATISTICS REPORT
                                        Date: FEB  1,1993
==========================================================================
INDIVIDUAL STATISTICS
--------------------------------------------------------------------------
Total Number of Individuals in Database:   28
              Number of Males:   14    50%
            Number of Females:   14    50%

              Number of deceased individuals:    7
Number of individuals with both birth and death dates:    7
              TOTAL Average Life Span:    71
              Male Average Life Span:     76
            Female Average Life Span:     68

Longest Life Span (Male)  :  78 yrs Hans Erik KNUDSEN
Longest Life Span (Female):  89 yrs Teresa Mary HANSEN

                    LIFE SPAN DISTRIBUTION
 Years: 0-10 11-20 21-30 31-40 41-50 51-60 61-70 71-80 81-90   90+
   Total   0    0     0     0     1     1     0     4     1     0
   Males   0    0     0     0     0     0     0     3     0     0
 Females   0    0     0     0     1     1     0     1     1     0

         Total Number of History Notes:    13
         Number of individuals with Notes:  3
         Average number of notes per person: 4

==========================================================================
MARRIAGE STATISTICS
--------------------------------------------------------------------------
     Total Number of Marriages in Database:   10
              Average age at marriage:   24
    Average Number of Children per marriage:    2

  NUMBER OF INDIVIDUALS WITH THE FOLLOWING NUMBER OF MARRIAGES
    No of Marriages:   0    1    2    3    4    5    6    7    8
    No of Individuals: 11   15   1    1    0    0    0    0    0

                     MARRIAGE AGE DISTRIBUTION
 Age at marriage: <15  15-20 21-25 26-30 31-40 41-50 51-60  60+
    No of individ:  0    3     2     5     0     0     0    0

              NUMBER OF CHILDREN PER MARRIAGE DISTRIBUTION
    No of Children:   0    1    2    3    4    5    6    7  8-12 13+
    No of Marriages:  1    5    1    2    1    0    0    0    0

==========================================================================
PLACE NAME STATISTICS
--------------------------------------------------------------------------
            TOTAL Number of Place names:    8
            Total number of place name uses:   28
         Average number of use per place name:   4
--------------------------------------------------------------------------
```

Cumberland Tree: Statistics report.

Everyone's Family Tree
Version 3.03A

Producer

The Dollarhide Systems
203 W. Holly St., Suite M4
Bellingham, WA 98225
800 733 3807 (orders only)

Basics

DOS
$169. Advanced version. Commercial; Free Demo ($99 Basic version 3.03B)
GEDCOM included in Advanced version only
Printed manual
Support by phone 206 671 3808; Prodigy XCVH42A
Purchase from producer or dealer

Data Entry

One database, but unlimited subfiles. Data entered in series of five screens: vitals — name, sex, title and reference (your own number or code); birth and christening — date plus four fields for location; residence — last known residence, date and address plus a field for date and location (LDS events appear here if you selected this option); death and burial — date and location; one all-purpose note area up to 64K (about 20 pages) per family and/or individual for biographical and source information. (Text editor does not support superscript, bold, underlining or italics.) LDS fields do not print in any reports. Marriage notes only print on the family group sheet. Names are entered individually, then linked via a pedigree screen. Name can be linked to spouse, father, mother or siblings. Linking correct person sometimes confusing if you have several people with the same name (manual suggests putting something unique in the reference field, linking the person, then deleting the reference). Macros for repeat information. Four date styles; supports "before", "after" and "about", other modifiers can be used to create "irregular" dates which may not display in Name List or transfer in GEDCOM.

Data Management

Three generation pedigree scanner screen to move up and down the generations. Name list displays all names in database. Can be sorted on surname, record number (assigned by computer) or reference number (user assigned). Can search for a surname or surname and given name (up to 28 characters searching from the left). Results of search can be printed. Name list can show surname and choice of two of the following: spouse, record number, reference number or one date (marriage, birth, christening, death or burial — selecting in that order with a date). Biography selection will produce a window with a biographical narrative including information from edit screens, spouse, parents and notes about the person. The notes can be edited from this screen. Family display will produce a screen identical to a printed family group sheet. The Descendancy selection produces a register format book on the screen. Further sorting of data, including by dates, can be done by transferring to GED (Genealogical Event Database). Children automatically arranged in a family by birth order.

Printed Charts

Pedigree charts (four or five generations) show full location, family group sheet, ahnentafel, individual summary, ancestor table, five blank forms, name finder lists and photo pedigree chart which can go from right to left or left to right. Descendancy report in book form with Register, Modified Register or Henry numbering systems. In narrative reports, the woman's maiden name will be placed in parentheses. In the descendancy report, only the name of a spouse and the spouse's parents print. Spouses' dates and individual notes do not print, but can be added to the notes for the family member. Reports can be sent to the printer, printed to disk in ASCII file or viewed on the screen. Blank charts are research log, reference (extract) sheet, research journal, correspondence log and individual record.

Other Features

Help screens. Research Log to record your sources of information. One line entry for book, page, event type (one letter code), year, place of event and type of record. Log can be printed for entire list, one person or group of persons from sorted list.

Comments

Hard drive is required for advanced version. The basic version will run on two floppies, but does not have GEDCOM or the Research Log and is limited to 1,200 people. Full credit is given if you want to upgrade from basic to advanced. Editor's Dark Horse selection in *Genealogical Computing*'s "Software to Beat" in 1991.

```
                Family Group - Louis and Carolina (Guth) Gressel
==================================================================
FATHER:

Louis Gressel
RIN #: 109
    b 9 Mar 1872 Scranton, Luzerne, PA
    d 31 Dec 1942 Philadelphia, Philadelphia, PA
    m Carolina (Lena) Guth Scranton, Lackawanna, PA

His Father: Johann Gressel    (1842-1884)
His Mother: Cecelia Kempter   (1851-1919)
==================================================================
MOTHER:

Carolina (Lena) Guth
RIN #: 110
    b 3 Apr 1876 Zweibruecken, Pfalz, Bav, Germany
    d 28 Apr 1929 Philadelphia, Philadelphia, PA
    m Louis Gressel Scranton, Lackawanna, PA

Her Father: Jacob Guth   (1848-1909)
Her Mother: Elisabetha (Elizabeth) Michel   (1857-1940)
==================================================================
CHILDREN:

1. William Joseph Gressel
   RIN #: 469
       b 23 Sep 1898 Scranton, Lackawanna, PA
       d 1976 St. Petersburg, Pinellas, FL
       m Marie Helnick
   ---------------------------------------------------------------
2. Frances Elizabeth Gressel
   RIN #: 468
       b 22 Nov 1900 Philadelphia, Philadelphia, PA
       d 1980 Philadelphia, Philadelphia, PA
       m John Roberts Philadelphia, Philadelphia, PA
   ---------------------------------------------------------------
3. Marie Cecelia Gressel
   RIN #: 91
       b 10 Nov 1901 Philadelphia, Philadelphia, PA
```

Everyone's Family Tree: Family group (part).

Descendants of Johann Peter Guth
==

1   Johann Peter Guth, son of Johann(es) Guth and of
        Catherine, born Jan 1719; died 1794 Zeiskam, Pfalz,
        Bavaria. He married (1) 15 Oct 1743, Zeiskam, Pfalz,
        Bavaria to Maria Barbara; and married (2) Zeiskam, Pfalz,
        Bavaria, to Eva Margaretha Frey, daughter of Abraham Frey
        and of Maria Margaretha; and married (3) Zeiskam, Pfalz,
        Bavaria, to Anna Apollonia von Gerichten, daughter of Johann
        Michael von Gerichten and of Anna Catherina; and married
        (4) Zeiskam, Pfalz, Bavaria to Anna Maria. !BIRTH,
        MARR 1,2,3,4, DEATH, BURIAL: Parish Register, Zeiskam;
        FHL #193,247.

        "The Palatine Immigrant", V. VIII, No. 4, p.213. Article,
        "The Guth Family of Zeiskam", submitted in 1988 by Ronald
        Guth of Ohio, a descendant through the 2nd wife.

        Occupation: Innkeeper

        Children of Johann Peter and Eva Margaretha (Frey) Guth
        were as follows:

        + 11   Johann Tobias Guth, born 8 May 1751.

        + 12   Eva Margaretha Guth, born 5 Jan 1753.

        + 13   Maria Eva Guth, born 12 Mar 1755.

        + 14   Johann Frederick Guth, born 10 Sep 1757.

        + 15   George Adam Guth, born 14 Jan 1760.

        + 16   Anna Catherina Guth, born 3 Apr 1762.

        Children of Johann Peter and Anna Apollonia (von Gerichten)
        Guth were as follows:

        + 17   Eva Catherina Guth, born 13 Feb 1764.

        + 18   Johannes Guth, born 28 Apr 1767.

        Children of Johann Peter and Anna Maria () Guth were as
        follows:

        + 19   Georg Guth, born 9 Jun 1774.

        + 1A   Johann Theobold Guth, born 30 Mar 1776.

==

Everyone's Family Tree: Descendancy report using the Henry numbering system.

Ancestors of Ernest Francis Neumann   printed February 11, 1993
==

                                                                        8 +-- Gustav Gottlieb Neumann
                                                                          | b 21 Mar 1831, Berlin, Brandenburg, Prussia
                                                                          | m Ruhla, Sach.-Co.-Gotha, Thu, Ger
                                                                          | d before 1879, Germany
                                                                          |
                                             4 +-- Berthold Neumann
                                               | b 17 Feb 1856, Ruhla, Sach.-Weim.-Eis., Thueringen, Ger
                                               | m Gotha, Sach.-Co.-Gotha, Thu, Ger
                                               | d 26 Mar 1921, Camden, Camden, NJ
                                               |
                                                                        9 +-- Adelheide Hossfeld
                                                                              b 21 Jul 1827, Ruhla, Thueringen
                                                                              d 4 Aug 1905, Philadelphia, Philadelphia, PA

                  2 +-- Ernst Franz Hugo Neumann
                    | b 23 Oct 1880, Gotha, Sachsen-Co-Gotha, Thueringen, Ger
                    | m Camden, Camden, NJ
                    | d 16 Feb 1941, Camden, Camden, NJ
                    |
                                                                       10 +-- Hermann Reinhold Wenige
                                                                          | b about 1821
                                                                          | m
                                                                          |
                                             5 +-- Anna Marie Minna Wenige
                                                     b 15 Dec 1857, Gotha, Sach.-Co.-Gotha, Thueringen, Ger
                                                     d 28 Sep 1898, Camden, Camden, NJ
                                                     |
                                                                       11 +-- Christiann Pempel
                                                                              b

1 +-- Ernest Francis Neumann
  | b 30 Jul 1904, Camden, Camden, NJ
  | m Marie Cecelia Gressel, Camden, Camden, NJ
  | d 5 Mar 1961, Camden, Camden, NJ
  |
                                                                       12 +-- Thomas William Watkins
                                                                          | b 1828, Southwark, Surrey, Eng
                                                                          | m Newington, Surrey, Eng
                                                                          | d about 1907, Eng
                                                                          |
                                             6 +-- George Nueces Watkins
                                               | b 23 Dec 1856, Newington, Surrey, Eng
                                               | m
                                               | d 5 Sep 1945, Lakeland, Camden, NJ
                                               |
                                                                       13 +-- Emma Cornock
                                                                              b 1829, Gloucestershire, England
                                                                              d after 1904, Eng

                  3 +-- Emma Cornock Watkins
                        b 4 Jun 1885, New York, New York, NY
                        d 4 Oct 1941, Camden, Camden, NJ
                        |
                                                                       14 +-- Patrick Ganly
                                                                          | b before 1825
                                                                          | m
                                                                          | d before 1885, Mayo, Ire
                                                                          |
                                             7 +-- Mary Elizabeth Ganly
                                                     b 17 Mar 1862, Aughamore, Mayo, Ire
                                                     d 23 Jun 1895, Stockton, Camden, NJ
                                                     |
                                                                       15 +-- Mary White
                                                                              b about 1829, Ire
                                                                              d 31 Oct 1884, Camden, Camden, NJ

Everyone's Family Tree: Pedigree chart showing full location details.

Family Connections

Producer

Quinsept, Inc.
P.O. Box 216
Lexington, MA 02173
800 637 7668

Basics

DOS
$125. Commercial
GEDCOM included
Printed manual
Support by phone 800 637 7668 (9AM-5PM M-F Eastern; off hours by appointment) by mail or CompuServe 72470,3027; GEnie S.VORENBERG; Prodigy CGMR62B
Purchase from producer or retail store

Data Entry

100,000 names, unlimited marriages per individual and children per marriage. No limit to number of events. Choice of events including user-defined and LDS. Notes and sources stored in separate unlimited size text file and displayed in biography. Supports foreign characters; no method of duplication of repeat information.

Data Management

Sorts by names, including Soundex, places, record numbers and dates. Relationship between two individuals can be shown in graphics form on the screen. On screen five generation pedigree chart from which you can select names for editing.

Printed Charts

Supports dot matrix, laser and inkjet printers. Prints family group sheets, alphabetical and chronological lists, including user-defined, five generation pedigree charts and cascading pedigree charts, calendars, historical events, tiny tafels. Reports can be sent to the printer, to a file on disk in ASCII format or viewed on the screen. Reports of less than 80 columns can be viewed on the screen can be edited and changes saved before printing.

Other Features

Help screens.

NOVEMBER 1992

Sun	Mon	Tue	Wed	Thu	Fri	Sat
1	2	3	4	5	6	7
8	9	10	11	12	13	14
15	16	17	18	19	20	21
22	23	24	25	26	27	28
29	30					

Birthdays

Day	Name	Age
17	MICHAEL GREGORY JOHNSTON	48
20	SUSAN CAROLYN VORENBERG	22
25	MARGARET RECTOR	108
26	LORRAINE SCHUMACHER	73

Family Connections: Birthday calendar report.

TIME-LINE for DUVALL DESCENDANTS

```
1851. . . . . . . . . . . . . . . . . . . . . . . . . . . 1851
  SEP 22 KATHERINE (KATE) RECTOR WAS BORN - FT SMITH AR
  SEP 22 The telegraph was first used by a railroad in Goshen, NY

1853. . . . . . . . . . . . . . . . . . . . . . . . . . . 1853
  JUN 30 SUSAN PAGE RECTOR WAS BORN - FT SMITH AR
  AUG 23 First bank clearinghouse was organized in New York City

1856. . . . . . . . . . . . . . . . . . . . . . . . . . . 1856
  JUN 17 Republican Party held first national convention (Phil.)
  JUL 22 HARRIET AMANDA RECTOR WAS MARRIED - FT SMITH AR

1858. . . . . . . . . . . . . . . . . . . . . . . . . . . 1858
  OCT 15 The Lincoln-Douglas debates ended in Illinois
  OCT 27 RH Macy & Co. opened its first store in New York City
  NOV 01 MARY W. (MINNIE) RECTOR WAS BORN - FT SMITH AR

1859. . . . . . . . . . . . . . . . . . . . . . . . . . . 1859
  JUN 11 A prospector found the Comstock Silver Lode in Nevada
  JUL 01 VIRGINIA DUVAL WAS MARRIED -
```

Family Connections: Time-line (FOOT.txt data merged with FOOTPRINTS IN HISTORY data).

Family History Program
Version 1.0

Producer

Brent Haberer
126 Crawford Circle
Golden, CO 80401
303 278 0988

Basics

DOS/WINDOWS
$35. Shareware
GEDCOM included
Help screens
Support by mail or on Prodigy TJJP55A
Purchase from producer; will be in shareware stores later in 1993

Data Entry

Newly developed program for Windows. Present version takes 10,000 names (next version one million), unlimited number of marriages per individual, 13 children per marriage (next version will be unlimited number of children). One note field per person; one per marriage and one reference field, each 4,000 characters. Reports can be sent to the printer, viewed on the screen or printed to disk in ASCII format.

Data Management

Sort by ID number or name. Custom query can be set up by user to sort on any field.

Printed Charts

Supports dot matrix, laser and inkjet printers. Prints pedigree charts (three generations per page) family group sheets, descendant charts, alphabetical lists and user-defined lists.

Comments

Windows is required to run this program. Setup procedure is for installation on a hard drive. Special request if you want to run from a floppy. Benefits of registration: automatically mailed fixes and enhancements and notified of new versions.

Family History System

Producer

Phillip E. Brown
834 Bahama Dr.
Tallahassee, FL 32311

Basics

DOS
$35. Shareware
GEDCOM included
Manual on disk
Support by mail or GEnie (Genealogy Roundtable, Category 2, Topic #7)
Download from bulletin boards

Data Entry

9999 records per file (see below for updated information). Surname, given name, ID number, sex, date and place of birth and death. Dates entered in numbers, i.e. 12/31/1992, but can also be in European style 31/12/1992. Very confusing as one cannot be sure which is the month and which is the day for first 12 days of a month: 3/9 could be March 9 or September 3. Place limited to 22 characters. Separate records for marriage, education, occupation, military, medical and address. Each record has a comment field which may be printed in family group report, indexed lists and ancestor, descendant and relative reports. Does not support "about", "circa", "after", or "before" dates. Can code primary source (*) or questionable (?). One field for indicating that a woman's surname be replaced by that of her most recent husband rather than maiden name in indexes and lists. Children and parents linked via record numbers. Hot key to repeat last used information in a field. Christening, burial and other event information can only be entered in comments area. Option to have adopted children treated as natural in printed reports.

Data Management

Search only on record number, surname or portion of surname, given name or a portion of the name, range of birth dates or range of death dates. Search for date based on numerical MM/DD format even though you may have selected the DD/MM format. Name search is case sensitive, i.e. if name is in database as JONES, it will not be found if you request Jones or jones.

Printed Charts

Some unusual and interesting charts. Ancestor, descendant and relative (ancestor and descendant together) reports in various formats including ahnentafel ("lineage number") and Henry ("bloodline") numbering systems. Descendant report can be grouped by families or generations. Relative report can also show relationship (common or civil rule) of each person to subject. Family group report in a fixed format or free form where all family information is together in a paragraph. Ancestor charts with four generations per chart or ancestor map with up to 53 generations. Map format compresses a lot of information onto one page. Descendant charts in boxes for up to 99 generations. Choice of information included in charts. Reports can be sent to the printer, to a disk file in ASCII format or viewed on screen.

Other Features

Built-in date calculator which will display a month and year, calculate numbers of years, month and days between two dates and convert between old style and new style dates. Two sample bases including British royal family.

Utility for verifying data: sex of spouses, dates, age, age at marriage, age of spouse, different name from father, marriage of parents at time of child's birth, etc. Can select part of a database for GEDCOM transfer.

Comments

Basic program with many limitations including limited choice of events, short place field, limited sorting fields and small number of charts. Long (99 page) manual on disk in 17 separate files as well as 12 other document files. Technical explanations on how program works which might be of interest after using the program for a while, but the user needs a short, to-the-point instruction on how to enter data. Moving around on menus usually has to be done using precise keys, usually function keys or tab and shift-tab. Cannot arrow down a list to make a selection or even move back in the date field with the arrow keys. When you press the wrong key, a buzzer sounds.

Available on CompuServe as FHSB1.ZIP and FHSB2.ZIP and on GEnie as FHSDSKB1.ZIP and FHSDSKB2.ZIP. These files must be unzipped onto floppies and then installed on your hard drive from the floppies. If installing from A to C (which is a hard drive), A must be the default, you must type (in caps) GO INSTALL HD A C. No other combination will work. This will create a directory on your C drive called FAMILY where the program will be installed.

Update: As this book was being packaged to go to the publisher, we received information on a new update that has just been released. The number of names has been increased to 32,000 with no limit on the number of children or marriages. When ordering from the producer, the basic program costs $10 for the disks with a manual on disk (118 plus 56 pages). The registration fee is $35. which includes an additional diskette with programs for extended options. (For registered users wishing to order the updated version, the charge is $15.) Reports from the basic system include ancestor (fixed, free and lifeline format), descendant (fixed and free format with either family or generation grouping) relative report (free format), blank family group worksheet, individual family group (fixed and free format), merged family group (fixed and free), blank ancestor chart, 4 generation ancestor chart, all generation ancestor MAP, descendant charts (vertical or horizontal arrangement), structure diagram descendant chart giving just the child number for an overall view of the family structure, horizontal box chart, family path chart showing path of relationships connecting two individuals and data validation report. The extended system adds an index for merged group reports, index sequence listing (list by surname, given name, birth date, death date or marriage date), summary reports by surname, ancestors, descendants or relationships and tiny tafel. The new version provides more complete controls over the formatting of the report page and an expanded address field. A chart summary report shows the basic structure of the chart and the number of "strips" required for the chart. More uniform use is made of function keys in the report printing programs. The basic program utility functions include change file name table, screen color and printer controls; GEDCOM import and export, validate file structure, dates and data relationships; interface to shareware HP Laserjet utility 4PRINT (allows landscape printing for the HP Laserjet, Deskjet and compatible printers — $49 registration fee to Korenthal Associates) and date calculator. The extended utility includes relationship calculator; extended search functions including Soundex; create sorted or relationship sequenced index files; tiny tafel files and reports, import/export using FHS GEDCOM format file and export name and address information to a mail merge ASCII file.

```
                  ++++ 64 Franz DUKE OF SAXE-COBURG-,b.15 Jul 1750,d. 9 Dec 1806 at age  56
              ++++ 32 Ernst I DUKE OF SAXE-COBURG,b. 2 Jan 1784,d.29 Jan 1844 at age  60
              |   ++++ 65 Auguste Caroline Sophie OF REUSS-EBERSDORF,b. 9 Jan 1757,d.16 Nov 1831 at age  74
          ++++ 16 Albert PRINCE CONSORT,b.26 Aug 1819,d.14 Dec 1861 at age  42
          |   |   ++++ 66 Emil Leopold August DUKE OF SAXE-GOTHA-A,b.23 Nov 1772,d.17 May 1822 at age  49
          |   ++++ 33 Dorothea Luise Pauline OF SAXE-GOTHA,b.21 Dec 1800,d.30 Aug 1831 at age  30
          |       ++++ 67 Luise OF MECKLENBURG-SCHWE,b.19 Nov 1779,d. 4 Jan 1801 at age  21
      ++++ 8 Edward VII KING OF UK,b. 9 Nov 1841,d. 6 Mar 1910 at age  68
      |   |       ++++ 68 George III KING OF GB (same as 44)
      |   |   ++++ 34 Edward DUKE OF KENT,b. 2 Nov 1767,d.23 Jan 1820 at age  52
      |   |   |   ++++ 69 Charlotte OF MECKLENBURG-STREL (same as 45)
      |   ++++ 17 Victoria QUEEN OF UK,b.24 May 1819,d.22 Jan 1901 at age  81
      |       |   ++++ 70 Franz DUKE OF SAXE-COBURG- (same as 64)
      |       ++++ 35 Victoria OF SAXE-COBURG-SAALF,b.17 Aug 1786,d.16 Mar 1861 at age  74
      |           ++++ 71 Auguste Caroline Sophie OF REUSS-EBERSDORF (same as 65)
  ++++ 4 George V KING OF UK,b. 3 Jun 1865,d.20 Jan 1936 at age  70
  |   |           ++++ 72 Friedrich Karl DUKE OF SCHLESWIG-HO
  |   |       ++++ 36 Wilhelm DUKE OF SCHLESWIG-HO,b. 4 Jan 1785,d.17 Feb 1831 at age  46
  |   |       |   ++++ 73 Friedericke Amalie VON SCHLIEBEN
  |   |   ++++ 18 Christain IX KING OF DENMARK,b. 8 Apr 1818,d.29 Jan 1906 at age  87
  |   |   |   |   ++++ 74 Karl LG OF HESSE-CASSEL,b.19 Dec 1744,d.17 Aug 1836 at age  91
  |   |   |   ++++ 37 Louise Caroline OF HESSE-CASSEL,b.28 Sep 1789,d.13 Mar 1867 at age  77
  |   |   |       ++++ 75 Louise OF DENMARK,b.30 Jan 1750,d.12 Jan 1831 at age  80
  |   ++++ 9 Alexandra OF DENMARK,b. 1 Dec 1844,d.20 Nov 1925 at age  80
  |       |       ++++ 76 Friedrich OF HESSE-CASSEL (same as 46)
  |       |   ++++ 38 Wilhelm OF HESSE-CASSEL,b.24 Dec 1787,d. 5 Sep 1867 at age  79
  |       |   |   ++++ 77 Caroline Polyxene OF NASSAU-USINGEN,b. 4 Apr 1762,d.18 Aug 1823 at age  61
  |       ++++ 19 Louise Wilhelmina OF HESSE-CASSEL,b. 7 Sep 1817,d.29 Sep 1898 at age  81
  |           |   ++++ 78 Frederik PRINCE OF DENMARK,b.11 Oct 1753,d. 7 Dec 1805 at age  52
  |           ++++ 39 Louise Charlotte OF DENMARK,b.30 Oct 1789,d.28 Mar 1864 at age  74
  |               ++++ 79 Sophie Frederike OF MECKLENBURG-SCHWE,b.24 Aug 1758,d.29 Nov 1794 at age  36
  ++++ 2 George VI KING OF UK,b.14 Dec 1895,d. 6 Feb 1952 at age  56
  |   |               ++++ 80 Friedrich Eugen DUKE OF WURTTEMBERG,b.21 Jan 1732,d.22 Dec 1797 at age  65
  |   |           ++++ 40 Ludwig Friedrich Alexander GENERAL OF CALVALRY,b.30 Aug 1756,d.20 Sep 1817 at age  61
  |   |           |   ++++ 81 Friedricke Sophie OF BRANDENBURG-SCHWE,b.18 Dec 1736,d. 7 Mar 1798 at age  61
  |   |       ++++ 20 Alexander OF TECK,b. 9 Sep 1804,d. 4 Jul 1885 at age  80
  |   |       |   |   ++++ 82 Karl Christain PRINCE OF NASSAU-WEI,b.16 Jan 1735,d.28 Nov 1788 at age  53
  |   |       |   ++++ 41 Henriette OF NASSAU-WEILBURG,b.22 Apr 1780,d. 2 Jan 1857 at age  76
  |   |       |       ++++ 83 Wilhelmina Caroline OF ORANGE & NASSAU-D,b.28 Feb 1743,d. 6 May 1787 at age  44
  |   |   ++++ 10 Francis PRINCE OF TECK,b.27 Aug 1837,d.20 Jan 1900 at age  62
  |   |   |   |   ++++ 42 Laszlo COUNT RHEDEY DE KIS-
  |   |   |   ++++ 21 Claudine COUNTESS VON HOHENST,b.21 Sep 1812,d. 1 Oct 1841 at age  29
  |   |   |       |   ++++ 86 Gregor BARON INCZEDY DE NAG
  |   |   |       ++++ 43 Agnes
  |   ++++ 5 Victoria Mary OF TECK,b.26 May 1867,d.24 Mar 1953 at age  85
  |       |           ++++ 88 Frederick DUKE OF EDINBURGH,b.20 Jan 1707,d.20 Mar 1751 at age  44
  |       |       ++++ 44 George III KING OF GB,b. 4 Jun 1738,d.29 Jan 1820 at age  81
  |       |       |   ++++ 89 Augusta OF SAXE-GOTHA-ALTENB,b.30 Nov 1719,d. 8 Feb 1772 at age  52
  |       |   ++++ 22 Adolphus DUKE OF CAMBRIDGE,b.24 Feb 1774,d. 8 Jul 1850 at age  76
  |       |   |   ++++ 45 Charlotte OF MECKLENBURG-STREL,b.19 May 1744,d.17 Nov 1818 at age  74
  |       ++++ 11 Mary Adelaide OF GREAT BRITAIN,b.22 Nov 1833,d.27 Oct 1897 at age  63
  |           |       ++++ 92 Friedrich II LG OF HESSE-CASSEL,b.14 Aug 1720,d.31 Oct 1785 at age  65
  |           |   ++++ 46 Friedrich OF HESSE-CASSEL,b.11 Sep 1747,d.20 May 1837 at age  89
  |           |   |   ++++ 93 Mary OF GREAT BRITAIN,b.22 Feb 1723,d.14 Jan 1772 at age  48
  |           ++++ 23 Auguste Wilhelmine OF HESSE-CASSEL,b.25 Jul 1797,d. 6 Apr 1889 at age  91
+++ 1 Elizabeth II QUEEN OF UK,b.21 Apr 1926
  |   ++++ 6 Claude George BOWES-LYON
  ++++ 3 Elizabeth Angela Marguerite BOWES-LYON,b. 4 Aug 1900
```

Family History System: Ancestor map showing ancestors of Queen Elizabeth II.

```
+++++++++++++++++   +++++++++++++++++   +++++++++++++++++   +++++++++++++++++   +++++++++++++++++
+++Edward III   | +++++1.Lionel of Ant+++++1.Philippa    | +++++1.Roger, Earl o+++++1.Edmund, Earl|
|  KING OF ENGLA| |  DUKE OF CLARE| |  COUNTESS OF U| |  MORTIMER     | |  MORTIMER     |
|b.13 Nov 1312  | |d. ??? 1368    | |d. ??? 1382    | |d. ??? 1398    | |d. ??? 1425    |
|d.21 Jun 1377  | |+++++++++++++++| |+++++++++++++++| |+++++++++++++++| |+++++++++++++++|
|+++++++++++++++| |s.Violante     | |s.Edmund, Earl | |s.Eleanor      | |s.Anne         |
|s.Philippa     | |  VISCONTI     | |  MORTIMER     | |  HOLLAND      | |  STAFFORD     |
|  OF HAINAULT  | |d. ??? 1404    | |d. ??? 1381    | |d. ??? 1405    | +++++++++++++++++
|b. ??? 1314    | |+++++++++++++++| +++++++++++++++++ +++++++++++++++++ |
|m.24 Jan 1328  | |s.Elizabeth    |                                     +++2.Anne         |
|d.14 Aug 1369  | |  DE BURGH     |                                     |  MORTIMER     |
+++++++++++++++++ |d. ??? 1362    |                                     |+++++++++++++++|
                  |+++++++++++++++|                                     |s.Richard      |
                  |+++++++++++++++| +++++++++++++++++                   |  EARL OF CAMBR|
                  +++2.Edward     | +++++1.Richard II   |               |d. ??? 1415    |
                  |  THE BLACK PRI| |  KING OF ENGLA|                   +++++++++++++++++
                  |b. ??? 1330    | |b. ??? 1367    |
                  |d. ??? 1376    | |d. ??? 1399    |
                  |+++++++++++++++| +++++++++++++++++
                  |s.Joan         |
                  |  OF KENT      |
                  |b. ??? 1328    |
                  |d. ??? 1385    |
                  |+++++++++++++++|
                  |+++++++++++++++| +++++++++++++++++   +++++++++++++++++   +++++++++++++++++
                  +++3.John of Gaunt+++++1.Joan        | +++++1.Cecily     | +++++1.George    |
                  |  DUKE OF LANCA| |  BEAUFORT     | |  NEVILLE      | |  DUKE OF CLARE|
                  |b. Mar 1340    | |+++++++++++++++| |+++++++++++++++| |d. ??? 1478    |
                  |d. 3 Feb 1399  | |s.James I      | |s.Richard      | |+++++++++++++++|
                  |+++++++++++++++| |  KING OF SCOTS| |  DUKE OF YORK | |s.Isabel       |
                  |s.Catherine    | |b. Dec 1394    | |d. ??? 1460    | |  NEVILLE      |
                  |  SWYNFORD     | |m. ??? 1424    | +++++++++++++++++ |d. ??? 1476    |
                  |b. ??? 1350    | |d.21 Feb 1437  |                   +++++++++++++++++
                  |m.13 Jan 1396  | |+++++++++++++++|                   |
                  |d.10 May 1403  | |s.Ralph        |                   +++2.Edward IV    |
                  |+++++++++++++++| |  NEVILLE      |                   |  KING OF ENGLA|
                  |s.Constanza    | +++++++++++++++++                   |b. ??? 1442    |
                  |  OF CASTILE   | +++++++++++++++++                   |d. 9 Apr 1483  |
                  |d. ??? 1394    | +++2.Philippa    |                   |+++++++++++++++|
                  |+++++++++++++++| |               |                   |s.Elizabeth    |
                  |s.Blanche      | |b. ??? 1360    |                   |  WOODVILLE    |
                  |  OF LANCASTER | |d. ??? 1415    |                   |b. ??? 1437    |
                  |b. ??? 1341    | |+++++++++++++++|                   |m. ??? 1464    |
                  |d. ??? 1369    | |s.John         |                   |d. ??? 1492    |
                  +++++++++++++++++ |  KING OF PORTU|                   |+++++++++++++++|
                                    +++++++++++++++++                   |+++++++++++++++|
                                                                        +++3.Richard III  |
                                                                        |  KING OF ENGLA|
                                                                        |b. 2 Oct 1452  |
                                                                        |d.22 Aug 1485  |
                                                                        |+++++++++++++++|
                                                                        |s.Anne         |
                                                                        |  NEVILLE      |
                                                                        |m. ??? 1472    |
                                                                        |d. ??? 1485    |
                                                                        +++++++++++++++++
```

Family History System: Descendant box chart.

```
Descendant Report for: Edward III KING OF ENGLAND
Prepared: 23 Jan 1993
    RELATION              NAME                          AGE  --- BORN --  --- DIED --

                  Edward III KING OF ENGLAND            64   13 Nov 1312  21 Jun 1377
Son             1 Lionel of Antwerp DUKE OF CLARENCE                      ??? 1368
gDaughter       . 1 Philippa COUNTESS OF ULSTER                           ??? 1382
ggSon           . . 1 Roger, Earl of March MORTIMER                       ??? 1398
g2gSon          . . . 1 Edmund, Earl of March MORTIMER                    ??? 1425
g2gDaughter     . . . 2 Anne MORTIMER
Son             2 Edward THE BLACK PRINCE               46   ??? 1330     ??? 1376
gSon            . 1 Richard II KING OF ENGLAND          32   ??? 1367     ??? 1399
Son             3 John of Gaunt DUKE OF LANCASTER       58   Mar 1340     3 Feb 1399
gDaughter       . 1 Joan BEAUFORT
ggDaughter      . . 1 Cecily NEVILLE
g2gSon          . . . 1 George DUKE OF CLARENCE                           ??? 1478
g2gSon          . . . 2 Edward IV KING OF ENGLAND       41   ??? 1442     9 Apr 1483
g2gSon          . . . 3 Richard III KING OF ENGLAND     32   2 Oct 1452   22 Aug 1485
ggSon           . . 2 Richard NEVILLE                                     ??? 1460
g2gSon          . . . 1 John NEVILLE
g2gSon          . . . 2 George, Archbishop of York NEVILL
g2gSon          . . . 3 Richard NEVILLE
ggSon           . . 3 James II KING OF SCOTS                              ??? 1460
g2gSon          . . . 1 James III KING OF SCOTS                           ??? 1488
ggDaughter      . . 4 Annabelle (Lady) STEWART
gDaughter       . 2 Philippa                            55   ??? 1360     ??? 1415
gSon            . 3 Henry IV KING OF ENGLAND            46   Apr 1366     20 Mar 1413
```

Family History System: Descendant report, family arrangement, fixed format.

```
                  Edward III King of England, Born 13 Nov 1312 in Windsor Castle, Died 21 Jun
                  1377 in London at age 64
        1         Lionel of Antwerp Duke of Clarence, Died ??? 1368
        2         Edward The Black Prince, Born ??? 1330, Died ??? 1376 at age 46
10>     3         John of Gaunt Duke of Lancaster, Born Mar 1340 in Ghent, Flanders, Died 3 Feb
                  1399 in London at age 58
        4         Edmund of Langley Duke of York, Born ??? 1341, Died ??? 1402 at age 61
    1   1         Philippa Countess of Ulster, Died ??? 1382
    2   1         Richard II King of England, Born ??? 1367, Died ??? 1399 at age 32
    3   1         Joan BEAUFORT
    3   2         Philippa, Born ??? 1360, Died ??? 1415 at age 55
    3   3         Henry IV King of England, Born Apr 1366, Died 20 Mar 1413 at age 46
    3   4         Catherine, Born ??? 1372, Died ??? 1418 at age 46
    3   5         John, Marquess of Dorset BEAUFORT, Born ??? 1373, Died 16 Mar 1410 in St
20>               Katherine by the To at age 37
    4   1         Richard Earl of Cambridge, Died ??? 1415
  1 1   1         Roger, Earl of March MORTIMER, Died ??? 1398
  3 1   1         Cecily NEVILLE
  3 1   2         Richard NEVILLE, Died ??? 1460
  3 1   3         James II King of Scots, Died ??? 1460
  3 1   4         Annabelle (Lady) STEWART
  3 3   1         Henry V King of England, Born ??? 1387, Died 31 Aug 1422 at age 35
  3 5   1         Henry, Earl of Somerset BEAUFORT, Born ??? 1401, Died ??? 1418 at age 17
  3 5   2         John, Duke of Somerset BEAUFORT, Born ??? 1403, Died ??? 1444 at age 41
30> 4 1 1         Richard Duke of York, Died ??? 1460
  1 1 1 1         Edmund, Earl of March MORTIMER, Died ??? 1425
  1 1 1 2         Anne MORTIMER
  3 1 1 1         George Duke of Clarence, Died ??? 1478
```

Family History System: Descendant report, generation arrangement, free form format.

Family Origins
Version 2.0

Producer

Parsons Technology
One Parsons Drive
P. O. Box 100
Hiawatha, Iowa 52233-0100
800 223 6925 (Orders only)

Basics

DOS
$49. Commercial; Free demo
GEDCOM included
Printed manual
Support by phone 319 395 7314 (8:30AM-9PM, M-F; 9AM-1PM Sat., Central), Fax: 319 395 9600; CompuServe 75300,631 (GO PCVENC forum, Parsons Technology section); GEnie T.PARSONS6 (IBM RoundTable, Category 31)
Purchase from producer, retail store or dealer

Data Entry

255 separate databases per directory, 30,000 individuals per database, 60,000 notes, 60,000 sources, 10 spouses per individual, 22 children per marriage. Supports mouse, LDS events (can suppress if not needed), accepts double dates. Does not support foreign characters. Main screen is three generation pedigree chart, which can be expanded to five generations. Highlight individual and select from menu to add spouse, children, parents or unlinked person. Individual screens have fields for surname, given names, sex, title, your own ID number/letters (optional), born, christened (can be changed to baptized, blesses, bar/bas mitzvah), died, buried date and place (63 characters). Date modifiers can only be ABT, AFT, BEF and BET. Choice of four date styles. Three user-defined fields for which the label can be selected from a list or create your own. Eight user-defined flags (for keeping track of family traits). Each event or the entire record can have three sources and a note each up to 20,000 characters. Marriage record asks for date, place, status and end date. Very easy to move around in the program. Main menu at the top must be displayed with [/] symbol. Status line at bottom for adding, editing, finding, moving to spouses or siblings or children, on edit screen for adding notes, sources, additional events. Help screens also refer to additional help screens. Hot keys can be created for duplicating information. Sources can be reused with a hot key. No checks on data quality (if person lived 150 years or died before his/her child was born).

Data Management

"Find" displays an alphabetical list on left of screen. On right is displayed name, birth, christening, death, burial information and parents' names. Search for duplicate records. Facility for rearranging order of children and spouses. Any other sorting comes under the print routine, customized report, which allows sorting on a field. Can also print a list of unlinked individuals. Function for merging two records.

Printed Charts

Supports dot matrix, laser, inkjet and deskjet printers. Pedigree charts (four generations on one sheet or multiple generations on cascading charts) in box charts, shadow boxes or no boxes; family group records with or without notes and sources; descendant chart with or without spouses with choice of boxes as above; ancestor chart (up to 30 generations with box choices as above) with eight generations or more on the width of one sheet without boxes (name, birth and death year only); summary for individual or family, custom design where you sort on different fields; modified register (book) form for descendants of one individual; ahnentafel (detailed ancestor report in narrative form). Modified register puts the event information in narrative style but does not incorporate notes or sources into the text. If notes/sources are included (optional) they are indicated with bracketed numbers [N2], [S1], etc. and notes and sources appear at the end. Alphabetical index refers to individual reference number, not page. List of unlinked individuals and index of data (list of every individual noting whether you entered a date, place, note and source for each individual event). LDS ordinance forms for temple submission and list of unfinished ordinances for individuals and marriages. Reports can be sent to the printer, saved to disk or viewed on the screen.

Other Features

Option to display surnames in uppercase or as they were entered. Can import and export text files from/to other word processors.

Comments

Very easy to use. Limited in searching capabilities. Register format a nice optional way to print information, but not satisfactory for a book as it does not incorporate text material. User could put biographical information in the notes file, then use a word processor to cut and paste into the report. Formerly marketed as AncestralLink by FormalSoft of Sandy, UT.

```
Charles Blaine Neister (1884-1960)
    │                   ┌─Edward Shipman (-1697)
    │               ┌─William Shipman (1656-1725)
    │               │   └─Elizabeth Comstock (1632-1659)
    │           ┌─Stephen Shipman (1698-1746)
    │           │   │   ┌─Benjamin Hand (-)
    │           │   └─Alice Hand (1669-)
    │           │       └─Elizabeth Whittier (-)
    │       ┌─Daniel Shipman (1732-1809)
    │       │   │   ┌─Thomas Pellet (-)
    │       │   └─Mary Pellett (1690-1746)
    │   ┌─David Shipman (1772-1827)
    │   │   │       ┌─Richard Haughton (1609-1682)
    │   │   │   ┌─Sampson Haughton (-1717)
    │   │   │   │   └─Catherine (-1670)
    │   │   ┌─EbenezerHorton/ Haughton (1699-)
    │   │   │   └─Sarah (-1760)
    │   │   └─Kezia Horton (1739-1807)
    │   │       └─Kasiah (-)
    │ ┌─Charles Shipman (1814-1895)
    │ │     │       ┌─Captain John Seaman (-)
    │ │     │   ┌─Jonathan Seaman (1647-)
    │ │     │   │   └─Elizabeth Strickland (-)
    │ │     │ ┌─Caleb Seaman (-1777)
    │ │     │ │   └─Jane (-)
    │ │     ┌─Caleb Seaman (1740-1820)
    │ │     └─ElizabethSimmons/ Seaman (1779-)
    │ │         └─Martha Jackson (1758-)
    └─Elizabeth Shipman (1849-1932)
      │             ┌─Richard Truesdell (1672-1707)
      │         ┌─William Truesdell (1700-1750)
      │         │   └─Mary Richards (1675-1732)
      │     ┌─William Truesdell (1722-1784)
      │     │   │   ┌─John Tyler (-)
      │     │   └─Martha Tyler (1702-)
      │     │       └─Hannah Stent (-)
      │   ┌─Justin Truesdell (1755-1803)
      │   │   │   ┌─William Jeason (-)
      │   │   └─Deliverance Jeason (-)
      │ ┌─William Truesdell (1797-1869)
      │ │     ┌─George Gardiner (1740-1816)
      │ │   └─Ann Gardiner (1774-1822)
      └─Ann Truesdell (1819-1891)
        └─Ann Nancy (-)
```

Family Origins: Ancestor chart without boxes.

Ancestors of Charles Blaine Neister   27 Jan 1993

```
          ┌─ Johannes Christian Nuchter (1771-)
    ┌─ Joseph Nichter (1805-1854)
    │     └─ Anna Katharina Wiegand (-)
 ┌─ Peter David Neister (1846-1914)
 │        ┌─ Jacques Philipp Ruch (1780-1838)
 │  └─ Salamina (Salome) Ruch (1813-1891)
 │        └─ Margaretha Lindenmann (1778-1823)
Charles Blaine Neister (1884-1960)
 │        ┌─ David Shipman (1772-1827)
 │  ┌─ Charles Shipman (1814-1895)
 │  │     └─ ElizabethSimmons/ Seaman (1779-)
 └─ Elizabeth Shipman (1849-1932)
          ┌─ William Truesdell (1797-1869)
    └─ Ann Truesdell (1819-1891)
          └─ Ann Nancy (-)
```

Family Origins: Ancestor chart with shadow boxes.

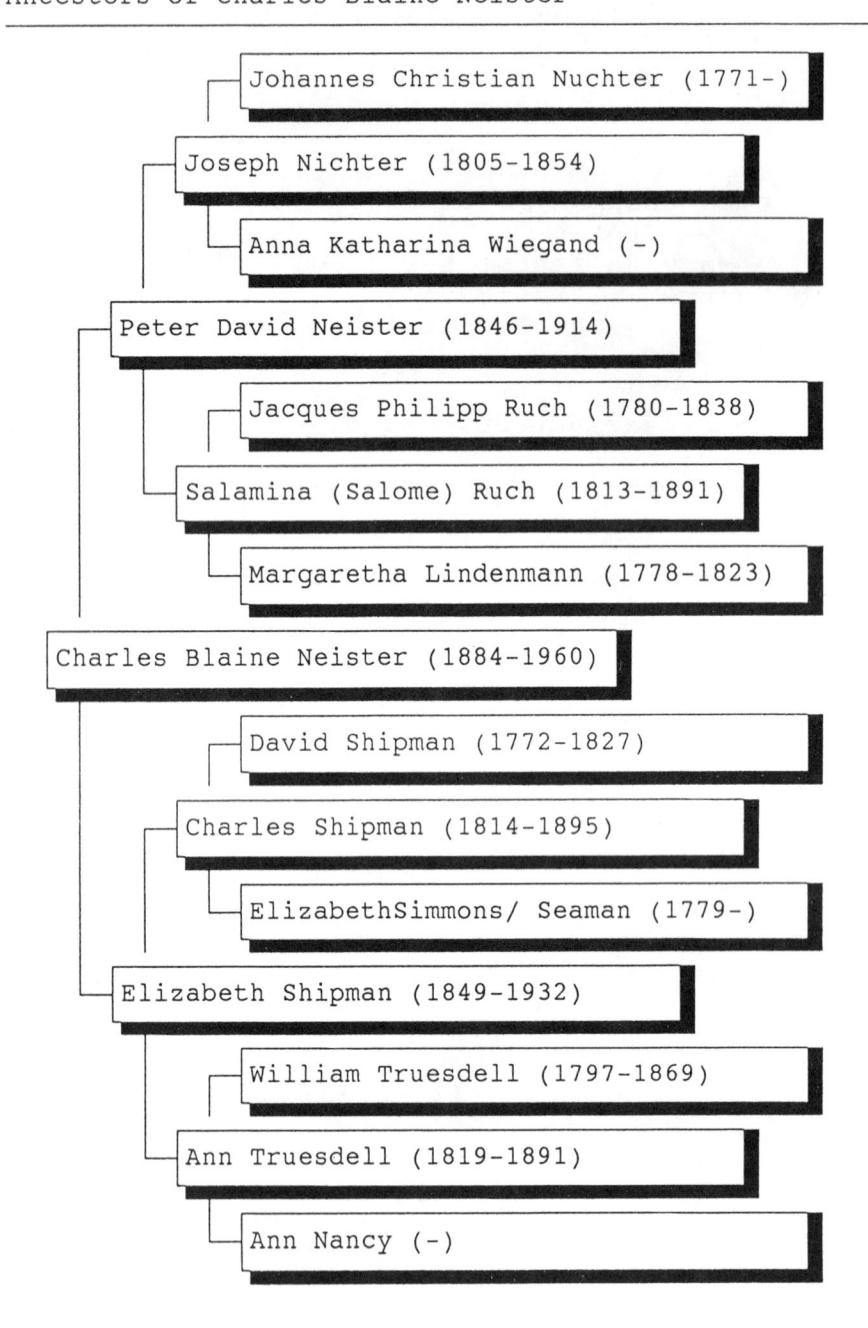

FIRST GENERATION

1. Daniel Shipman [S1] was born on 13 Mar 1732/1733 in E. Hartford, CT; died on 27 Apr 1809 in Leeds, Ont., Can.; buried in Augusta, Ont., Can..

He married Kezia Horton on 1759 in Colchester, CT [S2,S3]. Kezia Horton was born on ABT 1739; died on 21 Mar 1807 in Leeds, Ont., Can.; buried in Augusta, Ont., Can..

They had the following children:

2	i.	Levinia Shipman was born on 20 Nov 1760.
3	ii.	Ezekial Shipman was born on 17 Oct 1762 [S1]; died on 25 Jun 1843 in Leeds, Ont., Can. [S4]; buried in Brockville, Ont., Can., Read Cem..
4	iii.	Samuel Shipman was born on 17 Jan 1764; died on 8 Dec 1831 in Yonge, Ont., Can..
5	iv.	Keziah (Thirzah) Shipman was born on 5 Apr 1767.
6	v.	Daniel Shipman was born on 24 Jul 1769 [S1]; died on 8 Apr 1832 in Oxford, Grenville Co, Ont., Can..
+7	vi.	David Shipman

He also married Ann Chamberlain on ABT 1808. Ann Chamberlain was born on ABT 1758; died on 8 Jan 1839.

SECOND GENERATION

7. David Shipman was born on 7 Apr 1772 in E. Hartford, CT [S1]; died on AFT 1827.

He married Elizabeth Simmons/ Seaman on BEF 1799. Elizabeth Simmons/ Seaman was born on 1779 in Amenia, NY; died in Maitland, Ont.

They had the following children:

8	i.	David Shipman was born on 1800; died on 6 Mar 1879 in Leeds Co., Ont..
9	ii.	Sarah Shipman was born on BEF 1801.
10	iii.	Fanny Shipman was born on ABT 1805; died on ABT 1808.
11	iv.	Minerva (Minera) Shipman was born on AFT 1807.
+12	v.	Charles Shipman

THIRD GENERATION

12. Charles Shipman was born on 21 Mar 1814 in Maitland, Ont., Can.; died

---

Family Origins: Modified Register report.

Descendants of David Shipman

```
David Shipman
b 7 Apr 1772-E. Hartford, CT
d AFT        1827
 ||
Elizabeth Simmons/ Seaman
b 1779-Amenia, NY
m BEF        1799
d -Maitland, Ont
    |
    |---David Shipman
    |   b 1800
    |   d 6 Mar 1879-Leeds Co., Ont.
    |
    |---Sarah Shipman
    |   b BEF        1801
    |
    |---Fanny Shipman
    |   b ABT        1805
    |   d ABT        1808
    |
    |---Minerva (Minera) Shipman
    |   b AFT        1807
    |
    |---Charles Shipman
        b 21 Mar 1814-Maitland, Ont., Can.
        d 28 Jun 1895-Leeds, Ont., Can.
         ||
        Ann Truesdell
        b 25 Feb 1819-Quebec, Can.
        m 5 Oct 1846-Leeds, Ont., Can.
        d 6 Nov 1891-Leeds, Ont., Can.
            |
            |---Mary Shipman
                b 2 Sep 1847
                d 27 Dec 1869
```

Family Origins: Descendant chart with boxes.

Family Reunion

Producer

FAMware
1580 East Dawn Dr.
Salt Lake City, UT 84121
801 943 6908

Basics

DOS
$59.95 suggested retail; Demo $5.
GEDCOM additional $12.
Manual on disk
Support by phone 801 943 6908 (8:30AM-4:30PM Mountain, Mon-Fri)
Purchase at retail stores (may have discounted price) or mail order

Data Entry

32,768 names per database; up to 16 databases per path; three marriages per individual, 20 children per marriage. Eight fields with a choice of 113 events, including LDS and user-defined. Foreign characters supported. One note field.

Data Management

Sort on places, record numbers or any field. Utility to convert dates from one format to another.

Printed Charts

Supports dot matrix and laser printers. Prints pedigree charts (four-six generations per page) and can create a wall chart pedigree, family group sheets, descendant charts, alphabetical and chronological lists, ahnentafel and user-defined lists. Address labels and birthday lists. Printing can be done to disk in ASCII format.

Other Features

Help screens. Notepad feature.

Comments

Version 4.0 expected to be released in Spring, 1993 and will cost $89.95. It will include the Tree Easy program (see separate listing). Will handle twice as many records, have a larger surname field, database file for alphabetical access to records, mouse support. Improved reports include three, four, five and six generation pedigree charts, family group sheets, family facts sheets, descendant charts by generation and by family, multi-generation wall chart, new fancy screen displays, multi-generation "Extended Family" screen. Requires hard disk drive, color display and graphics adapter.

Family Roots

Producer

Quinsept, Inc.
P.O. Box 216
Lexington, MA 02173
800 637 7668

Basics

DOS, Macintosh, Apple II, Commodore 64, Commodore 128
$225.; MAC $180. Commercial
GEDCOM additional $35.
Printed manual
Support by phone 800 637 7668 (9AM-5PM M-F Eastern; off hours by appointment) by mail or CompuServe 72470,3027; GEnie S.VORENBERG; Prodigy CGMR62B
Purchase from producer or retail store

Data Entry

Eight million names, unlimited marriages per person and children per marriage. Choice of events, including user-defined and LDS. Supports foreign characters. Note field, unlimited size, for each event plus separate file for biographical information which prints on the family group sheet or person sheet.

Data Management

Sorts by name and record number.

Printed Charts

Supports dot matrix, laser and inkjet printers. Prints two types of pedigree charts with four or five generations on a page and cascading pedigree charts, two types of family group sheets, descendant chart, alphabetical and user-defined lists and ahnentafel. Add-on utility for box charts and multiple page wall chart style pedigree chart. Reports can be sent to the printer, to a disk file in ASCII format or viewed on the screen.

Other Features

Extensive customizing possible.

Comments

New version 4.0 due out in June 1993 for DOS and Macintosh. In addition to the standard events in the individual record, it will have 26 user-defined events and in the marriage record there will be four user-defined events in addition to the standard ones. There will be ditto and repeat keys and 36 function keys for rapid editing. Enhanced printing capabilities including user-defined templates for family group sheets, book form with modified register and Henry numbering systems. Will print to screen, printer or ASCII file. Source notes, database audit, show relationship between any two people, bold, underline and italics. Changer, a utility for re-sizing the files, will be built-in.

Utilities

Tree Charts. Changer for re-sizing files.

DESCENDANTS OF WILLIAM HENRY BICE (RN=3113)   01 Nov 1991

```
                        GREAT
                GRAND   GRAND
PERSON  CHILDREN CHILDREN CHILDREN
|       |       |       |
WILLIAM HENRY BICE (RN=3113)
|   B: 07 Apr 1860 @ KANSAS
|   M: 29 Sep 1881 to ELIZABETH YEAST (RN=3112) @ YORK NEB
|   D: 05 Oct 1886 @ SO.OF WILLIAMSBURG VA
|   (1: ^DIED OF TYPHOID FEVER)
|
|   LAURA BICE (RN=3114)
|   |   B: 03 Sep 1883 @ O'NEAL NEBRASKA
|   |   M: 06 Jun 1916 to ERNEST JACOB MAYER (RN=3110) @ KLAMMATH FALLS OREGON
|   |   D: 05 May 1970 @ LAS VEGAS NM
|   |   OCC: TEACHER
|   |   (1: ^A.B. DEGREE 1933 NMNU)
|   |
|   |   ESTHER JOSEPHINE MAYER (RN=3117)
|   |   |   B: 17 Oct 1920 @ KLAMATH FALLS, OREGON
|   |   |   2 Marriages
|   |   |   M: 20 Aug 1939 to HARRY MATTHEW VORENBERG (RN=3120) @ LAS VEGAS NM
|   |   |   Widowed
|   |   |   RM: 25 May 1979 to HOWARD JONES (RN=3121) @ AMARILLO TX
|   |   |   Living @ NURSING HOME, LAS CRUCES, NEW MEXICO
|   |   |   OCC: BOOKKEEPER
|   |   |   SOU: STEPHEN CARL VORENBERG (RN=1)
|   |   |   (1: HYDROENCEPHALITIS & ALZHEIMERS)
|   |   |
|   |   |   STEPHEN CARL VORENBERG (RN=1)
|   |   |       B: 13 Mar 1943^1 @ Las Vegas, NM^1
|   |   |       M: 09 Jan 1969 to PATRICIA JEAN MINGER (RN=2) @ NASHUA NH
|   |   |       Living @ LEXINGTON, MA 02173
|   |   |       OCC: PRESIDENT, QUINSEPT INC.
|   |   |       SOU: SELF (No RN)
|   |   |       (1: ^Birth Certificate)
|   |   |
|   |   |   MARILYN VORENBERG (RN=3122)
|   |   |       B: 30 Oct 1944 @ LAS VEGAS NM
|   |   |       M: 31 Aug 1968 to JAMES LAWLOR (RN=3123) @ TAOS NM
|   |   |       Living @ SILVER SPRING MD
|   |   |       OCC: BOOKKEEPER
|   |   |       (1: 301-649-5872)
|   |   |
|   |   |   JAMES DANIEL VORENBERG (RN=3124)
|   |   |       B: 17 Dec 1940 @ LAS VEGAS NM
|   |   |       3 Marriages
|   |   |       M: 11 Jun 1965 to PAULETTE PLANK (RN=3218) @ LAS VEGAS NM
|   |   |       Divorced
|   |   |       RM: 18 Oct 1973 to SHIRLEY ARY (RN=3203) @ LOVINGTON NM
|   |   |       Divorced
|   |   |       RM: 04 Nov 1983 to KATHRYN PHILLIPS (RN=3153) @ ROSWELL, NM
|   |   |       Living @ LAS CRUCES, NM
|   |   |       OCC: ARCHITECT
|   |   |       SOU: JAMES DANIEL VORENBERG (RN=3124)
|   |   |       (1: ADOPTED HORNAK CHILDREN)
```

Family Roots: Descendants chart, full information.

Family Scrapbook
Version 1.15

Producer

Christopher E. Long
632 Camelia St.
Atlantic Beach, FL 32233
904 246 4706 (before 10PM Eastern)

Basics

DOS
$40. + postage (in US $2).
GEDCOM included
Manual on disk; Printed with registration
Support by phone 904 246 4706 (9AM-10PM Eastern); Own BBS 904 249 9515; CompuServe 76500,2073
Purchase from producer, download from bulletin boards, purchase from shareware stores. Available on CompuServe as FSB106 (Ver. 1.06) and on GEnie as FSB106_A.ZIP, FSB106_B.ZIP and FSB_106.ZIP.

Data Entry

65,535 persons per database; supports multiple databases; seven marriages per person, 24 children per marriage. Supports foreign characters (selected from a menu — you don't have to remember the ASCII code), illegitimacy, adoption, cousin marriages as well as name changes (records birth name and new name). People entered in individual record screens and linked in marriage record. Events include born, died, buried, plus choice of two from a list of 10 (bar/bas mitzvah, baptism, LDS baptism, christening, confirmation, LDS confirmation, engagement, first communion, graduation). Choice of these two other events is for entire database, not on an individual record basis. Place consists of four fields, 27 characters each, coded town, county, state, country. Other screens for information on census, name change, last known address, immigration, passenger list, social security number, one line for source, occupation, religion, hobbies, military service, memberships. Marriage screen has field for separated as well as unmarried, divorced and annulled. Four lines of internal notes in one field. Install your own word processor within the program for entering unlimited additional text (should be able to accept a file name on the command line when executing the program and be able to save in ASCII). Macros for repeating information. Date codes for about, before, following, see notes, confirmed and unconfirmed.

Data Management

Can search by name, record number, date, event type. After adding new data you need to run re-index utility. Nice four generation pedigree chart displays on screen. Scroll through individual records by record number or alphabetically by name or marriage/divorce by date. Sorted lists from print routine can be displayed on the screen.

Printed Charts

Charts can be printed or sent to a file. Different types print in 10, 12, 17 or 20 cpi. (If your printer cannot print 20 cpi, some charts may not print correctly.) They include four and five generation pedigree (one page), six generation (two pages) and seven generation (three pages); address list which can be printed as mailing labels (choice of whether or not a name is included in printed list); ahnentafel; chronological report (list of dated events of a person's life or the entire database in chronological order); database statistics; database timeline (sorted list of all the events in the database that have a date); descendant chart (all descendants of one person in either boxed or unboxed form); family group sheet (one family, all families of the same name or every family in database; choice of including or omitting notes); family report (brief information on one family similar to Family Records screen; same options as family group sheet); family timeline (all dated events relating to a selected person and his/her relatives in date order); lineage chart (direct line relationship of two persons (ancestor-descendant relationship); missing information report (search for records with birth, marriage dates, burial place, etc. missing) pedigree report (same as pedigree search screen); person report (information on "person records" screen including data from "other information" screens; same options as family group sheet); relationship diagram (relationship between two persons); relationship report (lists all relatives of a given person (gives relationship, i.e., first cousin once removed, paternal or maternal side and if by marriage; also includes step and half relationships); sorted lists (one line of information per record); surname frequencies (statistical information — number of persons, males, females, percentage of database, etc. — for each surname); tiny tafel generator (create tiny tafel report for Tafel Matching System); blank forms to be used for research: 1790-1920 census, British census, census check summary chart, correspondence log, family group sheet (two pages), family inquiry form (for requesting information on a family), person inquiry form, relationship chart and research log. The blank forms are in ASCII format and can also be retrieved in a word processor. Choice of linking preposition — "in" or "at".

Other Features

Can code events such as H for hospital of birth of G for graveyard and can sort on this code. Will provide Soundex code (but does not correctly code names such as Szul where the z should be ignored as it is the same code as the initials). Hot key feature allows external programs to be linked to the program. If a name has been changed, you have a choice of which name to use in printed reports. Timeline file can be edited to include events that relate specifically to your database.

Comments

Well designed program that is very easy to use. Menus, status line and numerous relevant, informative help screens make the manual almost unnecessary but it should be read for many little extra features. Program requires 1.5 megabytes of free disk space. Supports quite a few printers. When reports are sent to disk, if the filename is already in use, the report will be appended. The program will not overwrite the file. GEDCOM file allows you to select one person, one person plus ancestors or descendants, one family, entire database. GEDCOM preview shows one line listing of names, sex, birth and death of people in file. New version which should be ready in early 1993 will include reverse register charts, ability to show calculated age, number of spouses increased to eight, cause of death field, drop box descendancy charts, indexes updated automatically (no need to re-index) and text editor. The producer hopes to include the following, but it is not guaranteed: ability to keep detailed source records, additional styles of family group sheets, additional blank charts and forms, a custom report generator, a match and merge feature.

Benefits of registration include serial number for support, printed manual and upgrade notices. Although registered users do receive a manual, the document on disk should also be printed as it contains additional information.

RELATIONSHIP DIAGRAM

Luther Collins (42)
Starry Woodard (41)

Doris Collins (141)
Odell Still (152)

Amelia Ann Still (153)
Roy Martin (155)

Madonna Martin (157)

Kellah Mae Collins (33)
born 6-Aug-1902, died 13-May-1982
married 10-Jan-1920
Thomas Matthew Johnston (32)
born 13-Jan-1902, died 5-Dec-1984

Mary Louvenia Johnston (6)
born 29-Mar-1921
married 26-Aug-1939
Grover Dewey Hutson (5)
born 4-Apr-1917, died 8-Sep-1979

Mary Frances Hutson (4)
born 6-Feb-1942
married 25-Dec-1964
Eugene Briand Long (3)
born 21-Jan-1942

Christopher Eugene Long (1)
born 6-Feb-1968

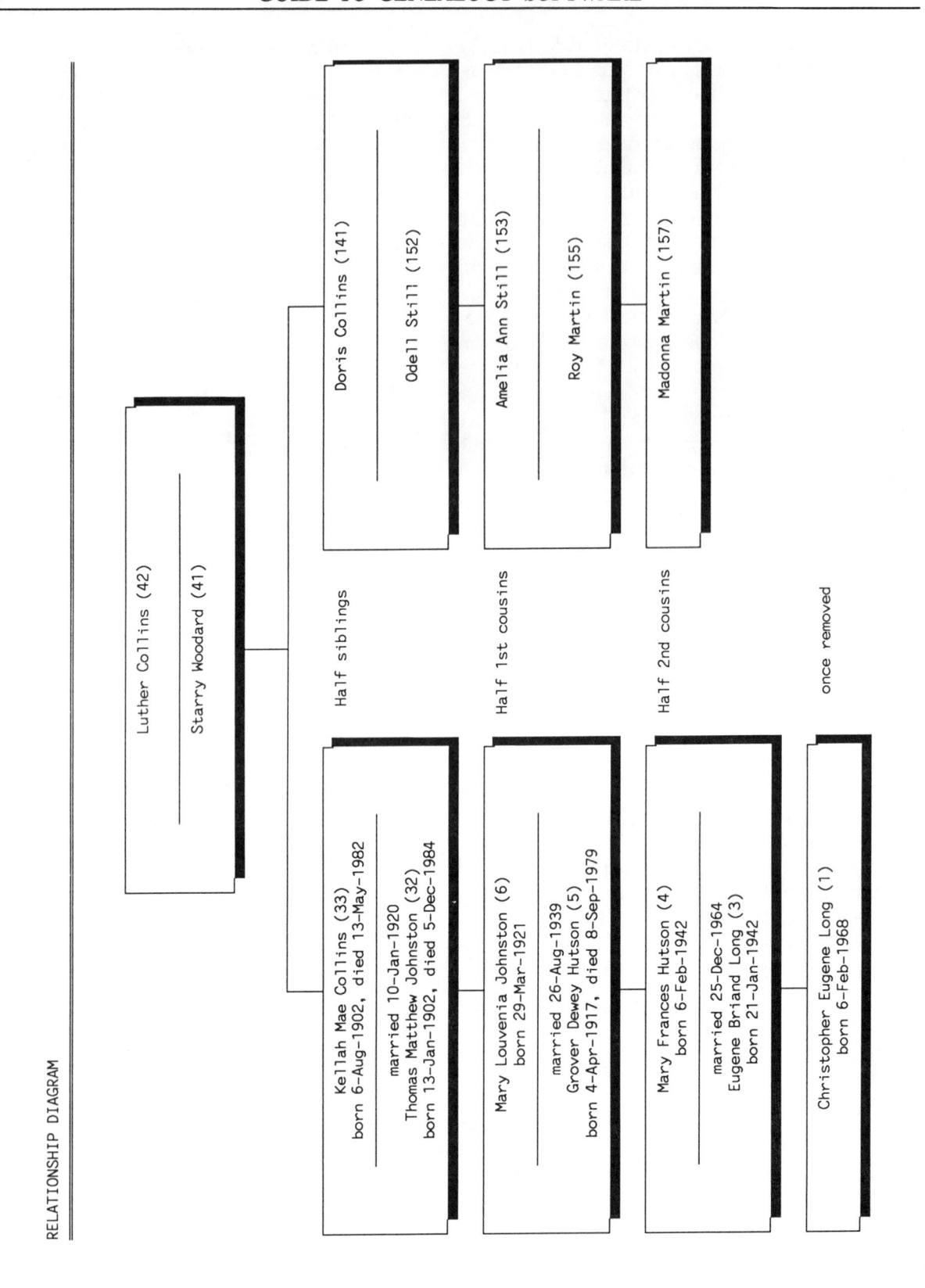

Half siblings
Half 1st cousins
Half 2nd cousins
once removed

Family Scrapbook: Relationship Diagram.

GEDCOM COMPATIBLE GENEALOGY PROGRAMS

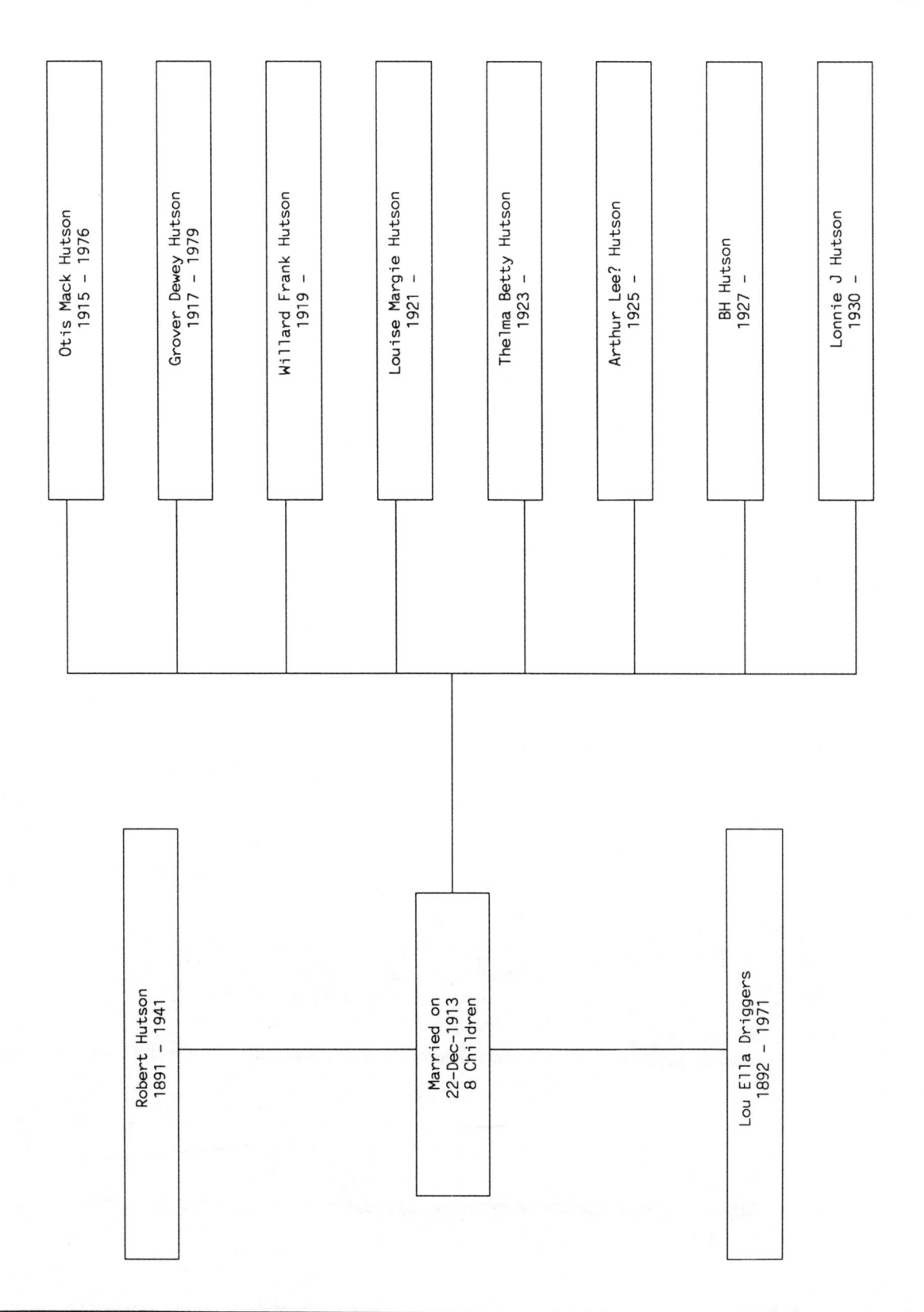

- Otis Mack Hutson 1915 - 1976
- Grover Dewey Hutson 1917 - 1979
- Willard Frank Hutson 1919 -
- Louise Margie Hutson 1921 -
- Thelma Betty Hutson 1923 -
- Arthur Lee? Hutson 1925 -
- BH Hutson 1927 -
- Lonnie J Hutson 1930 -

Robert Hutson 1891 - 1941 — Married on 22-Dec-1913, 8 Children — Lou Ella Driggers 1892 - 1971

Family Scrapbook: Family Chart.

LINEAGE CHART

```
            Mary Collins (40)
            Luther Collins (42)
                   |
       Kellah Mae Collins (33)
   born 6-Aug-1902, died 13-May-1982

          married 10-Jan-1920
       Thomas Matthew Johnston (32)
   born 13-Jan-1902, died 5-Dec-1984
                   |
        Mary Louvenia Johnston (6)
            born 29-Mar-1921

          married 26-Aug-1939
         Grover Dewey Hutson (5)
    born 4-Apr-1917, died 8-Sep-1979
                   |
        Mary Frances Hutson (4)
            born 6-Feb-1942

          married 25-Dec-1964
         Eugene Briand Long (3)
            born 21-Jan-1942
                   |
      Christopher Eugene Long (1)
            born 6-Feb-1968
```

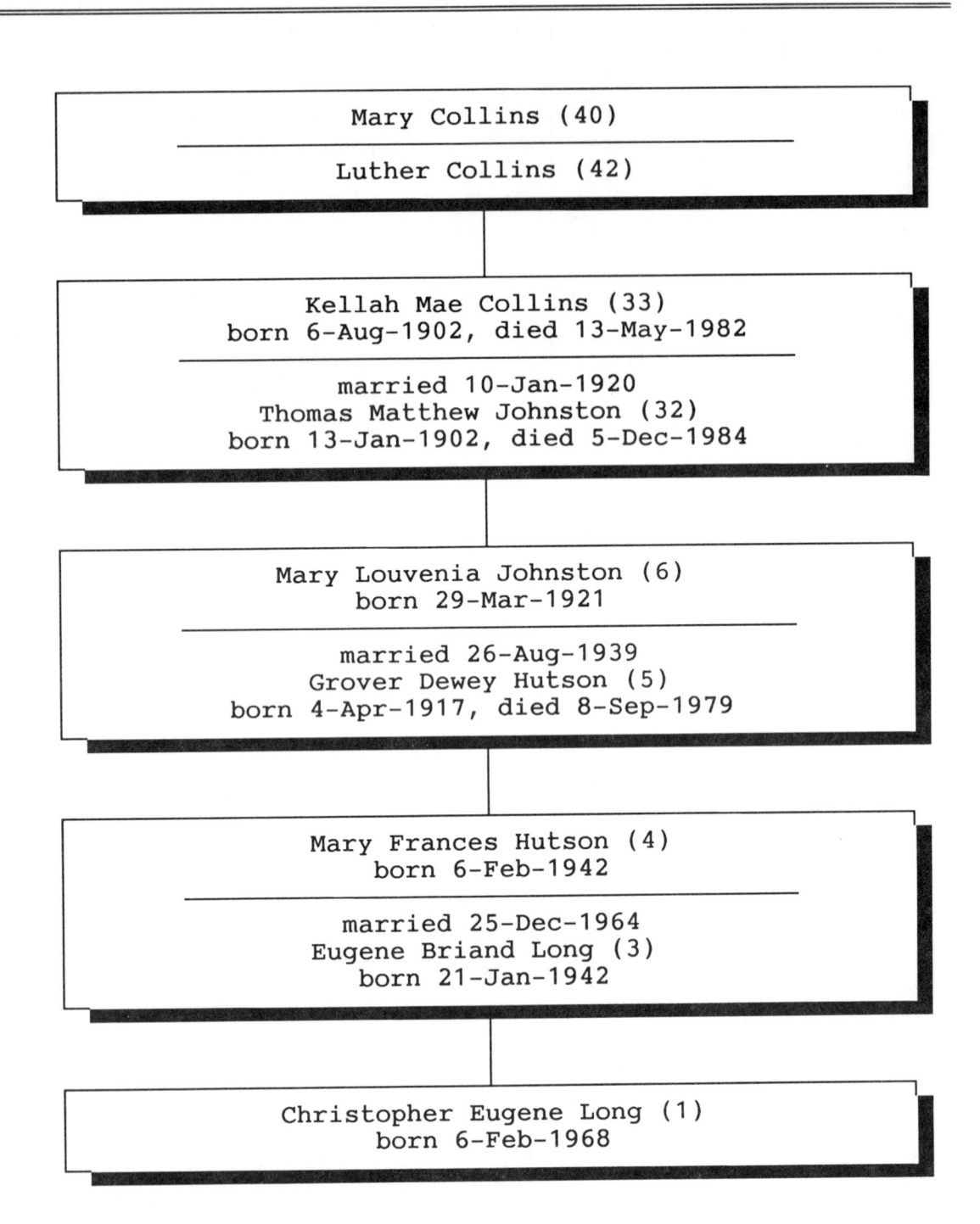

Family Scrapbook: Lineage Chart.

DESCENDANCY CHART for James Jonas Haskins

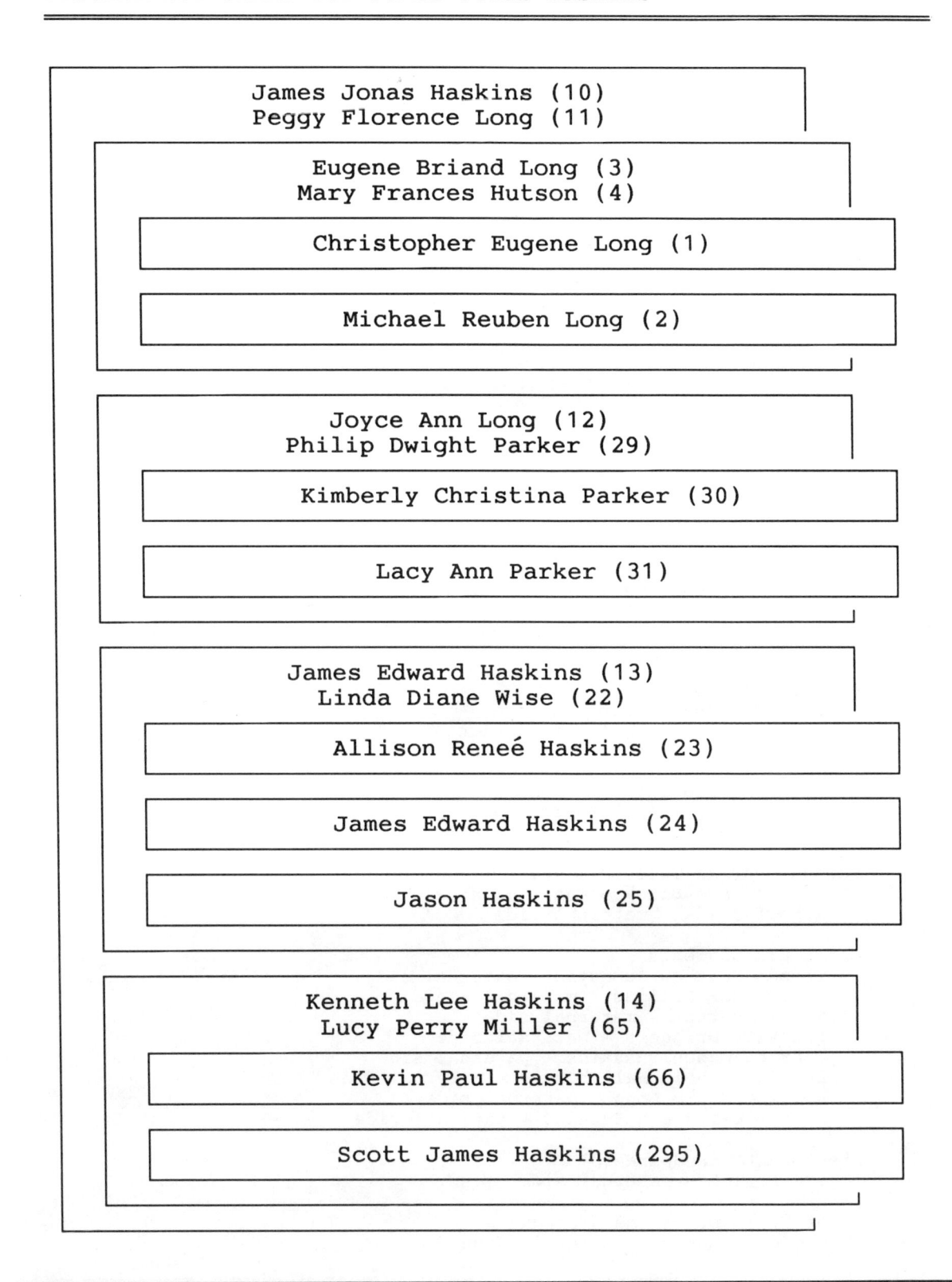

```
┌─────────────────────────────────────────────────────────┐
│              James Jonas Haskins (10)                   │
│              Peggy Florence Long (11)                   │
│   ┌─────────────────────────────────────────────────┐   │
│   │           Eugene Briand Long (3)                │   │
│   │           Mary Frances Hutson (4)               │   │
│   │   ┌─────────────────────────────────────────┐   │   │
│   │   │      Christopher Eugene Long (1)        │   │   │
│   │   └─────────────────────────────────────────┘   │   │
│   │   ┌─────────────────────────────────────────┐   │   │
│   │   │        Michael Reuben Long (2)          │   │   │
│   │   └─────────────────────────────────────────┘   │   │
│   └─────────────────────────────────────────────────┘   │
│   ┌─────────────────────────────────────────────────┐   │
│   │            Joyce Ann Long (12)                  │   │
│   │          Philip Dwight Parker (29)              │   │
│   │   ┌─────────────────────────────────────────┐   │   │
│   │   │     Kimberly Christina Parker (30)      │   │   │
│   │   └─────────────────────────────────────────┘   │   │
│   │   ┌─────────────────────────────────────────┐   │   │
│   │   │          Lacy Ann Parker (31)           │   │   │
│   │   └─────────────────────────────────────────┘   │   │
│   └─────────────────────────────────────────────────┘   │
│   ┌─────────────────────────────────────────────────┐   │
│   │         James Edward Haskins (13)               │   │
│   │           Linda Diane Wise (22)                 │   │
│   │   ┌─────────────────────────────────────────┐   │   │
│   │   │       Allison Reneé Haskins (23)        │   │   │
│   │   └─────────────────────────────────────────┘   │   │
│   │   ┌─────────────────────────────────────────┐   │   │
│   │   │       James Edward Haskins (24)         │   │   │
│   │   └─────────────────────────────────────────┘   │   │
│   │   ┌─────────────────────────────────────────┐   │   │
│   │   │           Jason Haskins (25)            │   │   │
│   │   └─────────────────────────────────────────┘   │   │
│   └─────────────────────────────────────────────────┘   │
│   ┌─────────────────────────────────────────────────┐   │
│   │          Kenneth Lee Haskins (14)               │   │
│   │           Lucy Perry Miller (65)                │   │
│   │   ┌─────────────────────────────────────────┐   │   │
│   │   │         Kevin Paul Haskins (66)         │   │   │
│   │   └─────────────────────────────────────────┘   │   │
│   │   ┌─────────────────────────────────────────┐   │   │
│   │   │        Scott James Haskins (295)        │   │   │
│   │   └─────────────────────────────────────────┘   │   │
│   └─────────────────────────────────────────────────┘   │
└─────────────────────────────────────────────────────────┘
```

Family Scrapbook: Descendancy Chart in boxes.

RELATIONSHIP REPORT for Christopher Eugene Long
===

    Half Granduncles and Grandaunts
        Dale Long - paternal side
        Getty Dale - paternal side, by marriage

    Second Cousins
        Michael Eugene Curtis - paternal side
        Matthew Oneal Darnell - maternal side
        Jimmy Pye - maternal side
        Catherine Pye - maternal side
        Christina McDonald - maternal side
        Lisa McDonald - maternal side
        Jason Pye - maternal side
        Dawn Johnston - maternal side
        Victoria Johnston - maternal side
        Drew Johnston - maternal side
        Jo Allison Johnston - maternal side
        Jace Johnston - maternal side
        Megan Johnston - maternal side
        Casey Warhoski - maternal side
        Edward Chesser Jr - maternal side
        Scott Chesser - maternal side
        Gina Varn - maternal side
        Matt Gibson - maternal side
        Sarah Gibson - maternal side
        Leslie Hutson - maternal side
        Scott Lancaster - maternal side
        Loren Lancaster - maternal side

    Half Second Cousins
        Rebecca Long - paternal side
        Jason Dale Long - paternal side
        Gary Dustin Lynn Long - paternal side

    Half Second Cousins Once Removed
        Steve Martin - maternal side
        Madonna Martin - maternal side

    Second Cousins Twice Removed
        Shannon Lee Black - maternal side
        Robert Black - maternal side

    Great Grandparents
        Thomas Matthew Johnston - maternal side
        Kellah Mae Collins - maternal side
        Robert Hutson - maternal side
        Lou Ella Driggers - maternal side
        Charles Manuel Haskins - paternal side
        Bessie Nichole Halliburton - paternal side
        William Henry Long - paternal side
        Jessie Elizabeth Suttles - paternal side

    Step Great Grandparents
        ??? Foster - paternal side

    Great Granduncles and Grandaunts
        George D Hutson - maternal side

Family Scrapbook: Relationship report showing step and half relationships.

Family Ties
Version 1.19g

Producer

E. Neil Wagstaff
Computer Services
1050 East 800 South
Provo, UT 84606
801 377 2100

Basics

DOS, Macintosh
$50 Shareware; ($55 with a copy of the program disk); free demo from bulletin boards
GEDCOM - Third-party program to only export data: See Family Tree Print Utility in Utility section
Manual on disk
Support by phone 801 377 2100 (8AM-7PM Mon-Fri; 8AM-12N Sat) or own BBS 801 374 8080; by mail from registered users for $3 plus a SASE.
Purchase from producer, shareware store or download from BBS

Data Entry

Multiple databases, each database limited to 32,766 lines of 80 characters each (including notes). Edit screen has place for last name plus three other names, birth, christening, death and burial date and location (town, state/country and county), marriage date and location, sex, father and mother. Every time you enter a new individual or state name, program will ask for confirmation that it is spelled right as incorrect entries can not be removed from the database. Delete and arrow keys do not work in edit screen. Ctl-S to move left and Ctl-D to move right. Delete by spacing out the letters with the space bar. Three codes used on dates: ? for doubtful, + for see notes and * for confirmed. In install are 14 letters that you can define as you want (after, before, circa, etc.). The number for names and locations shows on the right of the record and you can use these numbers for repeat. In install you can also enable LDS ordinance fields.

Data Management

A child without a spouse can be deleted. A spouse's record cannot be deleted, only blanked out. You can attach one of nine labels to a pedigree or family group sheet screen and you can return to the labeled record by using the jump command. The "back" part of the jump command allows you to move back through the last 10 moves made in the database. Free-form notes can be added, changed or erased. However, the erased line will still take up space in the database.

Printed Charts

Family group sheet and pedigree chart in regular or compressed font.

Other Features

Program also includes a demo that makes a good tutorial. Manual is arranged alphabetically by topic rather than step-by-step instruction on how to enter.

Comments

Benefits of registration, in addition to support, include a copy of FIX-NAME.EXE which will remove all unused personal and place names from the database and re-index the files.

Version 1.20 under development with enhanced printouts, ability to delete, change order, unlink, re-link unused entries. Registered users will be able to use their existing data with version 1.20 but the freeware version will not work with the data from prior versions. Available on CompuServe as FT119G.EXE and on GEnie as FAMTIES.EXE.

Utilities

Family Tree Print Utility for creating a GEDCOM file for exporting data only and printing box charts.

Family Treasures
Version 2.0

Producer

Family Technologies
7251 Sarsparilla Dr.
Corona, CA 91719
909 371 4764

Basics

DOS/WINDOWS
$49.95 Commercial; Demo available
GEDCOM included
Printed manual
Support by phone 909 371 4764 or CompuServe 71543,2760
Purchase from producer or retail store; dealerships being set up

Data Entry

Database of 1,000 names, 500 families (upgrade to unlimited number by April 1993), unlimited marriages per individual, 14 children per marriage. Supports foreign characters available in Windows; use cut and paste for repeat information. Four events (birth, death, burial and fourth field can be baptism, bar mitzvah, christening or confirmation) plus occupation. Single place field for place event scrolls to allow input of long place names. One all purpose freeform text area, unlimited size, for notes, sources, biographical information. Will accept one digitized photograph per person.

Data Management

Sorts on names, record numbers, events dates and places. Can view photographs of individuals on the screen, click on a portrait and jump to view the individual member with all relations, key dates and places shown.

Printed Charts

Supports dot matrix, laser, inkjet and color printers (will drive color printers, but only in black and white). Pedigree charts (four or five generations per page), family group sheets, descendant chart, alphabetical and chronological lists, user-defined lists, box charts and ahnentafel. Biography page includes digitized photo, all relations, events, occupation and unlimited biographical text area. Single page to wall-size multiple page timelines can be printed. Uses all Window's font capabilities. Can print to disk in any Window's print format.

Other Features

Built in timeline with 120 historical events which may be customized by the user. Photograph versions of pedigree, nameline (follows the history of a single surname) or single families can be displayed.

Comments

Requires hard disk, Windows and two megabytes of RAM. Unusual use of photographs in that you can display photographs on the screen and identify the record from the photograph and it will also print charts with photographs. Scanner required for photographs or producer offers a picture scanning service.

Sample Browser Printout

Charles Wellington Hardy II

Father: Charles Wellington Hardy
Mother: Honorine Mildred Page
Born: 3 Apr 1925
Birthplace: Utica, NY
Occupation: Computer Analyst, programmer

Married to: Carol Jane Fuller
   in: Portland, NY
   on: 20 Jun 1942
   Robert Winston Hardy
   Sandra Charol Hardy
   Charlynn Joy Hardy
   Charles Wellington Hardy

Died: 4 Jul 1991
Died in: Westfield hospital, Westfield, NY
Buried: 8 Jul 1991
Buried in: Evergreen Cemetary, Portland, NY

Charles spent his early childhood in Utica NY. He worked for US Steel during one war and also served in the Navy. He married Carol in Portland NY while working for Welchs grape juice company. He also taught drivers education in the local high schools.

Charles and Carol lived in Lincoln Nebraska for several years before moving to Westfield NY. Robert, Sandy and Char were born in Westfield. The family then moved to Detroit MI where Charles went to work for Chrysler. Charles the 3rd (Chip) was born in Detroit. After Chrysler, he worked for Blue Cross until his retirement.

Charles loved to garden and spend summer vacations in the Fuller home in Portland NY. After retirement, Charles gave many musical saw recitals (three times at Disneyland in CA) and won several sa competitions including a World Championship.

Family Treasures: Biography page with digitized photograph.

Nameline for George Elmer Ledden

7)
    Joseph Leddon
    Margery Leddon
        Benjamin Leddina
        Hensik Leddon
        Mary Leddon

6)
    Benjamin Leddina
    Birth: 16 Mar 1713
    Susan W Doffell
    Married: 4 Jan 1730 in Swedesboro
        Samuel Liddon

5)
    Samuel Liddon
    Death: 1 Jan 1795
    unknown Lorezer
    Birth: 1 Jan 1700
    Death: 1 Jan 1785
        Samuel Ledden Jr.
        Abraham Ledden
        Henry I Ledden

4)
    Henry I Ledden
    Birth: 21 Mar 1761
    Death: 1 Jan 1827
    Jane Rhodes
    Birth: 30 May 1772
    Death: 15 Oct 1857
        Moelita Ledden
        Abigail Ledden
        Samuel Ledden
        John 3 Ledden
        Mary Ledden
        Henry Ledden
        Sarah Ledden
        James R Ledden
        Elizah Ledden

3)
    Samuel Ledden
    Birth: 26 Sep 1796
    Death: 1 Jan 1854
    Hannah Dubois
    Birth: 9 Oct 1799
        Richard D Ledden
        Abigail S Ledden
        Rachael H Ledden
        Samuel D Ledden
        Joseph M Ledden
        Phineas J Ledden
        Joel D Ledden
        Hannah D Ledden

Family Treasures: Nameline Chart.

Family Tree Journal
Version 9.0

Producer

Rick Cherry
Cherry Tree Software
P. O. Box 964
Reynoldsburg, OH 43068
614 868 9184

Basics

DOS
$35. Shareware
GEDCOM included
Printed manual with registration
Support by phone 614 868 9184 (after 5PM Eastern), own bulletin board 614 868 9039 or by mail
Purchase from shareware store or download from bulletin board

Data Entry

Capacity of 32,767 names, four marriages per individual, unlimited children per union (unlimited number of family groups; marriage record not required to show parentage). Supports foreign characters. No hot key for repeat information. Parents must be entered on each individual record either by name or record number. Birth, death and four marriage events with date and location (limited to 30 characters); five user-defined fields (30 character limit). LDS, christening, burial, etc. would have to go into biography or user-defined event which would be too small for some dates and locations. Each field has note area, limited to total of 32,767 characters per individual. Additional biography section (32,767 characters). No word wrap in text editor, but does support bold, italic and underlining. You can also use any word processor that creates ASCII files for writing text. Choice of date format; supports circa, about, before and after.

Data Management

"Tree" screen shows individual, spouses, parents and children. Use function keys to move other people to key position or bring up record for editing. Search by name, dates, record numbers or all data and text files for any string of text. Function to tag records you want printed. Printed list sorted by surname, reference number or date of birth can be printed to the screen. Utility to combine two branches of a family into one group of files, split database, display relationships between two people, convert dates to different style, convert names to standard spelling, check for discrepancies in birth dates, check for two name spellings for one person.

Printed Charts

Supports dot matrix, laser and inkjet printers. Reports are in formats called books or booklets. Most charts are unique: tree and data includes born, died, age at death, marriages and other information from individual record, average lifetime of ancestors, ancestor chart in pedigree form and references; family group sheet (traditional), alphabetical name list, descendant chart, biographies, data forms, ahnentafel, missing information, time line and lists sorted by surname, reference number or date of birth. Reports can be sent to the printer, to disk in ASCII format or viewed on the screen. Option to print on both sides of the paper. Book form will print everyone in database (or those you have flagged) with choice of any or all of the following: introduction, family groups, trees and data, biographies (all biographical information prints together in a separate section under the person's name; it is not printed with the family information), name list, audit (missing information), miscellaneous (list of birthdays and information from user-defined fields), timeline of all events in database. Booklet produces same printouts, but for one individual.

Other Features

Section for address book which will also print labels. Will print boxes for inserting photographs or illustrations with caption below box. If you have a scanner, you can also print scanned photographs or documents directly into the biographies and references.

Comments

Minimum of two floppies required. Book is series of charts and not the register format. Can use a lot of paper (a 25 person database produced a 43 page book). Does not do a lot of sorting and analyzing. For the person who likes these unique reports. Benefits of registration: copy of the latest version, complete instruction manual on disk, full access to the bulletin board and notification of updates. Include a disk with your data files and it will be added to the Family Tree Journal Bulletin Board. Available on CompuServe (version 8.0) as FTJ80A.ZIP and FTJ80B.ZIP and on GEnie as FTJ82-1.ZIP and FTJ82-2.ZIP.

Daniel Truesdell (#3)

BORN: 1749 - Redding, CT
DIED: aft 1810 -
AGE AT DEATH: 61 years, 0 months, 0 days
MARRIED: Huldah Thorp (#4)
RESIDED: Kinderhook, NY; Ontario, Quebec
AVERAGE LIFETIME OF ANCESTORS: 63 years, 0 months, 0 days

ANCESTORS

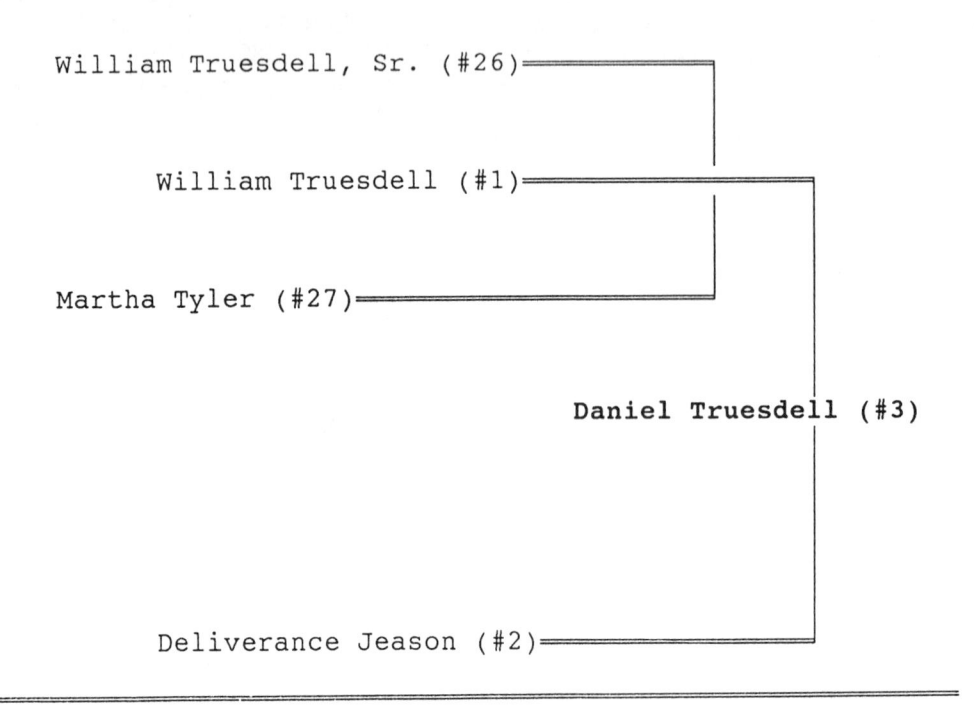

```
William Truesdell, Sr. (#26)═╗
                              ╠═╗
                              ║ ║
William Truesdell (#1)════════╝ ║
                                ╠═══╗
Martha Tyler (#27)══════════════╝   ║
                                    ║
                                    ╠═ Daniel Truesdell (#3)
                                    ║
                                    ║
Deliverance Jeason (#2)═════════════╝
```

DESCENDANTS

Cornelius Truesdell	(#7)	Born: bef 1785
Daniel Rankin Truesdell	(#9)	Born: 20 Jun 1805
Maria Truesdell	(#11)	Born: 1 Aug 1806
Sarah Caroline Truesdell	(#12)	Born: 24 Sep 1808
George Truesdell	(#14)	Born: ca 1810
Emily Truesdell	(#16)	Born: 1 Mar 1822

   GRAND CHILDREN (5)
CHILDREN (1)

Family Tree Journal: Trees and Data chart. (References on second page, not shown.)

APPENDIX D

FAMILY TIME LINE

29 Jun 1746	**William Truesdell (#1)** married **Deliverance Jeason (#2)**
1749	**Daniel Truesdell (#3)** was born
1755	**Justin Truesdell (#5)** was born
bef 1785	**Cornelius Truesdell (#7)** was born
ca 1794	**Ann Gardiner (#6)** married **Justin Truesdell (#5)**
ca 1796	**Samuel Truesdell (#17)** was born
ca 1797	**William Truesdell II (#19)** was born
24 Jul 1802	**Justin Truesdell II (#22)** was born
5 Jul 1803	**Justin Truesdell (#5)** died
20 Jun 1805	**Daniel Rankin Truesdell (#9)** was born
14 May 1806	**Ann Gardiner (#6)** married **Cornelius Truesdell (#7)**
1 Aug 1806	**Maria Truesdell (#11)** was born
24 Sep 1808	**Sarah Caroline Truesdell (#12)** was born
ca 1810	**George Truesdell (#14)** was born
aft 1810	**Daniel Truesdell (#3)** died
ca 1818	**Ann/Nancy (#20)** married **William Truesdell II (#19)**
1 Mar 1822	**Emily Truesdell (#16)** was born
ca 1823	**Sarah Purvis (#8)** married **Cornelius Truesdell (#7)**
6 Feb. 1828	**Stephen Shipman (#13)** married **Sarah Caroline Truesdell (#12)**

Family Tree Journal: Family Time Line.

APPENDIX B

MISSING INFORMATION

Ann/Nancy (#20):

    PLACE OF BIRTH _____
    DATE OF BIRTH _____
    FATHER'S NAME _____
    MOTHER'S NAME _____
    CORRECT DATE OF MARRIAGE (ca 1818) TO
        William Truesdell II (#19) _____

Adeline Dugas (#10):

    PLACE OF BIRTH _____
    DATE OF BIRTH _____
    FATHER'S NAME _____
    MOTHER'S NAME _____

Ann Gardiner (#6):

    PLACE OF BIRTH _____
    DATE OF BIRTH _____
    FATHER'S NAME _____
    MOTHER'S NAME _____
    CORRECT DATE OF MARRIAGE (ca 1794) TO
        Justin Truesdell (#5) _____

Justin Truesdell II (#22):

    CORRECT DATE OF DEATH (1872) _____

William Truesdell II (#19):

    CORRECT DATE OF BIRTH (ca 1797) _____
    PLACE OF DEATH _____
    CORRECT DATE OF MARRIAGE (ca 1818) TO
        Ann/Nancy (#20) _____
    CORRECT DATE OF MARRIAGE (ca 1840) TO
        Margaret Agnes McLeod (#21) _____
    PLACE OF MARRIAGE TO
        Margaret Agnes McLeod (#21) _____

Deliverance Jeason (#2):

    DATE OF BIRTH _____
    FATHER'S NAME _____
    MOTHER'S NAME _____

Family Tree Journal: Missing Information.

Family Tree Maker
Version 2.0

Producer

Banner Blue Software
P. O. Box 7865
Fremont, CA 94537
510 794 6850

Basics

DOS
$59.99 Commercial. Free demo planned for early 1993 to be available on CompuServe or America On-Line
GEDCOM additional $29.99
Printed manual
Support by phone 510 794 6850 (8AM-5PM Pacific) or by mail
Purchase from producer, widely available from software stores, often at a discount.

Data Entry

1200 individuals per file, multiple files supported, 99 marriages per individual, 99 children per marriage. Supports mouse and foreign characters. Data is entered on a family "card" which includes husband and wife's name and date and place of birth and death; marriage date, place and if divorced; children's names, sex and birth date. Individual cards automatically created from family card. Individual cards include four parts: 1) date and place of birth and death (automatically transferred from family card) five additional events, optional reference number, whether child is natural, adopted, foster or unknown; 2) occupation, personality/interests, place of residence, ethnic group/religion and four comment lines; 3) adult height, adult weight, cause of death, medical information as to whether person had heart disease, high blood pressure, stroke, cancer, addictions, alzheimer's, mental illness or diabetes; 4) five blank pages for free-form text created with the built-in word processor which supports bold, italic and underline. Six programmable keys for repeat information. One or two line source field for birth-/death/marriage and two other event fields. Five individual and one marriage event field as well as medical and comment fields can be renamed by user. The new name applies to all records. These user definable fields could be used for LDS data. Dates can be entered in almost any format and they will be converted to one form (preferred form can be selected). No double dates. Help screens. Card automatically saved when you move to another screen (which means you will not accidentally lose data, but you also cannot choose to not save an entry).

Data Management

User can easily move forward to child's family or back to parent's parents. Key clearly labeled for current record, "Parents of Richard", "Parents of Phyllis". Index of names will bring up alphabetical index by surname plus birth date. Type first letter of last name to move to that section of alphabet. You can also search by any field such as people born on, before or after a certain date; any type of illness, locations, sources. Kinship will tell relationship between two people. Facility to save selected descendants to form a new file or to join two files together. Utility to rearrange, insert, move or delete children within a family.

Printed Charts

Supports dot matrix, laser, inkjet and color plotter printers. Pedigree charts (three-five generations on one page) and multiple generations on continued sheets or large wall chart. Family group sheets. Alphabetical (name) and chronological (birthdate) lists. Dates, diseases, comments, etc. can be used as criteria for selecting people to be printed, but information on the list cannot be customized. It will always show name and birthdate. Birthday/anniversary calendar (either all people or just those living; with or without ages). Can change "about", "in", "husband" and "wife".

Very decorative box charts: photo tree (two or three generations per page), ancestor tree (all or two to ten ancestors of a person), descendant tree (descendants of an individual from two generations up to present) or direct descendant tree (shows only the direct line of descent, with or without siblings, between two people). Choice of style for ancestor and descendant charts: six styles of boxes — shadow, dashed, double, solid, notched and no lines — as well as seven border styles. Information contained in boxes can be customized with up to 20 items per box. Default is name, and date and place of birth and death. Other options are age at birth of first or last child, age at death, information from comments, religion, occupation, cause of death, etc. Birth and death date and place can be eliminated and re-selected with choice of five different date styles including birth and death year on one line. Blank fields can be selected to create space for a large picture tree. Text in boxes can be left justified or centered, selection of characters and lines per inch to help control size of tree. Four options for overall style of descendant chart from widest (horizontal format, putting each person into a box) to most compact (second most recent generation in each branch is in a vertical format with the most recent generation printed without boxes or dates). Charts can be viewed on screen prior to printing, but not printed to disk.

Other Features

With an adopted or foster child, there is the option to have the child treated as a natural child as far as printed reports are concerned. Option to use a dotted line instead of solid one to show you are unsure of link. Program can read a ROOTS III database so users of ROOTS III can use this program to produce the unique charts without having to use GEDCOM to transfer data.

Comments

Family Tree Maker says it is designed for the genealogy hobbyist, not the professional. It is easy to use and does provide for some documentation of sources and room for family stories. Its greatest strength is the attractive charts it will print. Many genealogists use this as a utility just for its charting ability. The 1200 name limit is somewhat of a problem, but since a chart of 1200 people would be too large to be practical, you can split your database into more than one file for generating charts. Named a favorite utility for charts in *Genealogical Computing*'s "Software to Beat" in 1992.

Utilities

FTMGEDFX

Direct Descendants of Heinrich Nüchter

Heinrich Nüchter
1657 - 1727
Age at first: 40 est.
Age at death: 70 est.

Children

Nicolaus Nüchter
1697 - 1746
Age at first: 27 est.
Age at death: 49 est.
=
Elisabetha
1702 - 1742
Age at first: 22 est.
Age at death: 40 est.

Grandchildren

Jakob Nüchter
1724 - UNKNOWN
Age at first: 36
Age at death: ?
=
Anna Schaeffer
1728 - UNKNOWN
Age at first: 33 est.
Age at death: ?

Great-Grandchildren

Johannes C. Nüchter
1771 - UNKNOWN
Age at first: 32
Age at death: ?
=
Anna K. Wiegand
1781 - UNKNOWN
Age at first: 22 est.
Age at death: ?

2nd Great-Grandchildren

Joseph Nichter
1805 - 1854
Age at first: 32 est.
Age at death: 49
=
Salamina S. Ruch
1813 - 1891
Age at first: 24 est.
Age at death: 77

3rd Great-Grandchildren

Peter David Neister
1846 - 1914
Age at first: 31
Age at death: 67
=
Elizabeth Shipman
1849 - 1932
Age at first: 29
Age at death: 83

4th Great-Grandchildren

Charles B. Neister
1884 - 1960
Age at first: 53
Age at death: 75

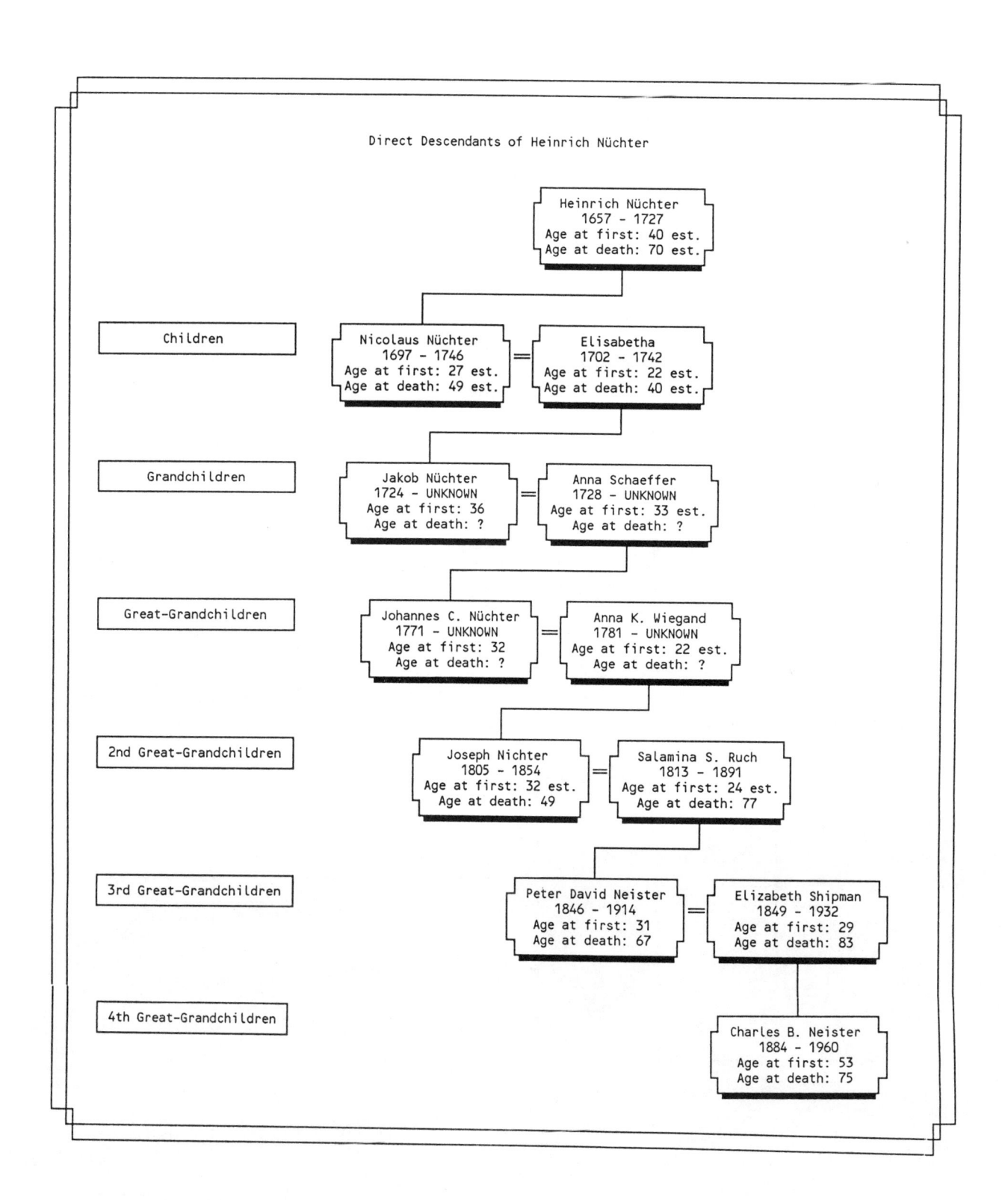

Family Tree Maker: Direct Descendants Chart, no siblings, notched boxes, decorative border.

March 1992 Birthdays and Anniversaries

Sunday	Monday	Tuesday	Wednesday	Thursday	Friday	Saturday
1	2	3 Catherine Nichter	4 Alicia Kelly Brown Maria Anna Frauziska Nüchter Nichter	5 Sarah Ann Trickey	6	7 Elijah Haughton Egrilona (?) Mallo
8 Martha Truesdell	9	10 Sarah Horton	11 Robert Edward Piippo Mary Shipman	12	13 George Meyers Ethel Riley Daniel Shipman	14
15 Dr. Samuel Shipman	16 Simon Nüchter	17	18 Wilhelm Magnus Nüchter	19 Katherine Haughton	20 Anna Maria Ruch Edward Shipman William Shipman	21 Dain Hormell Charles Shipman
22 Catharina Ruch Henrietta Trickey	23 Mary Abigail & Perry F Hormell	24 Bonaparte (Bonifatius) (Nüchter) Nichter Barbara Allison & Kirk Brown	25	26	27	28 Annie Meyers Johannes Christian Nüchter
29 Johann Nicolaus Lindenmann Joseph Nichter	30 Maria Regina Nüchter	31 Laurel Ruth & Toivo William Piippo				

Family Tree Maker: Birthday and Anniversary Chart, ages omitted.

Descendants of Johannes Christian Nüchter

Johannes Nüchter
born: March 28, 1771
died: UNKNOWN

Anna Wiegand
born: ABOUT 1781
died: UNKNOWN

- **Jakob Nüchter**
  born: December 13, 1803
  died: UNKNOWN
  - Anna Nüchter — born: October 23, 1824; died: UNKNOWN
  - Peter Nüchter — born: May 3, 1832; died: UNKNOWN
  - Anna Nüchter — born: May 3, 1832; died: UNKNOWN
  - Conrad Nüchter — born: November 13, 1833; died: UNKNOWN
  - Anastasia Nüchter — born: April 14, 1835; died: UNKNOWN
  - Julianus Nüchter — born: January 9, 1837; died: November 16, 1896
  - Mathilde Nüchter
  - Simon Nüchter
  - Emilie Nüchter
  - Josef Nüchter
  - Martina Nüchter

- **Peter Nichter**
  born: August 22, 1806
  died: May 20, 1868
  - Georg Nichter — born: April 5, 1836; died: June 13, 1905
  - Maria Nichter — born: March 4, 1838; died: UNKNOWN
  - Maria Nichter — born: March 30, 1840; died: April 27, 1840
  - Elisabeth Nichter — born: May 30, 1841; died: UNKNOWN
  - Theresia Nichter — born: April 28, 1843; died: UNKNOWN
  - Maria Nichter — born: February 7, 1846; died: UNKNOWN
  - Otto Nichter — born: December 27, 1847; died: August 13, 1895

Joseph Nichter
born: February 26, 1805
died: November 28, 1854

Salamina Ruch
born: July 19, 1813
died: July 1, 1891

- **Peter Neister**
  born: December 29, 1846
  died: March 26, 1914
  = **Elizabeth Shipman**
  born: January 10, 1849
  died: March 31, 1932
    - Charles Neister
    - Perley Neister
    - Mary Neister
  = **Mary Maxton**
  born: ABOUT 1850
  died: UNKNOWN

- **Elizabeth Nichter**
  born: ABOUT 1838
  died: UNKNOWN
    - Jake Bohner
    - Dan Bohner
    - (Female) Bohner
    - (Female) Bohner

- **Madalain Nichter**
  born: September 4, 1842
  died: June 26, 1926

Children

Grandchildren

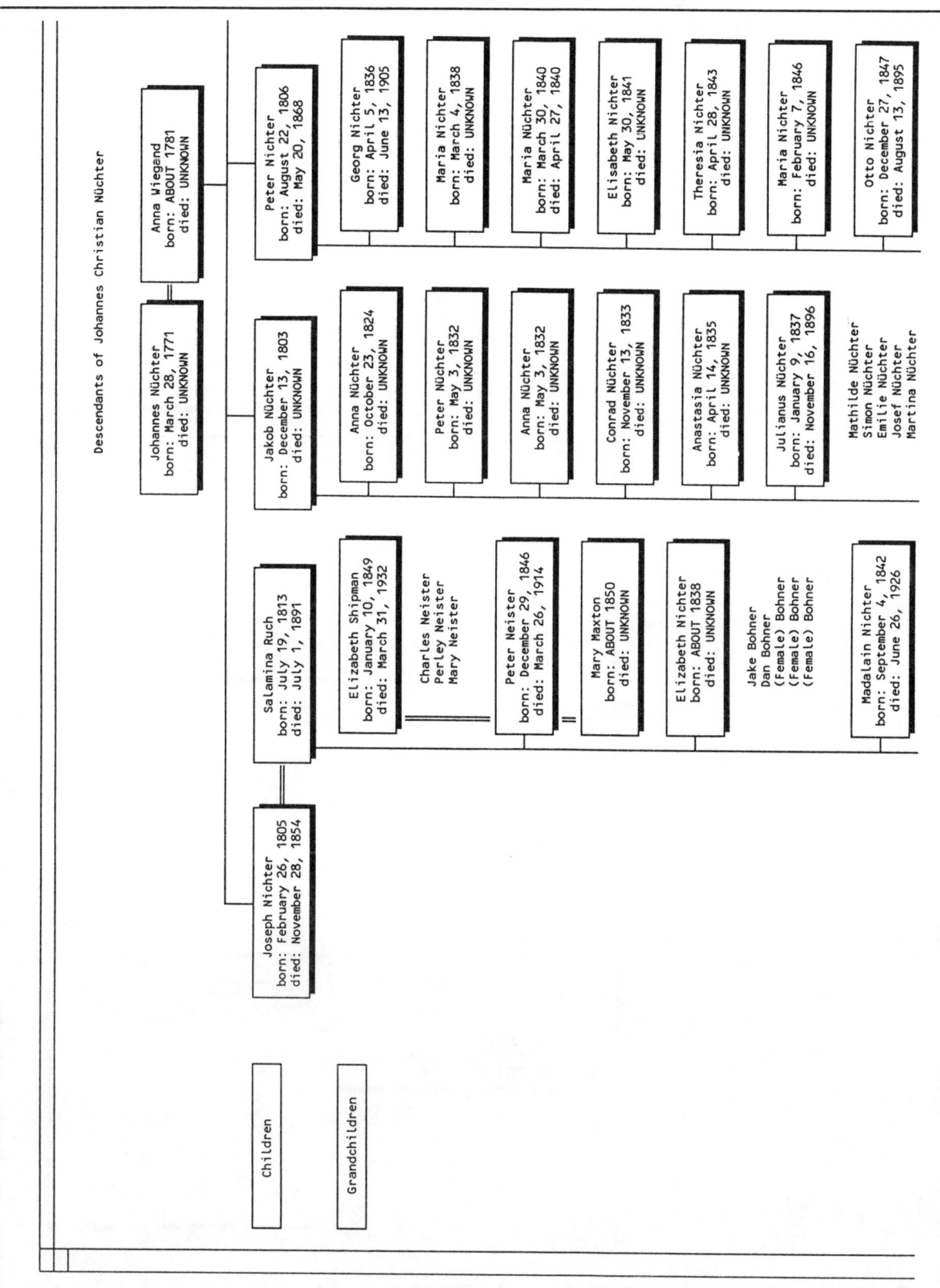

Family Tree Maker: Descendant Chart (partial), 4 generations, shadow boxes. First and second generation in horizontal boxes, third generation in vertical boxes, fourth generation unboxed.

Ancestors of Charles Blaine Neister

Parents / **Grandparents**

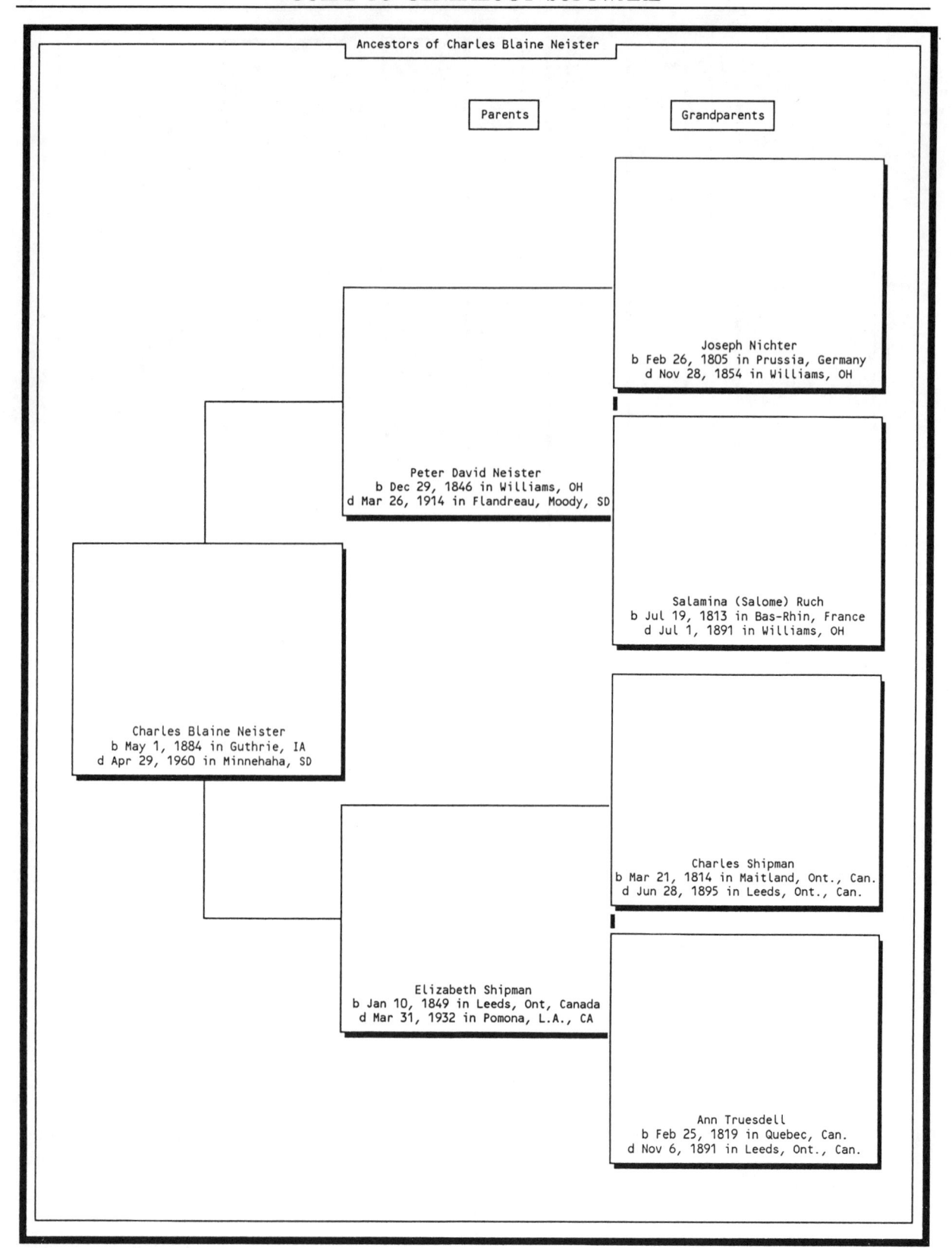

Charles Blaine Neister
b May 1, 1884 in Guthrie, IA
d Apr 29, 1960 in Minnehaha, SD

Peter David Neister
b Dec 29, 1846 in Williams, OH
d Mar 26, 1914 in Flandreau, Moody, SD

Joseph Nichter
b Feb 26, 1805 in Prussia, Germany
d Nov 28, 1854 in Williams, OH

Salamina (Salome) Ruch
b Jul 19, 1813 in Bas-Rhin, France
d Jul 1, 1891 in Williams, OH

Elizabeth Shipman
b Jan 10, 1849 in Leeds, Ont, Canada
d Mar 31, 1932 in Pomona, L.A., CA

Charles Shipman
b Mar 21, 1814 in Maitland, Ont., Can.
d Jun 28, 1895 in Leeds, Ont., Can.

Ann Truesdell
b Feb 25, 1819 in Quebec, Can.
d Nov 6, 1891 in Leeds, Ont., Can.

Family Tree Maker: Ancestor photo chart.

GENE-GENEX-GEDCOMG

Producer

Andrew Koppenhaver
13224 Old Chapel Rd.
Bowie, MD 20720
301 262 8993

Basics

DOS
$20. Shareware
GEDCOM included
Manual on disk
Support by phone 301 262 8993 (6-11PM Eastern); own BBS 301 989 8960; CompuServe 70476,521; GEnie ANDY-KOPPY; Prodigy NGDN81A
Download from bulletin boards

Data Entry

Basic genealogy program with a maximum of 3,000 entries, five marriages per individual, 16 children per marriage. Does not support foreign characters, no hot key for repeat information. Nine set events (no LDS ordinance fields). No notes.

Data Management

Sort on names, dates and record numbers.

Printed Charts

Pedigree (single page with three generations), descendant charts, alphabetical and chronological lists, ahnentafel, mother roots and father roots. Can print to disk in ASCII format.

Other Features

Help screens. Unique charts include children-grandchildren, parents-grandparents and list of living people in order of birthdate/marriage.

Comments

Author has no plans to update program. GENE is a limited genealogy program. No place information or notes supported. GENEX adds, deletes, modifies, and checks GENE date and GEDCOMG converts GENE data to and from a GEDCOM file. Benefits of registration include a copy of the GENE-PAF program, a utility to be used with a PAF database.

Genealogical Data Base Systems

Producer

Data Base Systems
P. O. Box 7263
Huntsville, Al 35807
205 881 6957

Basics

DOS, Apple II
Starter $19.95 (9.95)
MS-DOS $69.95 (34.95)
Apple II $99.95 (74.95)
Demo $10
Transfer (includes GEDCOM) $44.95 (22.95)
Commercial. Prices in parentheses available for limited period with purchase; application form obtainable from producer. Contact producer for additional costs for shipping, Alabama sales tax, shipments outside USA and non-cash payments.
GEDCOM additional
Manual on disk
Support by phone 205 881 6957 (9AM-5PM Central) and by mail
Purchase from producer, retail store or dealer

Data Entry

Starter system will take up to 200 records, regular MS-DOS program can handle 50,000 records while Apple version takes 8,000. Both versions allow 27 marriages per individual, 90 children per marriage. Eighteen events with choice of events which can also be LDS and five user-defined. Foreign characters not supported. Hot key for repeat information. Multiple 24 character note fields and one unlimited all-purpose note field.

Data Management

Sorting can be done on names, soundex, dates, places, record numbers and other events.

Printed Charts

Supports dot matrix, laser, inkjet and color printers. There are 24 types of ancestor charts tailored to suit the user's needs with 2-60 generations (MS-DOS, 2-75 for Apple II); six types of user-defined descendant charts with 2-60 generations (MS-DOS; 2-70 for Apple II). Apple charts can contain 1,000 people and MS-DOS 2,000. Family group sheet, two alphabetical and two numerical lists. Reports can be printed, sent to disk in ASCII format or viewed on the screen.

Other Features

Help screens. Book can be created with Genealogical Data Base Systems Book package. (See utilities section.)

Genealogical Information Manager (GIM)

Producer

D. Blain Wasden/Brian C. Madsen
2024 Club Pkwy
Norcross, GA 30093-5246
404 934 0774
Shareware

Basics

DOS
Price not available; in beta test
GEDCOM included
Manual on disk
Support by phone 404 934 0774

Data Entry

Up to 30,000 individuals per folder (database). One field for surname, one for given names. Date field will accept anything, even text. Events are birth, christening, death, burial, marriage, LDS ordinances. Single place field is 80 characters in length. Fields for Ancestral File Number and Reference number. Source and research (biographical) notes can be entered for each vital statistic and for each person and family. Supports foreign characters.

Data Management

Displays pedigree, all children of family, multiple spouses. Can cursor backward and forward through the chart selecting any person for individual information. Search by typing name; will display all similar spellings (uses soundex for search). Search for virtually any family history event or statistic imaginable and produce lists which can be displayed on screen or printed to disk or printer. Can search data for any grouping such as all persons born in California, all female ancestors who married more than once, all families with between four and seven children, the oldest man in the database, the longest marriage, etc. Can search for missing data, notes text, incomplete LDS ordinances. Place names can be sorted in six different ways. Can select whether search should be case-sensitive. Extensive custom sorting capability using and/or options.

Printed Charts

Four generation pedigree chart, family group chart (on blank paper or pre-printed LDS forms). All can be customized (select standard or ahnentafel numbering system, whether to show connecting lines for unknown ancestors, use of graphics characters, and inclusion of LDS ordinance data). More forms will be added as users request them. Set up allows printer selection and choice of fonts. "Vertical zoom" lets you control how chart will display on paper; adjusts chart for printing on European paper sizes, for example. Charts display on screen before printing; can zoom to enlarge sections for easier reading. Family group chart can have either husband or wife as person at top.

Other Features

Uses extended memory if available. Mouse support. Menu bar at top of screen, with additional selections by pressing <shift>, <control> or <alt>. Includes backup option which will first check for data errors and has option to fix corrupted data. On-line help and glossary. Hot key to shell to DOS. Can select novice or expert mode. GEDCOM import and export, full compatibility with FamilySearch databases and LDS temple submissions.

Comments

The program used nearly 1.7 megabytes of disk space. A 181-page manual (incomplete) is on disk, but the length would discourage printing it. Must type lengthy commands for sorts, but they can be saved in script commands to avoid re-typing. User should be comfortable with advanced DOS commands and some programming techniques to fully utilize the capabilities of this program.

HeartWood

Producer

HeartWood Software, Inc.
P.O. Box 5190, Bayview Station
Bridgeport, CT 06610
203 374 7481

Basics

Macintosh HyperCard 2.0
$75. Commercial. Free demo
GEDCOM included
Manual included
Support by phone 203 374 7481 (8AM-5PM Eastern)
Purchase from producer

Data Entry

Unlimited number of marriages per individual and unlimited number of children per marriage. Two note fields, 36,000 characters each. Photos can be kept in separate file (scanner required).

Data Management

Sorts on names, dates, places and other (such as father, mother, etc).

Printed Charts

Supports dot matrix, laser and inkjet printers. Prints family group sheets, descendant charts, alphabetical and chronological lists and pedigree charts (five generations per sheet and wall chart on multiple pages). Will also export in text format information on individual, family or all. Can send reports to printer or to disk in an ASCII file.

Other Features

Help screens. Draws graphical charts with icons and/or text. Links to photos and can also include a spoken history if you have sound recording equipment for your Macintosh.

Ancestors

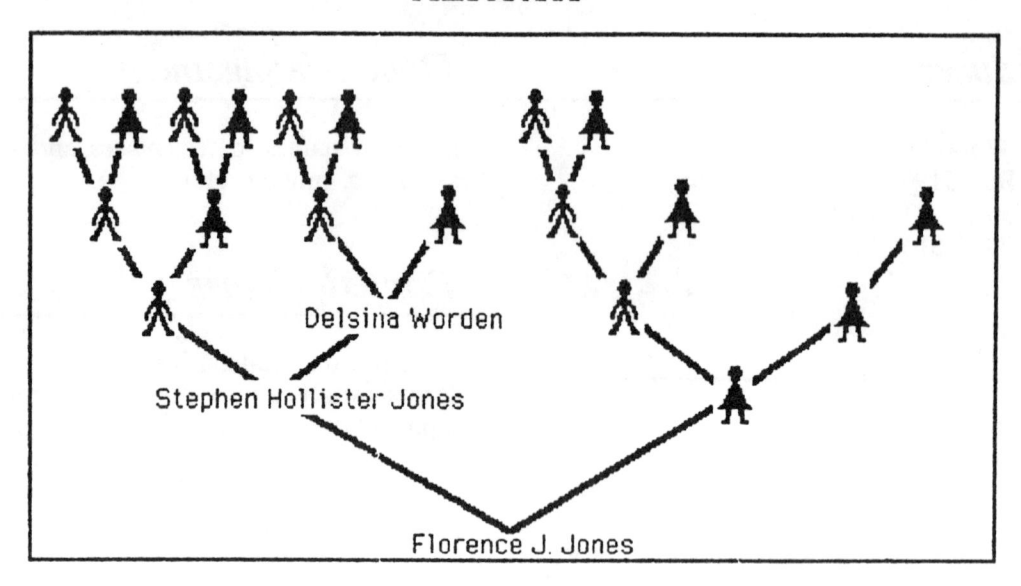

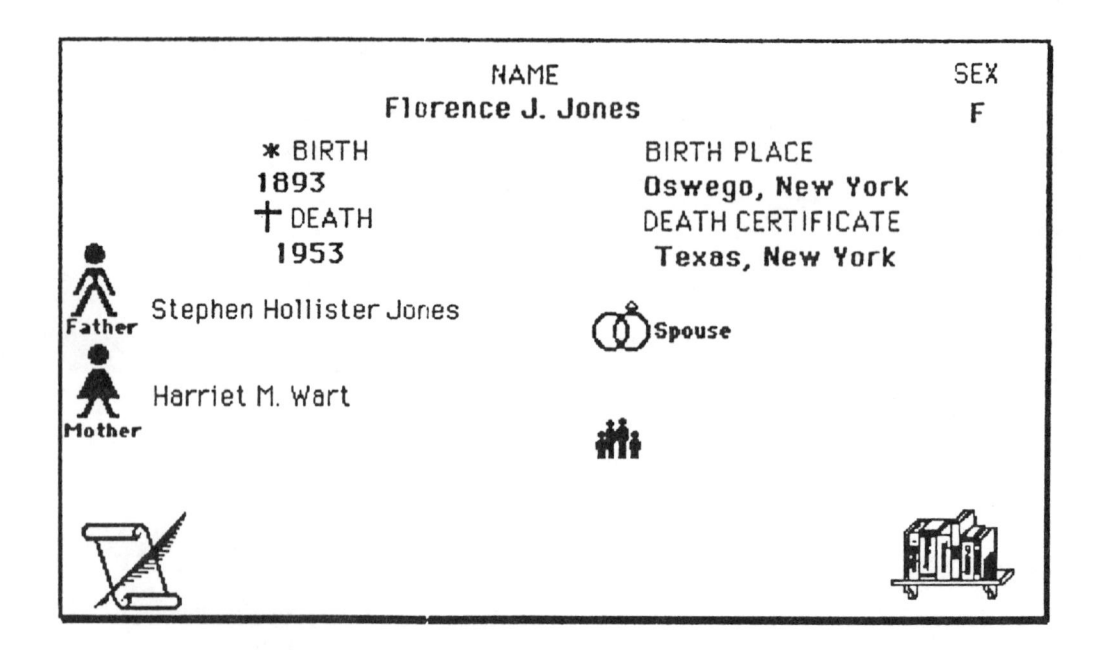

- Delsina Worden
- Stephen Hollister Jones
- Florence J. Jones

NAME: Florence J. Jones SEX: F

* BIRTH 1893 — BIRTH PLACE Oswego, New York
† DEATH 1953 — DEATH CERTIFICATE Texas, New York

Father: Stephen Hollister Jones
Mother: Harriet M. Wart

Spouse

HeartWood: Ancestor chart.

It's All Relative

Producer

Greg & Randall Kopchak
2233 Keeven Lane
Florissant, MO 63031
314 831 9482

Basics

Atari
$35. Commercial; Demo $5.
GEDCOM included
Printed manual with registration
Support by phone 314 831 9482 (7-10PM daily Central); CompuServe 73057,2312; GEnie Greg
Purchase from producer, retail store or dealer

Data Entry

Three marriages per individual, 15 children per marriage. Supports foreign characters. Preset events, no LDS or user-defined. One all purpose note field of unlimited size plus separate extended notes for biographical information which print on the personal record and in book form.

Data Management

Sorts by name, soundex, place, record numbers and dates (timeline or calendar).

Printed Charts

Supports dot matrix, laser and inkjet printers. Pedigree chart including wall chart, family group sheets, three types of descendant charts, alphabetical and chronological lists, two types of dropline charts, ahnentafel. Book form with register numbering system. Prints to disk in ASCII format and reports can be viewed on the screen. Book output can be tagged for direct importing and printing with Desktop Publisher ST.

Other Features

Abbreviator ST add-on for $19.95 allows use of hot key for repeat information.

Comments

Requires 500K or greater Atari ST or STe.

Lineages

Producer

Quinsept, Inc.
P. O. Box 216
Lexington, MA 02173
800 637 7668

Basics

DOS, Apple II, Commodore 64
$49. & $99. Commercial
GEDCOM $35 additional
Printed manual
Support by phone 800 637 7668 (9AM-5PM Mon-Fri; off hours by appointment); Prodigy CGMR62B; CompuServe 72470,3027; GEnie S.VORENBERG or by mail
Purchase from producer or retail store

Data Entry

Eight million names, unlimited marriages, unlimited number of children. Supports foreign characters; hot key for repeat information. Three set individual events plus marriage event. No LDS events. Each event has note area plus there is a separate file of unlimited size for biographical information.

Data Management

Sorts by name and record number.

Printed Charts

Supports dot matrix, laser and inkjet printers. Prints pedigree charts with four or five generations per page, does cascading pedigree charts and with an add-on utility will create a wall chart pedigree, family group sheets, alphabetical lists which can be user-defined. Box charts can be done with add-on. Only the $99 version will do descendant charts. Reports can be sent to the printer, printed to disk in ASCII format or viewed on the screen.

Other Features

Some customizing possible.

Utilities

Tree Charts.

MacRoots II

Producer

Itasca Softwords
P. O. Box 427
Bagley, MN 56621-0427
218 785 2745

Basics

Macintosh (MacPlus or higher)
$99. Commercial; Demo $5.
GEDCOM included
Printed manual
Support by phone 218 785 2745; by mail; America Online BruceM88
Purchase from producer

Data Entry

Maximum 10,000 names, 10 marriages per person, 35 children per marriage. Four event fields (one date and three place fields per event) per person and two per marriage with a choice from a list of 30, including LDS ordinance data. Two events per individual and two per family can be user-defined. Supports foreign characters; hot keys for repeat information; marriage label "common law". Note fields for 32K (about 10 pages) of data plus separate file for biographical information (also limited to 32K) which prints on family group sheet. Sources may be linked to each individual or family event field and/or the entire record. Supports "about", "estimated", "after", "before" and other dates. Global place changes. Hot key for repeat information. Option to automatically capitalize first letter of a word in a record entry for faster input.

Data Management

Sort by name or individual or family record numbers. Four generation on-screen ancestors chart for tracing lines. Mark Table for marking records for linking or finding. Search for text in notes. Option to find last saved and last found record. Global place changes.

Printed Charts

Supports dot matrix, laser and inkjet printers. You can select any font style and size in your own system or choose from wide variety within program. One page pedigree chart with up to 10 generations, family group sheets with choice of events, optional footnoted references and optional notes for the individual; individual history sheet; family summary; descendant charts with spouses, events and generation numbers optional; alphabetical lists; ahnentafel charts; list of major source records which is cross-referenced by event and record footnotes; unlinked individuals. Reports can be sent to the printer and some viewed on screen. Printing to disk not yet available.

Individual History   10/26/92   Page 1

Itasca Softworks, P.O. Box 427, Bagley, MN 56621, USA

Name: Abraham Bonnell Jr.[1]   Sex: M   Edit: 10/26/92
Born: 23 Nov 1731 Hunterdon Cty, NJ[2]
Died: 1 Nov 1797

Rec: 8
Birth: Legitimate
Parent: Natural

Marriage(s):

Date	Spouse	Place
1756	Elizabeth Foster	
	Status: Married	

References:

1 *New Jersey Archives*

2 Copy of Family Bible record: Philadelphia Historical Society. Vol. 2, PH 42.16. Taken from a Bible in possession of Arthur Franklin Bonnell of White House, Hunterdon Cty, NJ on 30 Nov 1914.

Officers of New Jersey Regiment in the French and Indian War, March and April 1758/59 Commissions issued by Honorable John Reading, Esq. Hunterdon Co.

Lieut. Abraham Bonnell

Book C2. Commissions in the Office of the Secretary of State of New Jersey.

New Jersey Archives, Vol. 9, pg 185.

It is evident from the record that Abraham Bonnell, Jr. was an ardent patriot. In the minutes of the Provincial Congress on the Committee of Safety of the State of New Jersey, (Trenton, New Jersey 1879, pg 184) is a list of the Deputies who attended the Session of the Month of August from Hunterdon County. Abraham Bonnell was one of the fifteen. On pages 563/5 *A Resolution passed July 18, 1776. An Ordinance for detaching two thousand of the Militia.*

BONNELL

Officers appointed to command the respective battalions;viz; in the counties of Sommerset, Sussex and Hunterdon, Mark Thompson, Colonel; Abraham Bonnell, Lieutenant Colonel.

Lt. Colonel Abraham Bonnell is recorded in the Adjutant's Office at Trenton, NJ and in Stryker's *Officers and men of New Jersey in the Revolutionary War*, as follows:

Page 336 : Lt. Col. in State Troops
Page 342 : Lt. Col. 2nd Regiment, State Troops
Page 357 : Lt. Col. in Militia in 3rd Regiment, Hunterdon County, N. Jersey.

These records make Lt. Col. Abraham Bonnell an eligible for membership in the Societies previously mentioned and also in the Daughters of the Revolution, Daughters of the American Revolution, Sons of the Revolution and the Sons of the American Revolution.

MacRoots II: Individual History Report with references and notes.

Origin
Version 1.26

Producer

Terrett Systems
1257 Nestor St.
Couitlam, B.C., Canada V3E 1H4
604 941 2819

Basics

DOS
$29. Shareware
GEDCOM included: Import only
Printed manual with registration
Support by phone 604 941 2819 or by mail
Purchase from producer or shareware store

Data Entry

Unlimited number of names, four marriages per individual, 20 children per marriage. Supports foreign characters; macros for repeat information. Edit screen includes fields for given name, surname, alias, gender, four set events (birth, baptism, died and buried), occupation, address and comments, place for parents' record numbers, marriage record number and children's record numbers. Separate unlimited text size area, one for notes and another bibliography; no word wrap in text editor. Four set events include date and place on one line limited to 35 characters. Date in numerical form only, either European (DD-MM) or American (MM-DD) style. Supports "circa", "before" and "after". Marriage record has fields for record number of bride and groom, marriage license number and separate fields for location (42 characters) and date. Records are automatically numbered using letters and numbers with the initial letters based on the person's first name. Linking is done by placing the appropriate record number for spouse, parents or children on an individual's record. The event history screen at the bottom of the screen contains the last 20 records you have worked on. It includes name of the individual or names of marriage partners and record numbers of everyone noted on that record. A record number can be "picked" from this screen and entered into the record on which you are working. Usually the newest person being entered can be linked to someone on this list so the record number for the link is usually easy to find. Concealed comments option for sensitive information. Warnings for unreasonable ages of individuals at marriage, parenthood, etc.

Data Management

Good sorting capabilities. Can sort on a name or any part of a name, including wild cards. Will also search on data in any field and position including specific characters throughout; specific characters at the beginning or end followed or preceded by wild cards; soundex search. Will search on multiple fields and can be set to select only those that match every field or only match any one field. Multiple searches also available. Tree screen shows four generations of ancestors. Memory resident clipboard can be used to maintain an index of records. Children and marriages automatically arranged chronologically.

Printed Charts

Pedigree charts (five generations per sheet), family group sheets, descendant charts, alphabetical and chronological lists, user-defined reports and lists, box charts, ahnentafel, missing data, inherited traits, book style ahnentafel and auto narratives. Although dates are entered in numbers, they will be printed in letters on some reports. Reports can be sent to the printer, to a disk file in ASCII format or viewed on the screen.

Other Features

Help screens. Date calculator to give you the day of the week for a date. Any clipboard selection can be saved to disk and restored at any time and can be resorted.

Comments

Will run under Windows. Files include Windows icon and PIF.

Pedigree

Producer

Pedigree Software
123 Links Drive
Solihull B91 2DJ
U.K.
(021) 704 2839

Basics

DOS
$89. Commercial; Demo available. $5
GEDCOM included
Printed manual
Support by phone 44 021 704 2839 (6-10PM UK time), by mail or CompuServe (100024,2470)
Purchase from producer

Data Entry

Up to 20 databases in a directory, each database will hold 10,000 names or one megabyte, 10 marriages per person, 20 children per marriage. Each individual record contains 45 fields including surname, forename, prefix, occupation, residence dwelling, phone, locality, county, post code; four events, birth, christening, death, and burial, all have fields for date, place, notes and source. Field names can be changed to suit the user. (LDS fields could be added.) Each event can be up to 255 characters and can have a note up to 4000 characters. Supports foreign characters. Separate records can be created for source documents and linked to specific events. Note pad for repeat information. Four generation pedigree chart on screen makes it easy to edit and add people.

Data Management

Indexes can be created on up to 20 fields and displayed on the screen. Up to four sorts can be made on any field, name, places, dates, record numbers or any field, allowing you to produce a list of "all Smiths born after 1810" for example. Soundex search supported.

Printed Charts

Supports dot matrix, laser, inkjet and color printers. Family group sheets, pedigree (five generations on one sheet and up to 30 generations on multiple pages), descendant charts, alphabetical and chronological lists, ancestor and descendant wide trees (dropline charts) with choice of brief, normal or full detail, descendant and ancestor tall trees (left to right charts with ancestor either on the right or the left) user-defined reports. Can view on the screen, send to the printer or print to disk. You can also design your own tables and reports.

Other Features

The screen lists function key choices across the top and bottom. Pull down menus guide you through many choices. Help screens for additional information. Demo comes with royal family database. You can add 170 of your own database, but cannot print.

Comments

The ancestor wide trees make a very nice dropline chart. The demo includes a tutorial to step you through the use of the program.

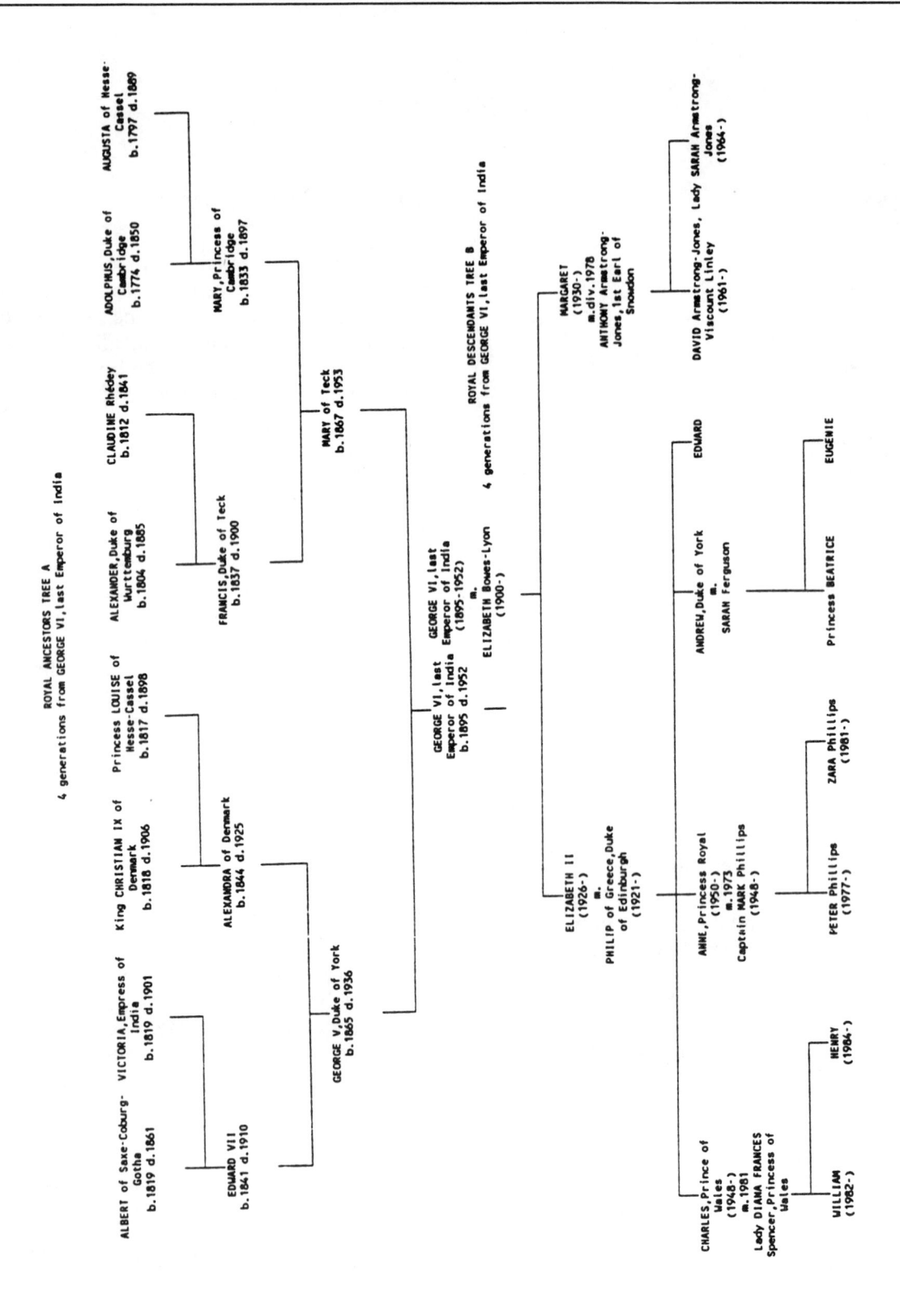

ROYAL ANCESTORS TREE A
4 generations from GEORGE VI, last Emperor of India

```
                                                                AUGUSTA of Hesse-
                                                                Cassel
                                                                b.1797 d.1889
                                                         ┐
                                              ADOLPHUS,Duke of
                                              Cambridge
                                              b.1774 d.1850
                                       ┐                 │
                                                         ├ MARY,Princess of
                                                         │ Cambridge
                                                         │ b.1833 d.1897
                                              CLAUDINE Rhédey
                                              b.1812 d.1841
                                                         ┘
                                              ALEXANDER,Duke of
                                              Württemburg
                                              b.1804 d.1885
                                                         ┐
                                                         ├ FRANCIS,Duke of Teck
                                                         │ b.1837 d.1900
                                                         ┘
                                       ┘
                                       MARY of Teck
                                       b.1867 d.1953
  ALBERT of Saxe-Coburg-                ┐
  Gotha
  b.1819 d.1861
                   ┐
                   ├ EDWARD VII
                   │ b.1841 d.1910
  VICTORIA,Empress of
  India
  b.1819 d.1901
                   ┘                   │
                                       ├ GEORGE V,Duke of York
                                       │ b.1865 d.1936
  King CHRISTIAN IX of
  Denmark
  b.1818 d.1906
                   ┐                   │
                   ├ ALEXANDRA of Denmark
                   │ b.1844 d.1925
  Princess LOUISE of
  Hesse-Cassel
  b.1817 d.1898
                   ┘                   ┘

                                       GEORGE VI,last
                                       Emperor of India
                                       (1895-1952)
                                           m.
                                       ELIZABETH Bowes-Lyon
                                       (1900-  )
```

ROYAL DESCENDANTS TREE B
4 generations from GEORGE VI, last Emperor of India

```
                                                      MARGARET
                                                      (1930- )
                                                      m.div.1978
                                                      ANTHONY Armstrong-
                                                      Jones,1st Earl of
                                                      Snowdon
                                                                    ┬ DAVID Armstrong-Jones,
                                                                    │ Viscount Linley
                                                                    │ (1961- )
                                                                    │
                                                                    └ Lady SARAH Armstrong-
                                                                      Jones
                                                                      (1964- )

   ELIZABETH II
   (1926- )
      m.
   PHILIP of Greece,Duke
   of Edinburgh
   (1921- )
           ┬ ANNE,Princess Royal
           │ (1950- )
           │ m.1973
           │ Captain MARK Phillips
           │ (1948- )
           │         ┬ PETER Phillips
           │         │ (1977- )
           │         └ ZARA Phillips
           │           (1981- )
           │
           ├ ANDREW,Duke of York
           │ m.
           │ SARAH Ferguson
           │         ┬ Princess BEATRICE
           │         └ EUGENIE
           │
           ├ EDWARD
           │
           └ CHARLES,Prince of
             Wales
             (1948- )
             m.1981
             Lady DIANA FRANCES
             Spencer,Princess of
             Wales
                     ┬ WILLIAM
                     │ (1982- )
                     └ HENRY
                       (1984- )
```

Pedigree: Ancestors Tree and Descendants Tree.

Pedigree Pursuit

Producer

Wes Landen
WL Futures Associates
613 Calle del Cerrito
San Clemente, CA 92672
714 492 4565

Basics

DOS
$129. + 5. s/h. Commercial. Free demo
GEDCOM included
Manual on disk
Support by phone 7-11PM Pacific

Data Entry

32,767 record maximum. Will handle BC dates. Date entry in format of your choice. Ditto key for surnames, places and source notes. Templates for sources notes. Search-and-replace for names. Supports foreign characters. Places are entered in four 16-character fields.

Data Management

Will list unconnected individuals. Relationships can be computed and printed on family group records. Has match and merge. Can check and change LDS temple codes. Search-and-replace for names.

Printed Charts

Family group options include printing other marriage information on the chart or in the notes, printing blank lines when there is no information or are no children, print charts in book style. Prints pedigree chart, descendant chart, birthday lists and blank forms. Family group charts print in alphabetical order for easy filing. Supports color printers. Can suppress printing of notes with sensitive information. Option to print notes only once among multiple family group sheets. Sorted lists: name, family, place, list of localities for a given surname, family group, pedigree. LDS entry forms, incomplete ordinances.

Other Features

Has option for Ancestral File submission. Backup option. On-line help. Rapid switching between printers. GEDCOM not necessary to run with Personal Ancestral File data; however, will not support notes in external files.

Comments

Free upgrade of next major release version sent automatically to each purchaser.

Personal Ancestral File
Version 2.2

Producer

The Church of Jesus Christ of Latter-day Saints
Family History Department
Ancestral File Operations Unit, 2WW
50 East North Temple Street
Salt Lake City, UT 84150
801 240 2584

Basics

DOS (Macintosh ver. 2.1 listed separately below)
$35. Commercial
GEDCOM included
Printed manual
Support by phone 801 240 2584 (6AM-4:30PM) Monday, 6AM-8PM Tuesday-Friday, Mountain; own BBS 801 240 3909
Purchase from
   Salt Lake Distribution Center
   1999 West 1700 South
   Salt Lake City UT 84101
   (Check to: Corporation of the President)
   800 537 5950 Visa or Mastercard

Data Entry

Data entered through individual entry screen and marriage entry screen. Maximum of 65,535 individuals, 60 marriages per individual, 30 children per marriage. Data entered in 16-character fields (four for name, one for title, four for each event place). Event fields for birth, christening, death, burial, marriage and LDS ordinances. Ditto keys to duplicate fields forward from previous entry and down within same entry. Hot keys to repeat previously entered fields, a list of the last 20 individuals entered, and shelling to DOS. On-line help includes lists of codes for states and temples. Pedigree Search screen allows adding and editing of data and notes, and links generations. Automatic checks and messages for errors in data entry, such as death before the birth. Verification check for spelling inconsistencies. Dates may be entered in any format and will convert to standard day-month-year; modifiers abt, bef, aft and double-dates accepted. One note file per database with up to 32 screens per individual for documentation of events and biographical and other notes; notes can also be entered in separate files using a word processor. Documentation notes are distinguished by a "!". Notes can be tagged for unlimited events or other categories of information.

Data Management

Pedigree Search screen displays three generations at a time and allows full browsing of all data, adding and editing of data and notes, linking generations, browsing alphabetical lists, display of five generation pedigree chart which scrolls to display all entered ancestors. Modify Family Structure has option to change child order or to change spouse order. Focus-Design Reports can be used to select groups of individuals by name, date or place of events, or any combination. Records with empty fields can also be identified, producing lists of everyone without a birthdate, without a county entered, etc. Notes can be searched for any string of characters and a list produced of individuals who have that note. Focus/Design lists are placed in a Focus List where they can be viewed, edited or printed. Match/Merge will search the database for possible duplicates and display them on the screen side-by-side for user analysis and merging if desired. A list can also be printed. If duplicates are already identified they can be selected and merged. Notes can also be merged. A second Match/Merge menu, accessed by setting the environment variable, will automatically merge individuals with matching ID fields, such as the Ancestral File Number which is placed in the ID field when importing from the Ancestral File.

Printed Charts

Configuration lists 44 printers and has option to create or modify an entry. Prints to printer, disk or screen, or pages to print can be selected. 35 pre-designed charts and reports. Pedigree charts (four, five, six generations), family group charts, both also cascading, with index. LDS or non-LDS options. Ancestry chart with option for wall chart in 12 or 20 cpi. Descendancy chart with birth-death years, ahnentafel with full dates and places for birth, marriage and death. Lists sorted by RIN, MRIN, name, place, ID number, family group, name code. Other lists include individuals with notes, end-of-line individuals, individuals without recorded parents, surname frequencies, and possible record problems (lists data that is outside demographic norms such as mothers over 46, husbands and wives with the same surname, etc. and children or spouses out of order). Prints individual summaries (listing all data for the individual, up to three marriages, parents, all notes) and family summaries. Summaries and family group records can be range printed. Blank charts and various forms can be printed in LDS or non-LDS format. Additional unlimited custom reports can be printed from the Focus/Design option.

Other Features

Relationship calculator also shows common ancestor. Date calculator has fields to enter first date, last date or the interval between; any two are entered and the third is calculated, with the first and last date displayed on two calendars. Dates before 1752 give message about possible inaccuracies due to change to Gregorian calendar in 1752. Soundex option displays all entries with the same soundex code as well as the code for the entered name. Other options are a descendancy count and name frequency report and a birth date graph (range for the whole database, not per individual). Two databases can be accessed and viewed at one time by switching between them. This is useful for comparing your data with data which has been received from someone else or from Family-Search. Data files can also be checked for possible corruption or other linking problems and problems can be fixed automatically. A backup routine is available from the exiting screen and the number of disks required in every size/density is shown. Configuration options can be changed on a temporary basis. Numerous choices include graphics lines on printouts and setting of colors and margins.

A Convert program is included which will change a database from all uppercase to first letter uppercase only, and also will change LDS temple codes previously entered in the two letter code, to the new three, four or five letter codes.

Research Data Filer (RDF) is included. This separate database program will store and manage your research notes and your research documentation. It provides an index to your paper files and gives you instant access to any information in any grouping or selection. Subgroups of data can be made and bibliographies maintained for any file. Reports can be printed.

The Genealogical Information Exchange (GIE) program is included, and has options for LDS temple submission and Ancestral File submission, both of which will screen the data for possible missing information and print lists of names submitted. GEDCOM option will create a GEDCOM file for export, and import either all or part of a GEDCOM file. GEDCOM files in original or paragraph format, and Listing Files, containing any data not converted, can be printed. A configuration option will put all Listing File information in the individual's notes, saving reading and re-entry of this data.

Comments

Personal Ancestral File is simple to use but very complex in features and performance. To augment the manual that comes with the soft ware, Joan Lowrey has written the *Personal Ancestral File Users Guide*. There are many user groups throughout the world. Finished second in *Genealogical Computing*'s "Software to Beat" balloting in 1992.

Utilities

Utilities for the DOS version include: AHNDES 1.7, Cascade 1.3, Descend 2.2, EDITPAF, FamilyPerfect, Family Records Utilities, Family Tree Print P22d (PAFP), FAMSORT 2.3, FOREST, FR_PRINT, GEN-BOOK, GENEPAF 8.1, GENENUM, GIPSI 2.2 and GIPSI Plus, Henry 1.3, HotNotes 2.2, HQ Pedigree Print 2.21, IMPORT 2.6, KinWrite, Lowcase 1.3, Marriage Search 1.3, NAMECLEN, NOTECLEN, NOTETOOL, PAF NOTES, PAF Toolbox, PAF Replace, PAF Viewer for Windows 1.2, PAF2PAF, PAFAbility 2.06, PAFAIDE, PAFNAMES, PAFSPLIT, PAFSTAMP, PEDIGREE, RDF Convert, RDF2GED 1.2, RECLAIM 3.0.

Personal Ancestral File 2.1 for the Macintosh

This version, released in December 1989, does not have all of the features given above for the DOS version. Match/Merge and Focus/Design Reports are not included. Charts that can be printed: pedigree (four or five generations), family group, sorted lists (RIN, MRIN, name, ID), incomplete LDS ordinances and sealings, four blank charts, LDS temple submission forms, descendancy (10 generation limit, shows birth dates only), individuals with notes, unconnected individuals and individual summaries. Only documentation notes will print with the family group chart. Unique features are the ability to browse entries in the name list and select a previous entry for duplication, cut-and-paste for field text and an index-reference help feature.

Utilities

A utility for the Macintosh version is GED-Companion.

FOCUS LIST OF TWINS IN THE DATABASE
Sorted by Birth Date

4 Feb 1993   Page 1

Name	Birth Date Death Date	Birth Place Death Place	Spouse or *Father Name
FOWLER,Minnie Lee-1925...............	....	....	Harold WASSON-1942.....................
FOWLER,Bennie D.-1926...............	....	....	*John W. FOWLER-1919....................
KOEPPEN,Christian Gottfried-861.....	18 Dec 1779 1780	Prenzlau,Brandenburg,Prussia,Germany.. Prenzlau,Brandenburg,Prussia,Germany..	*Johann George KOEPPEN-845..............
KOEPPEN,Johann Peter-860............	18 Dec 1779 1780	Prenzlau,Brandenburg,Prussia,Germany.. Prenzlau,Brandenburg,Prussia,Germany..	*Johann George KOEPPEN-845..............
KOEPPEN,Christiane Louise-815.......	8 Aug 1800 11 Aug 1800	Prenzlau,Brandenburg,Prussia,Germany.. Prenzlau,Brandenburg,Prussia,Germany..	*Christian Friedrich KOEPPEN-308........
KOEPPEN,Christian Friedrich-816.....	8 Aug 1800 18 Aug 1800	Prenzlau,Brandenburg,Prussia,Germany.. Prenzlau,Brandenburg,Prussia,Germany..	*Christian Friedrich KOEPPEN-308........
KOEPPEN,Henrietta-868...............	4 Apr 1836	Prenzlau,Brandenburg,Prussia,Germany..	*Adolph Friedrich KOEPPEN-839...........
KOEPPEN,Wilhelm-869.................	4 Apr 1836	Prenzlau,Brandenburg,Prussia,Germany..	*Adolph Friedrich KOEPPEN-839...........
SCOTT,James Thomas-2197.............	1848	,,MS..	*William SCOTT-2169.....................
SCOTT,Daniel W.-2196................	1848	,,MS..	*William SCOTT-2169.....................

Personal Ancestral File: Focus-Design report on twins in the database.

POSSIBLE RECORD PROBLEMS

4 Feb 1993   Page 1

Name	Problem
Mary (Polly)-32	Dual birth date spans 15 years
James WILKINS-37	Dual birth date spans 24 years
Catherine-38	Dual birth date spans 26 years
Ernest Francis NEUMANN-90	Christening is 12 years after birth
Catherine-157	Dual birth date spans 11 years
Rebecca LOWREY-221	Dual death date spans 15 years
Martha GUTH-397	Christening is 13 years after birth
Marie Elsie NEUMANN-409	Birth is 898 years later than death
GREEN-727	Dual birth date spans 52 years
PICKERING-728	Dual birth date spans 36 years
Richard Michael WATSON-955	Dual death date spans 11 years
AKIN-1284	Dual birth date spans 30 years
Lucy CULVER-1332	Birth is 892 years later than death
Laura Erving MORAN-1470	Death is 104 years after birth
Ellis BOYT-1997	Death is 103 years after birth
Crystal Pauline GREEN-3420	Dual death date spans 20 years
Francis Marion LOWREY-14	Spouse's (RIN=15) birth 16 years apart
James Abraham LOWREY-223	Born 1 years before parents' marriage
Francis Marion LOWREY-14	Child not listed in order of birth
Sarah LOWREY-225	Child not listed in order of birth
Mary Jane WATSON-957	Mother (RIN=28) was 46 when born
Sherod HOOD-1148	Born 2 years before parents' marriage
Mary L. (Polly) WILKINS-30	Mother (RIN=38) was 49 when born
Sarah (Sally) WILKINS-1884	Child not listed in order of birth
Edward HOOD-1134	Born 2 years before parents' marriage
Bedia (Bridget) HOOD-1144	Mother (RIN=40) was 46 when born
Elizabeth HOOD-1145	Mother (RIN=40) was 49 when born
Mary Etta GREEN-61	Child not listed in order of birth
Susan J. WHITE-760	Mother (RIN=71) was 46 when born
William KIMBELL-72	Spouse's (RIN=73) birth 24 years apart
Mary (Molly) KIMBELL-93	Born 1 years before parents' marriage
(female) MITCHELL-3050	Child not listed in order of birth
Martha MITCHELL-2019	Child not listed in order of birth
Mary A. MITCHELL-2026	Mother (RIN=75) was 46 when born
Susan Elizabeth BOYT-83	Only 12 when married to RIN 82
Henry W. GREEN-282	Mother (RIN=83) was only 14 when born
E. G. Urb? GREEN-1438	Child not listed in order of birth
Moses GREEN-1441	Mother (RIN=85) was 46 when born
William KIMBELL-72	Surname and spouse's (RIN=3382) surname same
Johanne Dorothea DREYSSE-178	Mother (RIN=177) was only 13 when born
Maria Barbara OTT-146	Only 13 when married to RIN 145
Jacob SCHMITT-169	Surname and spouse's (RIN=170) surname same
Johann Christoph DREYSSE-179	Only 15 when married to RIN 180
Maximilliane E DREYSSE-181	Mother (RIN=180) was only 14 when born
James Abraham LOWREY-223	Only 9 when married to RIN 228
Nancy-228	Only 0 when married to RIN 223
Sicily Angeline LOWREY-3080	Child not listed in order of birth
Joseph KEMPTER-131	Spouse's (RIN=262) birth 18 years apart
Johanna ZWICK-262	Marriage is 64 years after birth
Anne M. GANLY-691	Mother (RIN=314) was only 9 when born
Martin GANLY-694	Child not listed in order of birth
Johann MUELLER-322	Spouse's (RIN=323) birth 17 years apart
Geraldine Blanche CODORI-320	Child not listed in order of birth

Personal Ancestral File: Chart showing possible problems in the database.

Relativity
Version 1.80

Producer

Guardian Data Systems
516 Swain Ave.
Elmhurst, IL 60126
708 834 2534

Basics

DOS
$119. + $4.50 s/h
  limited version (500 records) - shareware - $39.00 + $4.50 s/h.
GEDCOM included
Manual: printed in commercial version and on disk in shareware
Support by phone 708 834 2534 and on CompuServe 76636,1711
Purchase from producer (by phone or CompuServe with VISA, Mastercard or American Express), download evaluation copy from bulletin boards

Data Entry

Unlimited number of data directories, 1,000,000 records per directory in commercial version, 500 in shareware version and 100 in evaluation copy; unlimited marriages per person, 24 children per marriage. Link from "navigation screen" which shows three generations. Record numbers not used. Unlimited number of marriages and children. Edit screen with many fields: first, middle and last name, sex, nickname, married name, title, Jr./Sr., alias. Birth field includes birth date prefix (c., cir., btw., abt.), date, city, state or province, county, country, multiple birth (yes or no), how many, adopted and by whom. Death field includes the same date and places as for birth, burial location and cause of death, age at death or current age if still living. Third field, History, has one user-defined field plus education, religion, military service, occupation(s), immigration date, method, country from and to. Alternate field label choices allow you to use one of the following in the birth field: birth date, baptism date, christening date or bar mitzvah date. In death field you can use death date, burial date, cause of death or tombstone inscription. No LDS fields. Will not accept a year or month and year by itself without a modifier, i.e., cannot enter the year 1816 alone. Four date fields, including three in numerical form (1/5/1892). One source note of 60 characters per data entry field. Text field up to 64K per individual using built-in word processor. Duplicate name warning. User-defined data fields can be created using macro keys. These fields can be included in the biographical text and the user can extract on anything in text.

Data Management

Good search capabilities. Name search will display an alphabetical list of surnames, then given names within the surname selected; press right arrow to see birth dates for names on list. Also will search on Soundex. Can search for all ancestors or descendants of a person. List displays names and relationship to key. Extract query will search on any field of the edit screen, multiple searches (and/or qualifiers) with choice of equal to, not equal to, greater than, greater than or equal to, less than, less than or equal to. Search results are in list of names with columns representing all fields in a record accessed by pressing the right arrow key. Pressing F6 allows you to edit the record. Feature to find common ancestor of two individuals and show their relationship.

Printed Charts

Supports many printers including dot matrix, laser, and inkjet; limited number of reports. Can only send reports to printer, not to disk nor display on the screen (this will be included in next update). Choice of surnames in caps or regular print. Reports include facts sheets (all information on an individual from the edit screen, plus parents' names and birth dates, siblings' names, birth order and birth dates, spouse and children with birth dates plus biographical information from text file), four generation ancestor chart (pedigree), complete ancestor chart (cascading pedigree), family group sheet, one page ahnentafel chart, complete ahnentafel chart and descendant report. Descendant report is in book style using the record numbering system. Compresses quite a bit of information into a small area, but does not include biographical information. User-defined report. User-defined and chronological lists.

Other Features

Help screens. Address book (commercial version only). GEDCOM very easy to use with several nice features: can display list of people in GEDCOM file before importing, can display a list of places in columns showing the field where they have been placed so you can move data to correct fields (if you only had a state in the original program, it may have been placed in the city field if fields from originating program not the same as Relativity), can tag records being imported and later delete if you don't want or untag if you want to keep.

Comments

Hard drive required; will not run under Windows, Deskvue or with TSRs. Easy to use. Edit screen has places for a great many fixed fields, but the majority of fields will not be used for any one individual. The fixed fields take up so much room that there is very little flexibility to add other fields that the user would find helpful. Reports are limited, but fact sheet and descendancy report are different from usual reports and very useful. Evaluation copy available on CompuServe and GEnie as RELSYS.EXE.

1. George Gardiner parents not on file
             Born: ABT 1740   Died: ABT 1816 in Leeds Co., Can., Ont.

   spouse (1)   Ruth Married: ABT 1797

             i. Emily Gardiner   Born: ABT 1799   Died: 14 Apr 1852
            ii. Nancy Gardiner   Born: 17 May 1800   Died: 04 Jan 1870

   cogenitor(2)

           iii. John Gardiner   Born: ABT 1766   Died: abt. 1829
            iv. Catherine Gardiner   Born: 14 Oct 1769   Died: 11 Jan 1830
      2.   v. Ann Gardiner   Born: ABT 1774   Died: ABT 1822   3 Children
            vi. George Gardiner   Born: 18 May 1782   Died: 06 Dec 1850
           vii. Jean Gardiner
          viii. Martha Gardiner

2. Ann Gardiner daughter of George Gardiner (#1)
             Born: ABT 1774   Died: ABT 1822

   spouse (1)   Justin Truesdell Married: ABT 1794 in Can.?

             i. Samuel Truesdell   Born: ABT 1796   Died: AFT 1861
      3.   ii. William Truesdell   Born: ABT 1797   Died: AFT 1869   10 Children
           iii. Justin Truesdell   Born: 24 Jul 1802   Died: abt. 1872

3. William Truesdell son of Justin Truesdell and Ann Gardiner (#2)
             Born: ABT 1797   Died: AFT 1869

   spouse (1)   Ann Nancy Married: ABT 1818 in Can.

      4.   i. Ann Truesdell   Born: 25 Feb 1819   Died: 06 Nov 1891   11 Children
            ii. Benjamin Truesdell   Born: ABT 1820
           iii. Mary Truesdell   Born: ABT 1822
            iv. Huldah Gertrude Truesdell   Born: ABT 1827   Died: 15 Mar 1890
             v. Sarah Truesdell   Christnd: 04 Mar 1832
            vi. William Henry Truesdell Born: ABT 1832   Died: 11 Apr 1885
           vii. Sarah Truesdell   Born: ABT 1839   Died: abt. 1914
          viii. Elizabeth Truesdell
            ix. John Truesdell   Died: abt. 1855

   spouse (2)   Margaret

             x. Margaret Agnes Truesdell   Christnd: 26 Jan 1837

4. Ann Truesdell daughter of William Truesdell (#3) and Ann Nancy
             Born: 25 Feb 1819 in Quebec, Can.   Died: 06 Nov 1891 in Leeds, Can., Ont.

   spouse (1)   Charles Shipman Married: 05 Oct 1846 in Leeds, Can., Ont.

Relativity: Descendancy Report.

Page 1   Q/E: 2

                          INDIVIDUAL FACTS SHEET
                                   For
                             Daniel Truesdell

       Age: Sex: M

BIRTH
        Birth Date: abt 1749
             City: Redding   ST/Prov.: CT
           County: Country:

DEATH
        Death Date: aft 1810
             City: ST/Prov.:
           County: Country:

HISTORY
        Education:
        Religion:
        Mil. Service:
        Occupation:
        Immigration: abt 1790   Method:
              From: New York   To: Canada

FAMILY
        Father: William Truesdell   Born: 21 Jul 1722
        Mother: Deliverance (Jeason)   Born: 01 Nov 1724

        Siblings:
           1) Justin Truesdell   Born: ABT 1755

- -
     Spouse #1: Huldah (Thorp)   Born:

     Marriage Date:
           Church:
             City: ST/Prov.:
           County: Country:

        Children:
           1) Cornelius Truesdell   Born: bef 1785
           2) Daniel Truesdell   Born: abt Aug 1785

===
BIOGRAPHICAL INFORMATION

    Daniel immigrated to Canada with his brother Justin and settled in Leeds
    County, Ontario. In 1810, he was living in Quebec. Many of his
    descendantss returned to New York.

===
Keeper of Records: Donna Przecha

Relativity: Individual Facts Sheet.

Reunion

Producer

Leister Productions
P. O. Box 289
Mechanicsburg, PA 17055
717 697 1378

Basics

Macintosh
$169. Commercial
GEDCOM included
Printed manual
Support by phone 717 697 1378 (10AM-5PM Eastern); by mail; CompuServe 71201,1105; America Online: LeisterPro
Purchase from retail store or dealer

Data Entry

Database size limited only by hard disk availability, nine marriages per person, 19 children per marriage. Supports foreign characters. Six events with choice of events, some of which can be user-defined. No LDS ordinance data. Three note fields with a limit of 30,000 bytes per note plus an all purpose note field of the same size for biographical information.

Data Management

Sorts by name, place, dates and other fields. Calculates relationships.

Printed Charts

Supports dot matrix, laser, inkjet and color printers. Pedigree charts with maximum of seven generations per sheet, cascading pedigree chart and wall chart on multiple pages; family group sheets, descendant charts, alphabetical and chronological lists and box charts (not dropline). Book style with legal numbering system. Reports can be sent to the printer, to disk in ASCII format or viewed on the screen.

Other Features

Help screens. Links high resolution color pictures to information.

ROOTS III

Producer

Commsoft, Inc.
P. O. Box 310
Windsor, CA 95492-0310
707 838 4300; 800 327 6687

Basics

DOS
$250. + s/h Commercial. Demo $10.
GEDCOM additional $40.
Manual included
Support: Phone: 707 838 4300 (9AM-4PM, Pacific); BBS: 707 838 6373; FAX: 707 838 6343; Prodigy: JJSR40A; GEnie: H.NURSE; CompuServe: 73710,773.
Purchase from producer, who periodically has special sales, dealers, who may have discount prices, and retail stores.

Data Entry

Data entered through individual edit screen and marriage edit screen. Maximum of 65,000 names but the larger databases require additional expanded memory. Names can be up to 60 characters and entered in any order. (Suitable for Oriental names where surname is first or Spanish compound surnames.) One name should be marked as surname for indexing and highlighting in reports. Each individual can have up to six events with a choice of 27 predefined labels (including LDS events) and four you can name yourself. Eight user-defined "flags" so you can tag records of particular interest. Each person can have up to 30 marriages and there is no limit to the number of children per marriage. Foreign characters are supported. Surname for child automatically entered. Hot key to complete previously used locations and footnotes. Also, fields to indicate illegitimacy and stillborn; adopted, foster children or unrelated; ancestor and descendant interest (for Tiny Tafel matching system); occupation; and date sure codes to show your opinion of the reliability of the information. Automatic checks and error messages for inconsistencies such as person over 100 at death, mother over 50 at birth of child, mother or father died before child was born, marriage after the birth of the child, etc. Automatically creates double dates for pre-1752 dates (or other change-over date you select). Arranges children and marriages chronologically by date. "Estimated" date that does not print on reports for approximated dates. Major footnote records for long footnotes (which can have a text file attached). Each event can be footnoted individually with a short footnote, a major footnote record or both. The entire record can also be footnoted. Four unlimited length text fields: biographical information (for the book form), research notes (for the family group sheet), footnote or source information and external file for text printed separately (i.e., not with a person's data). Text files are entered in a word processor or text editor and any that creates an ASCII file can be used. Most people use the text editor Roots Writer (see section on other programs) because it takes up a small amount of memory, is modified to work well with ROOTS III and is supported by Commsoft.

Data Management

Family group routine shows parents and children of one family. Function keys allow you to move forward or backward through the family line. Trace routine shows all ancestors of an individual. Kinship routine will show relationship between two people, check for possible duplicate records (no facility for merging two records; information must be copied and one record deleted), unlinked records, redundant ancestors (an ancestor that is related to a person through more than once descendant), ahnentafel number. The database can be searched and records isolated up to eight times on any combination of eight fields: vitals and flags (type of event); location; anniversaries (specific date), names, year (before, after or range), relationship (descendants or ancestors), modification history and footnotes. Each subsequent search only looks at those records from the previous search so a very specific group can be identified. Subject stack for storing up to 100 records (probably from a search) for further editing or viewing.

Printed Charts

Supports dot matrix, laser and inkjet printers. Pedigree chart (four, five, six generations with choice of included events) with cascading charts, family group sheet (LDS with set events or Commsoft with choice of included events), ahnentafel (with choice of events), descendant, heredity statistics (minimum, maximum and mean age at marriage, birth of first/last child, death, number of marriages and children for ancestors of any individual), genealogy format (book form for all ancestors or descendants of a person, all people related to a person arranged by family or generation), individual and marriage lists (choice of included events up to 130 characters per one line), major footnotes, calendar/anniversary (what event occurred on what date), relationship, summary data (information in individual edit record), mailing labels and index.

Other Features

Help Screens. Soundex coding. Utility programs Revent, Historiograph and Calendar can be installed to run within ROOTS. Reports can be printed to disk with formatting codes for WordPerfect format (WordPerfect, WordStar 6.0, Words for Windows) or Rich Text format (Ami Pro, Professional Write Plus, Word 5.0). Report can be finished in word processor where you can change fonts, page size, formatting and make use of all of the enhancements of your word processor.

Comments

Selected the "Software to Beat" by *Genealogical Computing* magazine in 1991 and 1992.

ROOTS' most important features are its ability to document sources in detail and to print in book form (genealogy format report). By putting the book into a word processor such as WordPerfect for final editing and printing, it produces a final product that is very professional looking. Its sophisticated sorting capabilities are extremely useful in analyzing your database.

ROOTS is a complex program and takes more time to learn. It is designed for the serious genealogist. Most people feel the need for additional manuals as the program manual is designed as a reference manual, not a learning manual. Additional manuals are *Getting Started with ROOTS III* by Kay Ingalls and *Understanding ROOTS III* and *More Understanding ROOTS III* by Donna Przecha. If you have 640K of RAM memory, you can enter about 2000-3000 people. After that you will need additional memory.

The GEDCOM program is a separate purchase but is necessary if you want to exchange data with anyone or download from the FamilySearch information available at most Family History Centers.

Utilities

Calendar, Dateline, DFoot, GEDCOM, Historiograph, PNames, R3Fix, R3MFNU, R3PST, Revent, R-Plot.

Note: Commsoft is working on a major new genealogy program which should be announced by the time this book is published. Call Commsoft for details.

Ancestors of: Donna Sue **Neister**

Generations: 47   Flags yield: 100.0%

	POP	MEAN	STD DEV	MIN	MAX	UNITS	RECORD NUMBERS MIN	MAX
MALE ANCESTORS: 185								
Age at christening	7	**2.7**	6.5	0.0	18.8	years	572	666
Age at first marriage	73	**27.4**	8.2	15.0	57.0	years	379	575
Age at birth of first child	106	**30.3**	6.3	15.5	48.5	years	379	368
Age at birth of last child	94	**38.6**	9.5	19.3	61.0	years	925	668
Age at death	92	**62.2**	14.9	0.3	98.0	years	660	628
Number of marriages	136	**1.2**	0.5	1.0	3.0		12	810
Number of children	185	**3.9**	3.5	1.0	16.0		327	1813
FEMALE ANCESTORS: 134								
Age at christening	4	**8.5**	12.8	0.0	30.6	years	644	7
Age at first marriage	60	**22.9**	6.0	2.0	42.5	years	1020	7
Age at birth of first child	68	**25.7**	5.6	17.2	43.1	years	553	7
Age at birth of last child	63	**35.0**	7.5	21.5	50.7	years	369	337
Age at death	44	**63.1**	16.7	26.4	88.5	years	407	7
Number of marriages	134	**1.2**	0.4	1.0	3.0		11	361
Number of children	134	**4.4**	3.3	1.0	13.0		7	1072
ALL ANCESTORS: 319								
Age at christening	11	**4.8**	9.8	0.0	30.6	years	572	7
Age at first marriage	133	**25.4**	7.5	2.0	57.0	years	1020	575
Age at birth of first child	174	**28.5**	6.6	15.5	48.5	years	379	368
Age at birth of last child	157	**37.1**	9.0	19.3	61.0	years	925	668
Age at death	136	**62.5**	15.7	0.3	98.0	years	660	628
Number of marriages	270	**1.2**	0.5	1.0	3.0		12	361
Number of children	319	**4.1**	3.4	1.0	16.0		327	1813
Age of all children at death	504	**47.9**	28.1	0.0	98.0	years	210	620
Age of non-infant children at death	465	**51.9**	25.5	1.0	98.0	years	12	620
Male children	1312	**54.7**				percent		
Female children	1312	**45.3**				percent		
Multiple birth events	319	**1.4**				percent		

ROOTS III: Heredity Statistics.

Relatives of Charles Blaine **Neister**

Parents
    Peter David **Neister**
    Elizabeth **Shipman**

Children
    Donna Sue **Neister**
    Mary Abigail **Neister**
    Elizabeth Ann **Neister**
    Laurel Ruth **Neister**

Grandparents
    Joseph **Nichter**
    Salamina (Salome) **Ruch**
    Charles **Shipman**
    Ann **Truesdell**

Siblings
    Perley Irwin **Neister**
    Mary Abigail **Neister**

Grandchildren
    Elizabeth **Przecha**
    Deborah Sue **Przecha**
    Kenneth Allen **Przecha**
    Steven William **Piippo**
    Robert Edward **Piippo**
    Blaine Richard **Smith**
    Barbara Allison **Smith**
    Gregory Wayne **Smith**

Great-Grandparents
    Jacques Philipp Jacob **Ruch**
    Johannes Christian **Nüchter**
    Anna Katharina **Wiegand**
    Margaretha **Lindenmann**
    David **Shipman**
    Elizabeth **Seaman/Simmons**
    William **Truesdell**
    Ann/Nancy

Aunts and Uncles
    Elizabeth **Nichter**
    Madalain (Lana) **Nichter**
    Catharine (Kate) **Nichter**
    John W **Neister**
    Mary **Nichter**
    Joseph **Nichter**

ROOTS III: Relationship Chart.

JUNE 1993

1	Tue	1755	(238 yrs)	Christening of Justin **Truesdell** in Redding, CT. (d. 1803).
		1746	(247 yrs)	Death of Maria Magdalena **Tuchman** in Mertzwiller, Bas-Rhin, France.
2	Wed	1670	(323 yrs)	Christening of James **Woodcock** in E. Harling, Norfolk, Eng. (d. 1678).
		1756	(237 yrs)	Burial of Thomas **Bruce** in Newchurch, IOW, Hants, Eng. (d. 1756).
3	Thu	1780	(213 yrs)	Christening of Phillis **Taylor** in Rodney Stoke, Som, Eng. (dec.).
		1850	(143 yrs)	Birth of Maria Josephina **Nüchter** in Margretenhaun, Hessen-Nassau, Prussia. (d. 1853).
		1790	(203 yrs)	Christening of Richard **Deane** in E. Harling, Norfolk, Eng. (d. 1825).
		1576	(417 yrs)	Christening of Thomas **Trusdale** in Boston, Eng. (d. 1637).
5	Sat	1748	(245 yrs)	Marriage of Thomas **Wavell** (d. 1770)

ROOTS III: Anniversary Report.

```
    Name: Henry Mumford                                                813
    Sex: M          BC: L    PC: N           AI: 0   DI: 0
    Ref:                     Occ: Shopkeeper         Entered: 26 Jul 1991
    Born:  9 Jan 1813        Rodney Stoke, Som, Eng.

    Died: 17 Jul 1879        Rodney Stoke, Som, Eng.

    Chr: 14 Feb 1813         Rodney Stoke, Som, Eng.

 Census:         1841        Rodney Stoke, Som, Eng.
           1841 census, Somerset, Winterstoke, bundle 968
 Census:  5 Apr 1851         Rodney Stoke, Som, Eng.
           1851 census, Rodney Stoke, Pt 114, p 68-79
 Census:         1861        Rodney Stoke, Som, Eng.
           1861 census, Rodney Stoke, Som.
  Flags: :*      :       :Edit+ :    :    :    :    :    :
 Father: William Mumford                                           810
 Mother: Ann [Taylor]                                              811
 RecFnt:
```

ROOTS III: Summary Report, Individual.

The Family Edge

Producer

Carl York
P. O. Box 3157
Knoxville, TN 37927
615 524 1702

Basics

DOS
$99. Commercial (The Family Edge Plus)
$19. Shareware (Version B5.A)
GEDCOM $20 additional
Printed manual (commercial version); on disk (shareware)
Support by phone 615 524 1702, by mail or on CompuServe 72571,2445
Purchase from producer, retail store or dealer (commercial); BBS or shareware store (shareware)

Data Entry

One major difference between the shareware and commercial versions is that the shareware version is limited to 500 names. The commercial version allows one million names per database, unlimited number of marriages per individual, 62 children per marriage. Nine set events, plus LDS, no user-defined. Main menu has surname, sex, given names, date and place for birth and death, burial place, occupation, father, mother, spouse and a one-line note. Pop-up screens if you use function keys to select burial, christening, immigration, marriage. Dates can be entered in any of 18 ways and will be converted to a standard format. Supports "after", "before", "circa", "roughly", question mark (?), "living" and a span of years (such as 1946-50) as structured dates. Other formats can be entered, but will be treated as unstructured and will not be recognized as a date when sorting, calculating and other manipulation of dates. Place fields for state (two letters only with pop-up menu for state abbreviations), county and city. If you insert "X" in state field, "county" becomes "country". City field is 60 characters long and is used for all data except country name in non-U.S. records. Pop-up screen for "history" (text field), alternate parents, source with space for 22 entries. Records are saved automatically as you complete them so you do not accidentally forget to save, but you also cannot ignore a record. It must be deleted or written over. The last entered surname plus two places (one for events while the person was alive, the other for death) are at top of the screen and can be entered into appropriate fields on the edit screen with the ditto key. Up to 24 macros can be created for other repeat information. Parents entered by record number. An asterisk in the father's or mother's field will add last entered person as the parent in the appropriate field. Otherwise number could be noted on scratch pad or located through search. Foreign characters supported with pop-up menu. Text editor for notes has word wrap, cut-paste feature. Notes can be created in other word processors if saved in ASCII format.

Data Management

"Find" feature locates a record after you fill in a portion of the edit screen — record number, name, partial name, soundex code or location. "Next" and "previous" will display other records. If the search was by number, the next record will be by number. If the search was by name, the next name will be in alphabetical order. Toggle to show different types of information at the bottom of the screen: children, full siblings, grandparents, first few lines of history notes, LDS ordinances or marriages. Tree selection allows you to scroll back through the records of seven previous generations. F2 will give you a name list on the screen where you can scan names alphabetically or by number, partial name, code or location. Location search is for state and county or foreign country only. List shows record number, person's name, birth date, death date, and record numbers for father, mother and spouse. This list can be accessed while editing a record so it is easy to see everyone in your database or a partial list at any time. Other function keys allow you to display a pedigree chart, family group sheet, ahnentafel, descendant chart or show blood relationship between two persons.

Printed Charts

Supports dot matrix, laser, inkjet and color printers. List of 14 printers plus four for custom installation. Printing not selected from a print menu but a different function key for each chart is listed on the first help screen. This permits printing in background while working in the edit screen. Name list (alphabetical, record number, location), pedigree chart (five generations with full data on one sheet), cascading pedigree chart for 33 generations (Plus version only). Family group has options of source and history notes for the husband and wife printed at end of the form, sources notes only for husband, wife and all children and grandchildren printed with family data, source notes for all with the family data plus history for husband and wife at the end of the form or no source or history notes. Extended family report (five generation group sheet) which includes names of grandparents, names, birth and death dates and locations of parents, all data for subject couple, full vital data on children and grandchildren. 23 generation ahnentafel, single surname ahnentafel and descendants chart (31 generations in Plus version). Reports can be sent to the printer, to a disk file or viewed on the screen.

Other Features

Scratch pad. Help key displays six pages of general help, including three pages of function key listings. Utility program for screen colors, cursor size, printer selection; clean data files, rebuild index files and recover corrupted data; audit to look for data entry errors (check for possible errors such as minimum and maximum age for mother or father, maximum years between birth and christening, will and death, etc. — parameters can be changed); convert PAF 2.xx files to Family Edge or import or export a GEDCOM file; merge databases. GEDCOM displays location fields where data will transfer and allows you to change. Most fields need editing when transferring from a program with single location field. Very easy to use menu to select from a wide variety of screen colors. Facility for saving screen "snapshots" to view or to save to disk.

Comments

Edit screen well designed in that you only have to look at burial, christening, immigration and other fields if you request them. Limited in sorting as there is no sorting by date. Location sorts only by state and county or, if a foreign country, only by country. Benefits of registration: technical support. Available on CompuServe as TFEB5A.EXE, UTLB5A.EXE and DOCB5A.EXE and on GEnie as TFEPRB5A.EXE, TFEUTB5A.EXE and TFEDOB5A.EXE.

The Family Edge Plus version offers several features not found in the shareware version: up to 57 unique relationships displayed in the blood relationship calculation (19 in the shareware version), 12 user-defined tags for each person, mass tagging of persons in some screens; searching, browsing and listing by those user-defined tags; sorting all or part of the person's file by birth, name, soundex of multiple combinations of the above; re-access to the previous location list, partial names list, tags list and sorted lists; automatic marriage record generation during spouse entry. Also four utility enhancements: split a portion of the database, utility for reporting on available memory, mass edit of county, city and note fields, ability to optimize a file group by removing extraneous data and compressing index files.

Ann Gardiner (#3) born circa 1774, USA; Married (circa 1794 Leeds Co., CANADA) Justin Truesdell (#4); died 1822 to 1824; child of George Gardiner (#1).
George Gardiner (#1) born abt 1733; Married (after 1797) Ruth ??? (#2); died 1816, Leeds Co., CANADA; occ. Farmer.
Deliverance Jeason (#15) born ___; Married (29 Jun 1746 Redding, CT) William Truesdell (#12).
Rachel Mallory (#8) born ___; Married (12 Jun 1832 Leeds Co., Ontario, CANADA) Samuel Truesdell (#5); died Leeds Co., Canada Co.
Rossinda Mallory (#11) born ___; Married Justin Truesdell (#7); Married (11 Apr 1832 Leeds Co., Ontario, CANADA) Justin Truesdell (#7).
Mary Manor (#25) born ___.
Margaret Agnes McLeod (#10) born circa 1815; Married (circa 1836) William Truesdell (#6); died after 1869.
Sarah Purvis (#23) born ___; Married (1822 to 1824) Cornelius Truesdell (#17).
Charles Shipman (#32) born 21 Mar 1814, Maitland, Ont., CANADA; died 28 Jun 1895, Lansdowne, Leeds Co., CANADA; buried Ebenezer Cemetery; occ. Farmer.
Huldah Thorp (#27) born ___; died 11 Jul 1810, Lanora, Quebec, CANADA; buried St. Andrews Cemetery.
Polly Tollman (#29) born ___; Married (25 Jan 1809) Daniel Truesdell (#28).
Ann Truesdell (#31) born 25 Feb 1819, Quebec, CANADA; died 6 Nov 1891, Leeds Co., CANADA; buried Ebenezer Cemetery; child of William Truesdell (#6) and Ann/Nancy ??? (#9).
Cornelius Truesdell (#17) born ___; Married (1822 to 1824) Sarah Purvis (#23); died after 1835; child of Daniel Truesdell (#26) and Huldah Thorp (#27).
Cornelius Truesdell (#24) born Dec 1824, Montreal, Quebec, CANADA; died 7 Jul 1887, Lucky Valley, IA; child of Cornelius Truesdell (#17) and Sarah Purvis (#23).
Daniel Truesdell (#26) born 1749, Redding Co CT; died after 1810; child of William Truesdell (#12) and Deliverance Jeason (#15).
Daniel Truesdell (#28) born 1785, CT; Married (25 Jan 1809) Polly Tollman (#29); died 7 Jun 1867, Colton, NY; buried Pierrepont Cemetery Cem; child of Daniel Truesdell (#26) and Huldah Thorp (#27).
Daniel Rankin Truesdell (#18) born 20 Jun 1805, Sorel, Quebec, CANADA; died 1872; child of Cornelius Truesdell (#17) and Ann Gardiner (#3).
Emily Truesdell (#22) born 1 Mar 1821, CANADA; child of Cornelius Truesdell (#17) and Ann Gardiner (#3).
George Truesdell (#21) born circa 1810, Lower Canada, CANADA; died after 1881; child of Cornelius Truesdell (#17) and Ann Gardiner (#3).
Justin Truesdell (#4) born 1755, Redding, CT; Married (circa 1794 Leeds Co., CANADA) Ann Gardiner (#3); died 5 Jul 1803, Sorel, Quebec, CANADA; occ. Miller; child of William Truesdell (#12) and Deliverance Jeason (#15).
Justin Truesdell (#7) born 24 Jul 1802, Sorel, Quebec, CANADA; Married Rossinda Mallory (#11); Married (11 Apr 1832 Leeds Co., Ontario, CANADA) Rossinda Mallory (#11); died 1872, Leeds Co., CANADA; buried Yonge Mills Cemetery Cem; occ. Farmer; child of Justin Truesdell (#4) and Ann Gardiner (#3).
Maria Truesdell (#19) born 1 Aug 1806, Berthier, Quebec, CANADA; child of Cornelius Truesdell (#17) and Ann Gardiner (#3).
Samuel Truesdell (#5) born circa 1796, Upper Canada, CANADA; Married (12 Jun 1832 Leeds Co., Ontario, CANADA) Rachel Mallory (#8); died after 1861; occ. Farmer; child of Justin Truesdell (#4) and Ann Gardiner (#3).
Sarah Caroline Truesdell (#20) born 24 Sep 1808, Sorel, Quebec, CANADA; child of Cornelius Truesdell (#17) and Ann Gardiner (#3).

The Family Edge: Name list in record number order showing all information from edit screen.

```
FAMILY EDGE              EXTENDED FAMILY REPORT              1 Feb 1993
================================================================================
HUSBAND: Justin Truesdell (#4)
   BORN: 1755                    Redding, CT
CHRIS'D: 1 Jun 1755              Redding, CT
   MARR: circa 1794              Leeds Co., CANADA
   DIED: 5 Jul 1803              Sorel, Quebec, CANADA
    OCC: Miller
 FATHER: William Truesdell (#12) born 21 Jul 1722, North Branford, CT; died after 1784.
 MOTHER: Deliverance Jeason (#15) born ____.
================================================================================
   WIFE: Ann Gardiner (#3)
   BORN: circa 1774              USA
   DIED: 1822 to 1824
 FATHER: George Gardiner (#1) born abt 1733; died 1816, Leeds Co., CANADA; occ. Farmer.
 MOTHER:
================================================================================
1  | NAME: Samuel Truesdell (#5)
M  | BORN: circa 1796             Upper Canada, CANADA
   | MARR: 12 Jun 1832            Leeds Co., Ontario, CANADA
   | DIED: after 1861
   | WIFE: Rachel Mallory (#8)
   |   BORN:                      DIED:
   --------------------------------------------------------------------------------
2  | NAME: William Truesdell (#6)
M  | BORN: circa 1797             Upper Canada, CANADA
   | MARR: circa 1818             Lower Canada (Quebec), CANADA
   | DIED: after 1869
   | WIFE: Ann/Nancy ??? (#9)
   |   BORN:                      DIED: before 1836
   | ALSO: Married circa 1836 Margaret Agnes McLeod (#10);
   --------------------------------------------------------------------------------
   |           Grandchild by Ann/Nancy ??? (#9)
   |  1  NAME: Ann Truesdell (#31)
   |  F  BORN: 25 Feb 1819        Quebec, CANADA
   |     MARR:
   |     DIED: 6 Nov 1891         Leeds Co., CANADA
   |      BUR: Ebenezer Cem, Lansdowne, Leeds Co., CANADA
   --------------------------------------------------------------------------------
3  | NAME: Justin Truesdell (#7)
M  | BORN: 24 Jul 1802            Sorel, Quebec, CANADA
   | MARR:
   | DIED: 1872                   Leeds Co., CANADA
   |  BUR: Yonge Mills Cemetery Cem, Leeds Co., Ontario, CANADA
   | WIFE: Rossinda Mallory (#11)
   |   BORN:                      DIED:
   | ALSO: Married 11 Apr 1832 Rossinda Mallory (#11);
================================================================================
HISTORY NOTES: Justin Truesdell (#4)
      Justin fought on the American side in the Revolutionary War, but he and his
      brother probably can to Canada to get free land.
================================================================================
```

The Family Edge: Extended family report showing 5 generations.

The Master Genealogist

Producer

Bob Velke
Wholly Genes Software
6868 Ducketts Lane
Elk Ridge, MD 21227
410 796 2447

Basics

DOS
$99. Commercial; Free demo
GEDCOM included
Printed manual
Support by phone 410 796 2447 (9AM-9PM Eastern); BBS 703 823 5216; by mail; CompuServe 76366,1760; GEnie B.VELKE; Prodigy pending.
Purchase from producer or dealer

Data Entry

There are no limits on the following: databases, people per database, names per person, events per person, types of events per person, witnesses to a single event, parents per person, children per person, length of each name and place, number and type of source citation and length of descriptive notes. Primary name, birth and death event names (tags) marked with an asterisk to designate as primary tags for producing traditional reports. List of 100 predefined tags plus unlimited number of custom designed tags can be created. There are data entry screens for name, event (birth, marriage, death, other) parental relationship, address, history, add person (quick entry screen for name, date and place of birth and death plus one source citation). Fields appearing on various data entry screens include principle ID numbers, tag type, date, place (detail, city, county, state, country), memo and source citation. It also supports scanned images (PCX, GIF, BMP, TIF and TGA formats) and has surety levels to show your opinion of the quality of the source. Dates can be entered in several forms and converted to the default format. Supports "circa", "before", "after", "ante" "post" and "between". You can also enter irregular dates in a format that will not be converted and the date will be displayed as entered. Source screen for full documentation details. The program assigns a number for future use of this source on other records. Navigation can be done with pull-down menus or hot keys. Functions take place in windows, many of which can be re-sized, zoomed or moved around the screen. Supports foreign characters from ASCII table (using Alt key plus numeric keypad) and hot keys or macros for repeat information. F3 will repeat last location entered, press again for previous up to 15 entries. Can also display a list of all place fields entered and you can select location from list. Events will automatically be sorted in chronological order. Area for biographical information which will print on the family group sheet. Memo field for notes which can be suppressed from person view screen or reports. Unique witness field which can attach a single event to any number of individuals in the database, including unrelated ones. Can also include historical events, such as Chicago fire, and have person a witness to this event which will place person in a location and a time when you may not have any other information on the individual.

Data Management

Three display screens: person, family and tree (pedigree screen). Name list (called a picklist) is a pop-up list of all people in the database: can be filtered by name (surname, given, soundex of surname, soundex of given name, aliases), sex, birth date, death date or ID number. List can be sorted on one parameter and arranged according to another. Will search on a portion of a name. Sort process based on Boolean logic (and/or/not). Relationship calculator. Flags (preset and user-defined) can be set on records to designate certain characteristics or to mark person for inclusion in a special group. Able to display text and images, including color photographs, on the same screen.

Printed Charts

When tested, the printing feature was not activated. You will be able to send reports to the printer, view on the screen, create a GEDCOM file or delimited file for ASCII, DIF, MOD, SDF, SYLK, SK1, WKS, WR1, WRK or XLS. It will print four and five generation pedigree charts, ahnentafel, cascading descendancy, family group sheets, anniversaries and address labels. The book style will not be included in the first release, but is planned for ver. 1.1 with support for WordPerfect formatting versions 4.2 through 5.1.

Other Features

Help screens. Research Log which can be tied to particular people, sources or repositories. Text editor with cut and paste, search and replace, tabs, word wrap and other features. Time lines on world events in various categories which you can create yourself. Date calculator and calendar.

Comments

This program was still in the testing stage when this book went to press. It is designed for the serious computer genealogist. The hardware requirements are quite high so be sure it will run on your computer before obtaining a copy. It requires a hard drive; a 386 or higher computer is strongly recommended; the program needs about three megabytes of hard drive space and 2.5 megabytes of extended or expanded RAM to run. DOS 4.0 or later with 5.0 highly recommended. Also recommended is four megabytes, rather than 2.5, of extended or expanded memory, a color monitor, a mouse and disk cache software such as Microsoft SMARTDRV. This version will not run under Windows, but a true Windows version is under development. The program is designed to be easy to operate, but like any program that will do so many things, it will take longer to learn.

Tree Easy

Producer

FAMware
1580 East Dawn Dr.
Salt Lake City, UT 84121
801 943 6908

Basics

DOS
$24.95 Commercial
GEDCOM additional $12.
Manual on disk; help screens
Support by phone 801 943 6908 (8:30AM-4:30PM Mountain) or by mail
Purchase from retail store or producer

Data Entry

20,000 names, birth, death, burial and three marriages per individual, 20 children per marriage. Cross referenced to parents' and children's record numbers.

Data Management

Three generation pedigree chart displays family and locates records for editing.

Printed Charts

Supports dot matrix, laser and color printers. Pedigree, individual data sheets, photo charts and sorted surname indexes with choice of date formats and line drawing characters. Reports can be sent to the printer, to a disk file or viewed on the screen.

Other Features

Brief data entry tutorial.

Comments

Described by the producer as a very simple beginner genealogy program system which has been thoroughly tested on both children and adults. Material can be transferred to FAMware's more sophisticated program, Family Reunion.

Your Family Tree
Version 2.0

Producer

MVP Software
P. O. Box 458
Aliquippa, PA 15001
412 378 0411

Basics

Amiga
$79.95 suggested retail price. Commercial; Demo free from BBS or $2 by mail
GEDCOM separate purchase; cost to be announced
Printed manual
Support by phone 412 378 0411 (9AM-9PM daily Eastern) or by mail
Purchase from producer, retail store or dealer

Data Entry

16 million families and 16 million individuals with eight marriages per individual and 40 children per marriage. Supports foreign characters and has a hot key for repeat information. Five set event fields (no LDS). One all purpose text field for notes and biographical information which prints on a separate page with an individual or family record. Accepts various dates forms and converts them to one standard form.

Data Management

Can sort by name, dates, places, record numbers and other fields. Multi-field and multi-conditions search.

Printed Charts

Supports dot matrix, laser and inkjet printers. 30 printed reports include pedigree charts (five generations on one page) including cascading charts, family group sheets, descendant charts, alphabetical, chronological and user-defined lists, calendar of birthdays and anniversaries, ahnentafel and mailing labels. Blank forms for field research. Wall type pedigree charts and book style planned for future versions. Reports can be sent to the printer, to a disk file in ASCII format or viewed on the screen.

Other Features

Can link IFF (digitized) pictures to individuals and families. Pull down menus. Built-in "Remember" function serves as a scratch pad. Tutorial.

Comments

Requires Amiga WB 1.2 or higher with one megabyte of RAM. Your Family Tree Companion (price to be announced) will provide GEDCOM import/export, tiny tafel, soundex listings and reports, data validation and recovery utilities, a relationship calculator and separate report printing program with over twice the number of reports and improved on-screen viewing. An updated version of the program is planned for late 1993 release which will support user definable events, fields and reports as well as other improvements. Formerly marketed by MicroMaster, now being marketed by the primary designer and programmer, Michael A. Pasterik, as MVP Software.

Non-GEDCOM Programs

Non-GEDCOM Programs

The following programs do not support GEDCOM, although some of the developers have plans to incorporate it into the next version. You may still want to use these programs if they have a special feature of interest to you, but you cannot bring data in from another program or transfer it out at this time. Unless otherwise noted, these programs are for DOS systems.

If you find a shareware program you like and use, please remember to send in your registration fee!

EZ-Tree 1.0/2.0

Jim Hass
P. O. Box 447
Richfield, OH 44286-0447
314 756 8081
$39. Shareware; Demo $10.

Very simple, easy to operate genealogy program. (We tried version 1.0, producer provided information on version 2.0.) Edit screen includes first, middle and last name and maiden name, date and place of birth and death, sex and three comment lines. Names are limited to 16 characters each name; birth and death information, 32 characters; and personal comments and marriage and divorce notes, 144 characters. Supports foreign characters and a mouse. Dates, locations can be entered in any format. Use function keys to add parents, spouse, or children to person highlighted on tree on screen and to find and edit records. Reports, which will appear on screen or can be printed, include highlighted person, all records and descendants of one person. According to producer, version 2.0 also has alphabetical lists, pedigree charts, chronological lists and a dropline chart. Manual on disk and help screens. Registered users receive printed manual and latest updates. GEDCOM to be included with next revision, registered version only. Producer provides support by phone or on CompuServe (73057,3113). Version 1.0 available on CompuServe as EZTRE1.ARC and version 2.0 on GEnie as EZTREE20.ZIP.

Family Heritage File

Star-Com Microsystems
25 West 1480 North
Orem, UT 84057
801 225 1480 (9AM-6PM Mountain)
$149. + $5. s/h Commercial. Demo $7.

MACINTOSH

Program available from producer, dealers and retail stores. Comes with printed manual and help screens. Program will accommodate 10,000 individuals per data folder. There is no limit to number of marriages; each marriage can have 30 children. Supports foreign characters. Producer says the number of events is unlimited and they can be user-defined, but examples only showed birth, christening, death and burial. Separate note fields can be type coded by user and are unlimited in size. Notes print on family group sheet. Sorting can be done by names or places of birth and death and sorted lists can be printed. Printed reports include family group sheets, alphabetical lists, user-defined lists, four generation pedigree chart and descendant charts. Print to disk in ASCII format. Supports dot matrix, laser and inkjet printers. Support provided at number and times listed above. Version due out about February 1993 will support GEDCOM.

GENP

GENP
37 Charles St.
Cheltenham, Victoria 3192
Australia
61 3 584 2765 (9AM-6PM; 8PM-10PM local time)
$99.95 US (includes airmail postage)

AMIGA

Multiple databases which can be linked, unlimited number of people per databases, marriages per person and children per marriage. Supports foreign keymaps and keyboards (uses full Amiga character set). Nine user-defined fields, 12 footnotes per person, supports patronymic naming system, 20 hot keys for duplicating information. Can store one graphic (picture, map or document) per person. Use your own word processor to write text data. Search on most fields and multiple fields. Supports dot matrix and laser printers. Print reports to screen or printer. Includes tutorial, three sample databases with pictures, 138 page manual and 150 help screens. Requires Amiga computer with 1 megabyte of memory and one extra disk drive. German language version available. Utility: GENP MultiMedia.

KinQuest

Orelle Corporation
Box 643
LaGrange, IL 60525
708 352 3020
$79. Shareware

Multiple databases, maximum two billion names, unlimited marriages per person, unlimited children per marriage. Enter names on a profile screen. Pop-up screen for entering first, middle and last name, sex, tag and comment. You must supply a supporting document to enter a name. Document categories are primary, secondary, correspondence and photographs. Automatically capitalizes the first letter of names. Place for birth, death and marriage date and place (town, county, state and country). Also shows one spouse and one child. Press enter for menu at various points in the record and, depending on the field you are in, different menus will appear. Linking for spouses and children done from a pop-up menu. Can build a search category on name, birth, marriage, death or document. Locations can be city, county, state or country; dates can be exact year, before or after. Will only display records (one at a time) that fit that criteria. Five printed reports: family record, family record blank form, ahnentafel, list of source documents, name list for all names in the database. Reports are first printed to a file, and can be printed from the print menu later. A simplified, entry level version called KinQuest Archivist is sold commercially at magazine stands for about $7. Support available on CompuServe (71760,2613) or by mail.

My Family 2.2

PractiComp
6490 Dubois Rd.
Delaware, OH 43015
614 548 5043
$25. Shareware

Producer is working on a major update which will incorporate many new features including GEDCOM. Benefits of registration include a copy of the latest version, notice of updates and support by phone and on CompuServe.

Parents

NickelWare
P. O. Box 393
Orem, UT 84059
$25. Shareware

WINDOWS

One of the few genealogy programs that operates under Windows. Requires a 286 or higher computer and Windows. A fairly basic program with space for birth, christening, marriage, death and burial dates and places. One notes field, unlimited size. People are linked via a three generation family tree into which names can be dragged and dropped. Uses Windows clipboard for repeat information. Sort by name. Prints all or part of a pedigree chart, multiple pages if necessary. Can print to disk in ASCII format. Manual on disk and help screens. Supports dot matrix, laser, inkjet and color printers. GEDCOM planned for next release. Available on CompuServe as PARWN2.ZIP. Support by author on CompuServe (72730,1002).

Photo Family Genealogy Version 1.0

Genealogy Software
1764 S. Henkel Circle
Mesa, AZ 85202
602 897 0415 (after 6PM)
$39.95 Commercial; Demo $9.95

Requires a VGA or SVGA monitor and scanner for photos. Lineage-linked program with choice of events which can also be user-defined. Unlimited marriages per individual, 99 children per marriage. Database size only limited by disk size. Does not support foreign characters or

LDS fields. One note field of 64,000 bytes per person created with built-in text editor. Will sort on names and record numbers. Prints family group sheets, descendant charts, alphabetical lists, user-defined lists, pedigree charts (four generations per page), cascading pedigree charts and book format. Supports dot matrix, laser and inkjet printers. No printing to disk or viewing reports on the screen. Displays photographs of individuals with birth and death dates underneath photo and has a slide show for each family. Available from producer.

Roots and Relatives

Gateway Software
639 Consol Avenue
Winnipeg, Manitoba, Canada R2K 1S9
204 667 2721
$99.50 + $2. s/h

APPLE II

Requires a dot matrix printer and PRODOS operating system. Data entered in family group sheets, not individual records. Each record contains 113 fields of information. A 3.5" floppy can store 800 family records. In addition to date and place for born, baptism, died, buried and marriage, it also has place for occupation, settled at, moved to, religion, code for source and notes (four lines, 63 characters per line). Parents are cross-referenced to their parents' family record and the family record number for each child is noted. By linking families in this way, it allows you to print pedigree and descendant charts. Will also do an index of the husbands and wives from the family group sheets. A word processor can be used to add text.

Visual Genealogy

Tristan Mark Williams
1361 Eastside Rd.
El Cajon, CA 92020-1420
$20. Shareware

Has the look and feel of a Windows application. Supports mouse use. Manual on disk and as a help message. Can handle as many individuals as memory allows. Data entry screen has fields for name, sex, date and place of birth and death, the record number of the individual's father and mother, and flags to link spouses, divorce spouses, sons, daughters; occupation, comment field, and name of separate notes file. Name, place and comment fields scroll to 128 characters each. Displays ancestry chart (similar to a descendants chart, not graphic chart format), descendants chart and personal data (notes). Note editor uses Wordstar keystrokes. Can view two displays on screen at once, scroll through either, and re-size any display. Individuals' numbers must be known to edit, link, etc. Displays alphabetical list. Also can print to disk or printer. Stores all data in each record in ASCII format, which will take up a lot of disk space. Deviates from norm by asking for woman's surname to be her married name, with the maiden name at the end, as /Jones/, so it is difficult to find females in alphabetic list or to locate all female children of a given surname.

Utilities

Utilities

For the purposes of this book, a utility is defined as one of two types of programs, both of which are designed to supplement a regular program. A utility refers to a program that does not involve data entry.

It may be a program that will accept data from another program or a GEDCOM file for the purpose of printing additional charts or processing the data in ways not available in the primary program.

Or, it can be a program that primarily provides information such as a Soundex code, calendar or birth date. You may enter a minimal amount of data, such as a date, to receive information back but you do not permanently enter data into these programs. Some event database programs can be edited and you can add your own information, but they have been included under this category since their primary purpose is to provide information, not to enter data.

The GEDCOM import/export programs that are a separate purchase but produced by the same company as the main program for which they are written will be listed with the program in the first section. GEDCOM programs in this section are those written by someone other than the primary program producer. Unless otherwise noted, these programs are for DOS systems.

If you find a shareware program you like and use, please remember to send in your registration fee!

AHNDES 1.7

Jack Chandler
812 Vermillion Dr.
Henderson, NV 89015
702 565 3158
Donation requested. Shareware

Utility for Personal Ancestral File. Prints an Ahnentafel with dates and places for birth and death for up to 52 generations. Also prints a chart showing the direct line of descent from any ancestor to any descendant, with dates and places for birth, marriage and death. Can handle large databases; tested to 45,000 individuals, but it depends on how big it is in the lower generations. Prints to printer or disk. Available on CompuServe as AHNDES.EXE (version 1.0).

Bdate 2.0

Dave Maynard
19 Brookfield Rd.
Binghamton, NY 13903
Freeware

Utility to calculate date of birth based on death date and age at death. Screen displays fill-in format for you to enter, in numbers, the month, date and year of death and the age at death in years, months and days. It will display the date of birth. If you enter a wrong number, you cannot go back and correct. Ctl-C will exit the program and you can start again. Program dated 1988, available on CompuServe as BDATE2.ARC and on GEnie as BDATE.ARC. Producer can be contacted on Compuserve: 76657,1510 or GEnie: D.MAYNARD1.

Calendar 1.0

Commsoft, Inc.
P. O. Box 310
Windsor, CA 95492-0310
707 838 4300; 800 327 6687
$40. Commercial (Includes Historiograph 1)

Stand-alone calendar or utility that works within ROOTS III. Displays one month at a time. The Gregorian calendar (after Oct. 15, 1582) is on the right and a choice of Hebrew, Julian (before Sept. 13, 1752) or French Republican (Sept. 22, 1792-Dec. 31, 1805) can be displayed at the same time on the left. Use cursor to move backward/forward through months and years or type in a specific date. Will also calculate birth date from a person's age at death. When installed within ROOTS will run in the lower portion of the screen. Includes manual. Available from producer, who periodically has special sales, dealers who may have discount prices, and retail stores. Support: Phone: 707 838 4300 (9AM-4PM, Pacific); BBS: 707 838 6373; FAX: 707 838 6343; Prodigy: JJSR40A; GEnie: H.NURSE; CompuServe: 73710,773.

Calendar 1.1

Dan and Leonard Devoe
46 Buena Vista Ave.
Salem, MA 01970-1042
508 745 1689
$7. Shareware

Calendar utility. Well written program, operates from a command line: Type CAL plus any year from 1 to 65,535, or prompt appears if you just type CAL. The calendar for the first six months of the year will be displayed in color on the screen. Press any key to see the second six months. Press the space bar to print entire year on 8.5"x11" sheet, P for the previous year and <enter> for the following year. It changes from Julian to Gregorian calendar in 1582, the year it was initially adopted. The Gregorian calendar was officially adopted in the U.S. and

British Empire in 1752, but most dates before 1752, such as Washington's birthday, have been converted to the Gregorian, "new style" date. Available on CompuServe as CAL11.ARC. Producer can be contacted on The Witch City BBS: 508 745 1689 CompuServe: 73030,446; GEnie: D.DEVOE1.

Calendar 2.2

Judson D. McClendon
329 - 37th Court N.E.
Birmingham, AL 35215
205 853 8440
$10 Shareware

Calendar utility. At the prompt, enter any year since 1582 and the program will print the calendar for the year on an 8.5" x 11" sheet of paper or to a file on disk (not on the screen). Holidays are in bold and major American holidays listed at the bottom. (Knowing the date for Martin Luther King Day, Washington's Birthday, Memorial Day, etc. in 1612 really is irrelevant though!) Available on Compuserve as CALNDR.ARC. Author available on Compuserve: 74415,1003

Cal.exe

Durwood Gafford
14609 NE 45th E12
Bellevue, WA 98007
$10. Shareware

Calendar utility. Operates from a command line. Will display a calendar on the screen either for one month of a given year (current month and year if you just type CALENDAR) or an entire year, depending on the command. For a year calendar, six months display on the first screen, press any key for the remainder of the year. Changes from Julian to Gregorian in 1582. No facility for printing except screen print. Available on CompuServe as CAL.ARC. Producer can be contacted via CompuServe: 71531,2261.

Cascade 1.3

Patrick J. Waldron
39 Park Dr.
Dublin 6, Ireland
IR £10, or donate to favorite charity

Utility for Personal Ancestral File. Prints descendants charts up to 99 generations. When cascading descendants of all ancestors of root person, collateral relatives to a maximum of six generations will be listed. Option to select male line only. Includes full dates and places and an index. Batch file must be edited to access data files. Available on CompuServe as CASCAD.ZIP and on GEnie as CASCADE.ZIP.

COLA 4.1
(Cost of Living Adjustment)

Rick Mendosa
5700 Via Real, #126
Carpinteria, CA 93013
$15 Shareware

This program was obviously designed for purposes other than genealogy but genealogists can certainly make use of it. It adjusts money amounts for the years 1749-1990. If your great uncle left someone $50 in his will of 1898, you can translate that into its value today or any other year. If someone paid $800 for a farm in 1820, what would be the comparable price in 1940? Just enter the years and one amount and it converts it. Includes instructions on how to update the program with monthly cost of living statistics from the Bureau of Labor Statistics. Benefits of registration: copy of the program that displays COLA data graphically. Available on CompuServe as COLA.ZIP.

Dateline 1.0

Patrick C. Deatherage
755 South Iowa Ave.
League City, TX 77573
713 332 3268
Freeware. $3 by mail

Utility for ROOTS III. It takes the Calendar report of ROOTS III which lists events by month and day and rearranges it to print events in chronological order (by year). Available on CompuServe as DATELN.ZIP.

DESCEND 2.2

John C. Barron
510 E. Braker Lane
Austin, TX 78753
$20. Shareware

Utility for Personal Ancestral File. Prints descendancy charts for up to 16 generations, with full dates and places and an option to include no notes, all notes or just source notes (those with the !). Option to print parents of spouses. Can select up to 30 ancestors at one time. Limit of 5000 marriages, five marriages per person, 20 children per family. Includes an index which is limited to 5200 entries. Prints to printer (at 17 cpi), screen or disk. Available on CompuServe as DESCEN.ZIP and on GEnie as DESCEN21.ZIP.

DFoot

Richard Cleaveland
2373 N. Fillmore St.
Arlington, VA 22207
$5.00 shareware

Utilty for ROOTS III. Operates from a command line to produce a sorted or unsorted list of all detail footnotes used in a ROOTS III database. It can be obtained from the producer or a bulletin board. It contains a manual on disk. Benefits of registration include free updates (if any) for one year. Producer provides support by mail, on Prodigy (PTGW13A) or CompuServe (72077,357). Program available on GEnie as DFOOT4.ZIP.

Dropline 1.1

Carl Jarnberg
Legacy Software
3111 S. Valley View, Suite A214
Las Vegas, NV 89102
$49.95. Commercial

Utility for GEDCOM. Prints descendancy box charts in four sizes and with four choices of box outlines. Separate boxes for spouses. All persons in the same generation are printed on the same horizontal line. Whenever possible, boxes are printed in closest available space on that line, resulting in less white space and a reduced horizontal chart length. Limits: up to 30 spouses per person, unlimited children, three to 150 generations, 2000 boxes per row. Option to print row numbers and column numbers. Produces an index. Supports daisy wheel, dot matrix and laser printers. See example of chart on p. 164.

Easter

No producer information

No documentation included. Program dated 1988. Operates from a command line, but prompt appears if you omit the year. Type EASTER plus a year from 1753 to 6753 and it will display the date for Ash Wednesday, Palm Sunday and Easter. Available on CompuServe as EASTER.ZIP.

EDITPAF

Robert J. Scott
4521 Moraga Ave.
San Diego, CA 92117
619 273 5908
Freeware

Utility for Personal Ancestral File. Will move an individual's notes from the PAF Note File to a word processor for editing, then put the notes back into the PAF Note File in one easy operation. Can also be used to create notes in a word processor and to delete notes. Currently compatible with WordPerfect 4.2/5.0/5.1 and First Choice, but other word processors will be added to the list. Macro capability in the word processor can be utilized for duplication of frequently-used notes, such as source documentation.

EstiDate

Andrew J. Morris
P. O. Box 535
Farmington, MI 48332
Freeware

Will give you an estimated range of dates of birth, marriage and death for a person based on the information you know. Screen has place for name, sex, born, died, first married, last living, first child born, last child born, father's and mother's birth and death year. There are two categories of estimated dates: logical, the widest possible range, and probable, more likely dates. There are settings you can change. The default male maximum age is 105 (logical) or 85 (probable). Female logical ages are 110 and 90. You can also change the probable and logical ages for both males and females for age at birth of first or last child and age at first marriage. The range for birth, marriage and death is quite wide. When asked probable range for a female whose first child was born in 1795 and was last living in 1822, it calculated the logical birth range at 1740-1783 (probable at 1750-1779) and logical death range at 1822-1893 (probable 1822-1869). This would help researchers, especially those who dislike math, avoid making bad assumptions (like a 72 year old mother) as it does give the outside limits.

EVENTS

Craig L. Sturgeon
100 Lyons Ave.
Brantford, Ontario
Canada N3R 4R4
$5 (Canadian) Shareware

Event database utility. When you type "EVENTS" a list of historical happenings and birthdays on that day appear on the screen. If more than one screen you need to type "events ¦ more" to see one screen at a time. No instructions on how to view other dates. You can update the events file with your own information. Windows version also included but you need another file (VBRUN100.DLL) which is not included. Available on CompuServe as EVENTS.ZIP.

Family Attic 2.01A

David Kleiman & Alan Kobb
Up-A-Tree Software
P. O. Box 2270
West Paterson, NJ 07424
$25. Shareware

Collection of utility programs, some especially helpful for people doing Eastern European or Jewish research. The soundex menu will code a name in U.S. Soundex (National Archives Coding System), Daitch/Mokotoff, HIAS (Hebrew Immigrant Aid Society) Case Name Indexing System and the New York Health Department system which is a modification of the standard U.S. system. List can be created and printed. You can also add names to the list from other files including ASCII, Xbase delimited, DBF and GEDCOM. Languages menu displays a keyboard for the appropriate language and will allow you to display and store a name in English, Hebrew, Yiddish, Russian/Cyrillic, Polish and Czech. If you enter in the Hebrew/Yiddish field only, it will transliterate into English. The glossary displays genealogical terms in up to 16 European languages including Hebrew and Yiddish. List is in alphabetical order by the English word so of limited use in translating from the foreign language. GEDCOM menu allows you to view the contents of a GEDCOM file, convert it to a DBF file or replace information in the file. It also includes a phone book which can double as an auto-dialer and a research calendar. Support provided by mail, on CompuServe (71600,375) and MCI Mail (DKLEIMAN:386-3087).

Family Records Utility (FRU)

Steven M. Cannon
1065 West 10210 South
South Jordan, UT 84065
801 254 0160
Freeware (v. 1.8)
$20. Commercial (v. 2.1)

Utility for Personal Ancestral File. This menu-driven program has many options. A search-and-replace feature will globally change any name or place to another spelling, abbreviation, or new entry. You can clear fields, such as all ID fields, all LDS fields, or remove the word "Submitted" from LDS fields. Printed reports include all events on a certain day and month, everyone in birthday (month and day) order, unconnected individuals, and an index to all data (requires 20 cpi). Lists can be printed of individuals who have a selected tag in their notes, as well as the contents of the tagged note. Using this feature, address labels can be printed, as well as phone lists. Also converts data to ASCII for use with other database software (dBase, Paradox, etc.). Version 2.1 includes options to temporarily change the configuration and to edit data that Personal Ancestral File's GEDCOM couldn't handle, as well as a printed manual and support. Freeware versions available on CompuServe as FRU16.ZIP and on GEnie as FRU18.ZIP.

Family Tree Print (FTP)

Keith R. Wehmeyer
Common Sense Software
P.O. Box 50941
Indianapolis, IN 46250
317 594 0820
$25 + $2.50 shipping. Shareware

Utility for Family Ties v. 1.17/1.2 (FTP v. 1.20c), Personal Ancestral File 2.1/2.2 (FTP v. 2.2d) or any GEDCOM-compatible program (FTP v. GEDc).

Prints a wall-size box chart of ancestors, descendants or all data; includes "pruning" capability to select only a portion of the database and prints an index based on row and column locations. Allows you to browse the database to locate families to include. Prints a three generation family box chart, showing children, parents and grandparents. Also prints a Register book form with index and a Family Group Chart. Converts a Family Ties database to GEDCOM for use with other programs. Any type of printer can be used, including Postscript. Also prints to disk. With a database of 3,700 people, it took over 15 minutes to process the layout for the wall chart. Fortunately, before printing, it also produces a display showing how many pages wide and long the wall chart will be and the total number of pages that are to be printed. In the test case in which "all data" was selected, the wall chart would have been 670 pages. There are options to quit throughout the program. (See sample charts on pp. 163 and 165). Also serves as a GEDCOM creating utility for Family Ties. Support by phone 6PM-10PM (Eastern) or on Prodigy: VMSR09A or CompuServe: 70274,3020. Available on CompuServe as FTPG.ZIP (GEDCOM files), FTPF.ZIP (Family Ties) and FTPP.ZIP (PAF) and on GEnie as FTP.ZIP (GEDCOM), FTP120C.EXE (Family Ties) and FTP22C.ZIP (PAF).

Family Viewer

Robert Lott Billard
34 Forest Ave.
Lynbrook, NY 11563
$10. Shareware

Utility for GEDCOM. Converts a GEDCOM file and allows you to view the data in family relationships. To select a subject, type in a name or surname and it will display the person at the top along with parents and one spouse. If you select that person one screen will display the children, a second shows siblings and a third aunts and uncles. The fourth screen displays more information about the subject including the day of the week and date of birth and death, how many children, age when parents died, age at birth of first and last child. You can print a report for an individual which will show all of this information combined plus grandchildren and brothers- and sisters-in-law. When entering dates we sometimes overlook their significance in a family setting. If you see a report on a woman that says her mother died when she was 11, her father died when she was 12 and at 14 she married a man who was 30 years older than she, the dates begin to tell a different story.

FamilyPerfect

Steven M. Cannon
1065 West 10210 South
South Jordan, UT 84065
801 254 0160
$20. Commercial

Utility for Personal Ancestral File. Requires WordPerfect for Windows 5.1/5.2, Microsoft Windows and a mouse. Works with existing PAF data files to produce books and other high-quality output. Will print pedigree charts, list-type family group records and a narrative book report with an index. From inside WordPerfect for Windows, you can view PAF data in pedigree format or individual or marriage lists and select individuals to include in the report. Uses modified Register format and generates the index after you have finished editing the text.

FAMSORT 2.3

Larry M. Rayburn
2519 E. Meredith Dr.
Vienna, VA 22181
703 281 4030
Freeware

Utility for Personal Ancestral File. Produces alphabetical listings from the marriage file arranged with surname first and sorted by MRIN, Soundex, husband's name or wife's name. A config program must be run to identify the path to the data files if other than the default. Print to disk or printer. Available on CompuServe as FAMSOR.ZIP.

Fan Chart Generator 1.02

Christopher E. Long
632 Camelia St.
Atlantic Beach, FL 32233
904 246 4706 (9AM-10PM Eastern)
Freeware

This is not a circular or semi-circular type fan chart. It prints a blank pedigree box chart with one person at the bottom and boxes for each generation of ancestors above. Thus the chart "fans" out getting wider at the top. You have a choice of box size (number of characters, not inches) and height as well as vertical space between boxes. It will print up to 14 generations. The chart is first imaged to disk then printed so you may need quite a bit of free disk space for large charts. Can be printed to disk and edited in a word processor (boxes can be filled in with your own data). Supports 53 printers. Prints 78 characters per line or 130 characters for wide paper. Will also print left to right style pedigree charts. Version 1.01 available on CompuServe under FCG101.ZIP. Program requests $10 registration but author advises it is freeware. Author can be reached on CompuServe: 76500,2073.

Feast

Marc Millier
Free (Public Domain)

Very simple program for people doing Norwegian genealogy. In Norwegian parish records before 1814 a date is usually recorded by the name of the church feast day celebrated on that day or by the number of Sundays after that feast day. Operates from a command line, but prompt appears for proper entry form. Type the name of the feast day in Latin or English, the year between 1582 and 1824, and +/- the number of weeks and it will give you the modern date. Available on CompuServe as FEAST.ARC.

Forest

Ann Turner
418 Gilbert
Menlo Park, CA 94025
$5. Shareware v. 1.1; Commercial v. 2.1

Utility for Personal Ancestral File. Checks a database for unconnected individuals or trees and gives lists showing how many individuals are in each tree as well as the name, RIN and tree number of each individual in trees other than the largest tree. The files that are created can be imported into a database program for sorting by name or tree number. Version 2.1 runs faster than 1.1 and puts the files it creates into the database directory; it is included on the disk with the PAFSPLIT program. This utility is essential for anyone who receives data from another source, such as relatives or FamilySearch. Shareware version available on CompuServe and GEnie as FOREST.ZIP.

FR_PRINT

Robert J. Scott
4521 Moraga Ave.
San Diego, CA 92117
619 273 5908
Freeware

Utility for Personal Ancestral File. Descendancy reports are printed in Family Group Record format. The option to exclude empty fields results in a more compact report. Notes are printed immediately after each chart on the same page. The next chart is printed without a page break and there is an option to print on both sides of the paper. Pages are numbered and listings for married children include the page number where the child is shown as a husband or wife. These page number cross-references permit tracing generations without using the index. An index is printed at the end of the report. You can specify the number of generations to include.

FTMgedFX

Brian Harney
111 Willowcrest Dr.
Frankfort, KY 40601
Freeware: No cost if copy obtained from BBS. If ordered, $5. donation (payable to Kentucky Genealogical Society)

Utility for Family Tree Maker GEDCOM. Makes changes in the GEDCOM file created by Family Tree Maker in some fields so that the transfer into ROOTS III and PAF is smoother. Identifies possible problems in advance and makes global changes which saves editing later. (Commas inserted in location fields after 16 characters to accommodate ROOTS requirements, eliminates blank medical history fields.) If you want to make a GEDCOM file from Family Tree Maker and do not want to buy the GEDCOM, Brian Harney will make a GEDCOM for you for the nominal cost of $7. per disk.

GCFiler 1.1

Philip Cain
Orelle Corporation
Box 643
LaGrange, IL 60525
$15. Shareware

Utility for converting a GEDCOM file to a standard ASCII file so you can then move the information into a spreadsheet or database file. Works with dBASE, PC-File, Paradox, etc. Also converts from ASCII to GEDCOM. Menu-driven, easy to use, mouse compatible. Program available on CompuServe and GEnie as GCF11.EXE (self-extracting with built-in install program) and documentation in separate file, GCF11.ARC.

GED2TT F1

Andrew Koppenhaver
13224 Old Chapel Rd.
Bowie, MD 20720
301 262 8993
$20 Shareware

Converts a GEDCOM file to a Tiny Tafel. Initially it will select a list of surnames from which you can delete those you don't want. It will prompt you to insert a location (country, at least) where required and request other information. Program needs disk space equal to 50% of size of input GEDCOM file so you may not be able to run on a floppy. Will accommodate 20,000 names. An almost painless way to create a Tiny Tafel. Also will make changes in a GEDCOM file: change all names to capitals, convert all names to first letter capitals and abbreviate state names. Allows you to specify exact spelling for up to six unique capitalizations such as McDonald, O'Brien, etc. On the initial try it would not accept a three level directory as location of the GEDCOM file and there was no escape except to reboot. Benefits of registration: later version of the program and copies of GENE, GEDCOMG, GENEX and GENE-PAF programs. Available on CompuServe and GEnie as G2TTF1.ZIP.

Author can be reached on Prodigy at NGDN81A; CompuServe at 70476,521 and GEnie at ANDY-KOPPY

GEDCOM (for Family History System)

John Steed
6907 Childsdale Rd.
Rockford, MI 49341
616 866 9422
Free

Utility for Family History System releases prior to April 1992. Creates a GEDCOM file from a Family History System database. For export only; will not import data into the program. Not needed for Family History System April 1992 or later release which contains its own GEDCOM. Available on CompuServe as FHSGED.ARC. Author can be contacted on his own bulletin board at 616 364 1127; CompuServe: 75745,1371 or GEnie: J.STEED1.

GEDCOM (for Genealogy on Display)

John Steed
6907 Childsdale Rd.
Rockford, MI 49341
616 866 9422
Free

Utility for Genealogy on Display. Creates a GEDCOM file from a Genealogy on Display database. For export only; will not import data into the program. Available on CompuServe as GGED.EXE and GGED.ARC on GEnie. Author can be contacted on his own bulletin board at 616 364 1127; CompuServe: 75745,1371 or GEnie: J.STEED1.

GEDCOM (for Linkages)

John Steed
6907 Childsdale Rd.
Rockford, MI 49341
616 866 9422
Free

Utility for Linkages. Creates a GEDCOM file from a Linkages database. For export only; will not import data into the program. Available on CompuServe as LNKGED.ARC. Author can be contacted on his own bulletin board at 616 364 1127; CompuServe: 75745,1371 or GEnie: J.STEED1.

GEDCompanion

Mark Taylor
P. O. Box 2034
Cupertino, CA 95015-2034
$20 incl. shipping. Commercial

MACINTOSH

Utility for GEDCOM. Converts GEDCOM files from Personal Ancestral File and other genealogy programs into formats that can be read by word processors, spreadsheets, databases and outline programs, making any kind of sorting possible. Displays data in the file in modified spreadsheet format which can be sorted by name, RIN, birth date or death date and can be printed. Prints an ahnentafel with dates and places for birth, marriage and death, and a "Family History", which is a descendants chart with dates and places for birth, christening, death, burial and marriage and full spouse information including parents, with Henry numbering. Supports More from Symantec Corporation and Org Plus by Banner Blue Software, Inc., which when used with GED-Companion will produce box charts. Each box is re-sizable and will contain as much data as the box size you select will display. Box sizes can be mixed, corners rounded, fonts changed.

GEDPST

Richard Cleaveland
2373 N. Fillmore St.
Arlington, VA 22207-4953
$5. Shareware

Utility for a GEDCOM file. See listing for R3PST for description of program and example.

GEN-BOOK

Rex Clement
Clement Custom Programming
2105 Country Lane
Auburn, CA 95603
916 889 8801
$59.95 included shipping. CA residents add tax.
Commercial

Utility for Personal Ancestral File. Prints a narrative book directly from Personal Ancestral File data and notes files. Creates a WordPerfect 5.0/5.1 file which can then be edited as desired. Text and boxes for photos, maps, documents, etc., can be inserted. Scanned images can be incorporated into the report. Fonts and margins, tabs, etc. can be easily changed. Register, modified Register, Henry and descendancy numbering systems can be selected. Option to print descendants of selected individuals or ancestors of a selected descendant. Draft option shows blank lines for missing information. The index in two or three columns is created after editing. Prints a title page. This program can be used with any word processor which can read a WordPerfect file. All options are on one screen in this very easy to use program. (See example on p. 31.)

GENCHECK

Keith R. Wehmeyer
Common Sense Software
P. O. Box 50941
Indianapolis, IN 46250
317 594 0820
$12.50 Shareware

Checks the integrity of the data in your database. Will read Family Ties (Ver. 1.17-1.20), Personal Ancestral File (Ver. 2.1-2.2) or any PAF-compatible GEDCOM database. Will check for corruptions caused by computer viruses, system failures or program "crashes"; verify correct information as entered in the database by date and relationship link tests; and verify all LDS information. Output can be sent to the printer, screen or disk. Will display "errors" (christening date earlier than birth date) and "warnings". A warning indicates a possible error such as age at death over 100, mother over 50 when child was born, etc. The warning messages can be suppressed. Support for registered users by mail, phone (6-10PM), CompuServe (70274,3020) or Prodigy (VMSR09A).

GENE-PAF 8.1

Andrew Koppenhaver
13224 Old Chapel Rd.
Bowie, MD 20720
301 262 8993
$20. Shareware

Utility for Personal Ancestral File. Several reports can be printed. In the Ahnentafel, RINs are optional and ID numbers can be used; notes (all or tagged) can also be included. The Children chart shows all the children and grandchildren of a selected couple. In the Roots chart, an ahnentafel showing only the male line or only the female line can be printed with ahnentafel or sequential numbering; another option is to print labels that can be used under pictures, giving name, dates and spouse. The Parents option shows the parents, paternal grandparents and maternal grandparents of the selected individual. Sorted lists have several options. Output to screen, ASCII file, spreadsheet/DB file, printer.

Genealogical Data Base Systems Book

Data Base Systems
P. O. Box 7263
Huntsville, AL 35807
205 881 6957
$44.95

Utility for Genealogical Data Base Systems. Produces a book from Genealogical Data Base Systems program data. Ancestor or descendants books can be printed to disk or screen and edited. Includes cover page, table of contents, preface, ancestor or descendant charts, family group sheets, names and place locations, indexes and, for descendants book only, an address and telephone list.

GENENUM

Craig Miller
2115 Haena Dr.
Honolulu, HI 96822
$2. Shareware

Utility for Personal Ancestral File. RINs are placed in the ID fields. This was written to preserve the RINs after GEDCOM conversion, as importing data will assign new RINs to the incoming data but the ID numbers do not change.

GENKIT

Richard A. Pence
3211 Adams Court
Fairfax, VA 22030
703 591 4243
Freeware

Useful menu-driven utility program. The date section will tell you the day of the week for a specific date and will give a birthdate from the age at death. Fill in day, month and year at the prompt so you don't have to guess which format to use for the date. Soundex section displays the Soundex equivalents and codes a name. The Ahnentafel menu lists starting and ending ahnentafel numbers for 14 generations, tells relationship of descendant to ancestor (based on ahnentafel numbers) and gives chart number and position for ahnentafel number. Displays a sample five generation pedigree chart showing ahnentafel numbers. Relationship menu shows your relationship to cousins of ancestors/descendants or relationship of any two descendants of common ancestor. You have to pick position of individuals on a numbered chart. The Henry menu tells the relationship of the individual to the progenitor based on the Modified Henry number. Information screens describe the calendar changes from "Old Style" to "New Style", the soundex coding system, ahnentafels and Tiny Tafels with samples, Henry number system, relationship chart, table for conversions of linear and area, land measurements and land descriptions and typical township layout showing section numbering. Easy to use. Available on GEnie as GENKIT16.ZIP and GENKIT.ARC on CompuServe.

GENP MultiMedia 1.0

GENP
37 Charles St.
Cheltenham, Victoria 3192
Australia
61 3 584 2765 (9AM-6PM; 8PM-10PM
  local time)
$35. US

AMIGA

Utility for GENP. Allows user to incorporate several text files from other word processors and in different fonts, if desired, as well as graphics and sound into GENP data. Supports color printers. Integrates ARexx programs into GENP. Includes manual on disk and tutorial.

GIPSI 2.2 & GIPSI Plus

Research Services
797 East 5050 South
Ogden UT 84403
801 479 3553
$25 ($35 with disk). Shareware v. 2.2
$45 (incl shipping). Commercial, GIPSI Plus

Utility for FamilySearch. Genealogical Index Processing System & Interpreter (GIPSI) is used with International Genealogical Index (IGI) and Social Security Death Index (SSDI) files downloaded in GEDCOM format from FamilySearch. Data is converted to a database that can be accessed by the user's database management program, such as dBase II, dBase III, dBase IV, Lotus 1-2-3, PC-File, Reflex, DataPerfect, Paradox, etc., and also Research Data Filer which comes with Personal Ancestral File. More sorting is then possible, such as by place, events in a certain range of years, all children of specified parents, etc. Also can search in many ways, including partial names. Can process multiple GEDCOM files at once. GIPSI Plus will also process Ancestral File and Military Death Index GEDCOM Files as well as "generic" GEDCOM files. It will directly convert Personal Ancestral File data files to a database without the need to first convert to a GEDCOM file. This is a DOS program, but an icon and .PIF file are included for running under Windows. An update to GIPSI Plus is scheduled for release in the Spring of 1993. It will include RDF to/from GEDCOM conversion. Shareware version available on CompuServe and GEnie as GIPSI12.ZIP.

Graftree 2.0

Bill Beinert
P. O. Box 1974
Peter Stuyvesant Station
New York, NY 10009
$10. Shareware

Well written, very useful menu-driven program for handling a GEDCOM file. When you receive a GEDCOM file you don't really know what you have until you gedcom it into your own program and print some type of chart. The GEDBROWS part of the program puts family groups together on the screen. Select a record number and it displays the individual and names of spouse(s), parents and children. You can browse through the generations by selecting father or mother of the individual displayed, previous or next person on the GEDCOM file or select an individual by number. Record numbers appear next to children so it is easy to move to a child, but there is no facility for searching by name. GRAFTREE prints a box chart (sideways) of descendants of the person you select. You can limit the number of generations from two to 42. Printing can take a while and it takes as long to "print" a blank page as one with data. There is an option to set up the charts in a file for later printing which could be done at a time when you are not using the printer. Seven generations fit on one banner style page. Supports charts up to 100 pages wide with 2000 individual and 1000 family records. As with most box charts, it takes up a lot of paper. If an individual has seven children who in turn have no children, the columns below these seven will remain blank for the depth of the chart. Preview feature shows you each individual box as it is selected, not the entire chart. Available on CompuServe as GRAFTR.V20 and GEnie as GRAFTR.V2A. CompuServe: 76407,132. (OS/2 version allows you to search by name, selecting the person from a list box. Other enhancements planned for the OS/2 version.)

Henry 1.3

Ann Turner
418 Gilbert
Menlo Park, CA 94025
$5. Shareware

Utility for Personal Ancestral File. Prints a sorted list showing the Henry number for all individuals and spouses. Henry numbers show generation and order in the generation, such as 1865 is the fifth child of the sixth child of the eighth child of the ancestor. Can be used to audit a database for order of marriages and children as well as continuity of surnames. Has a limit of 16 generations. Author can be reached on CompuServe: 71336,1610 and GEnie: A.TURNER1. Program available on CompuServe as HENRY1.ZIP and GEnie as HENRY13.ZIP.

Historiograph 1
Historiograph 2

Commsoft, Inc.
Box 310
Windsor, CA 95492
707 838 4300
$40 per program. Commercial
(Historiograph 1 part of Utility Package 2 with Calendar)

Utility for ROOTS III. While in the Trace routine in ROOTS III, a time line can be displayed for up to six of the direct line ancestors. Historiograph will display a timeline at the bottom of the screen for the category selected. If you select composers, it will show the life span of the major composers which will allow you to see who was living at the same time as the ancestors. Categories on Historiograph 1 are world conflicts, composers, U. S. Presidents (and events of their terms) and European royal rulers. Historiograph 2 has seven additional categories: arts, biology and medicine, chemistry and physics, jurisprudence, religion and education, transportation and communication, and world demographics. Available from producer, who periodically has special sales, dealers who may have discount prices, and retail stores. Includes a printed manual and help screens. Support: Phone: 707 838 4300 (9AM-4PM, Pacific); BBS: 707 838 6373; FAX: 707 838 6343; Prodigy: JJSR40A; GEnie: H.NURSE; CompuServe: 73710,773.

HOTNOTES 2.2

Jan Unter
Silicon Roots! Associates
P.O. Box 20541
San Jose, CA 95160-0541
408 268 5192
800 645 8808   PC Gear (credit card orders)
$29.95 + $2 shipping ($3 international).
$3 to upgrade from 1.0/1.1 (mail only).
Commercial

Utility for Personal Ancestral File. HotNotes is a TSR (memory-resident) program to use with PAF notes. The earlier shareware version (1.1) has a menu of tags for notes which can be selected and/or edited. Version 2.2 also has hot key commands to save and insert sources, a small word-wrapping editor (will word-wrap up), cut-and-paste from screen, import of external text files directly into PAF notes, and user-defined keyboard macros. Has 58 tags with 15 user-defined tags. Has on-line help screens. Many options within each feature. Both versions include a text file on how to document sources. Version 2.2 uses less memory than the shareware version. Support on CompuServe 70313,2522. Shareware version available on CompuServe as HOTNOT.ZIP and on GEnie as HOTNT102.ZIP.

HQ Pedigree Print 2.21

Steven M. Cannon
1065 West 10210 South
South Jordan, UT 84065
801 254 0160
$20.   Shareware

Utility for Personal Ancestral File. Prints a five or eight generation pedigree chart on one 8.5"x11" sheet of paper. Requires a 24-pin Epson-compatible dot matrix printer which can print at 20 cpi. Author can be reached on CompuServe at 76340,3630. Program available on CompuServe as HQ.ARC.

IGI255 3.0

Patrick C. Deatherage
755 South Iowa Ave.
League City, TX 77573
713 332 3268
Freeware. $5 by mail (Also see below)

Utility for FamilySearch. Takes data saved in text (not GEDCOM) format from the International Genealogical Index (IGI) and allow you to print it using 55 single line entries per page rather than the 12-13 entries per page in the FamilySearch format. Data can be sent to the printer, printed to a disk file or viewed on the screen. It also gives you four different fixed sorting options and a custom sort allowing nine additional sorts as well as a filtering option. It will also create a DBF file. There is no charge for the program, but it is copyrighted. The author asks that you repay him by thanking the volunteer at your local family history center and sending him a picture postcard from your area. Otherwise, the cost is $15! Available on CompuServe as IGI255.ZIP.

Import 2.6

Jack Chandler
812 Vermillion Dr.
Henderson, NV 89015
702 565 3158
$5-10. Shareware

Utility for Personal Ancestral File. Any ASCII (text) file with line length no greater than 78 characters can be imported directly into any individual's notes. You are asked for the file path and name and the RIN. Very easy to use. Available on CompuServe as IMPORT21.ZIP and on GEnie as IMPORT22.ZIP.

JCAL - The Jewish Calendar

Lester Penner
25 Shadow Lane
Great Neck, NY 11021
516 466 5574 (H)
516 273 3100 (W)
$18. Shareware

Converts a date from the Gregorian calendar to the Jewish calendar and vice versa. Runs from a command line and you can only request one specific date at a time, but can request an unlimited number of successive years. Results can be printed to a file. Also provides the Torah reading for the Sabbath following the date entered. Available on CompuServe as JCAL75.EXE and GEnie as JCAL.ZIP. Author can be reached on CompuServe: 75236,1572.

KinWrite

Keith Webber
LDB Associates.
8305 E. Morris
Wichita, KS 67207-2435
316 683 6200
316 651 0204
$59.95. Commercial

Utility for Personal Ancestral File. Prints a narrative book with index from Personal Ancestral File data files. Can select descendants by generation, descendants by family line, or ancestors. User selections include margins, page lengths, type sizes, page headers. Has option to include or exclude certain tagged notes. Notes tagged FOOTNOTE:X will print as end notes. Photos with captions can be added, but picture space cannot be less than 6" high, and can be a half or full page in width. Photos are interleaved. One-column index can show page numbers or person number. Descendants are numbered consecutively or by RIN. Prints a table of contents, document pages, ancestor charts, lifespan report, list of unconnected individuals. Prints to printer or disk. If you print to disk and edit the report in your word processor, you will have to enter the new pages numbers in the index.

Lowcase 1.3

Jack Chandler
812 Vermillion Dr.
Henderson, NV 89015
702 565 3158
Freeware

Utility for Personal Ancestral File. Data that has been entered in all uppercase can be accurately converted to first-letter-uppercase-only. State codes and Roman numerals are not converted. Names with Mc, Mac, O' are followed by an uppercase letter. This program is more efficient than the option in FRU or the CONVERT program in Personal Ancestral File. Available on GEnie as LOWCASE.ZIP.

Marriage Search 1.3

John C. Barron
510 E. Braker Lane
Austin, TX 78753
$20. Shareware

Utility for Personal Ancestral File. Can search marriage data by location, by low date or high date, or bride's or groom's name. Output to screen, disk or printer. Available on CompuServe as MSRCH.ZIP.

NAMECLEN 1.0

Jack Chandler
812 Vermillion Dr.
Henderson, NV 89015
702 565 3158
Donation requested. Shareware

Utility for Personal Ancestral File. Removes unused names, places, etc. from the Name File. These result from misspellings as well as deleted individuals. Is much faster and easier than using GEDCOM to accomplish this. Available on CompuServe as NAMCLE.EXE.

NOTECLEN

Jack Chandler
812 Vermillion Dr.
Henderson, NV 89015
702 565 3158
$5. Shareware

Utility for Personal Ancestral File. Eliminates the empty space occupied by deleted notes. Makes each individual's notes contiguous. This results in faster access to notes and in reduced size of NOTES2.DAT file. Available on GEnie as NTSCLE.EXE.

NOTETOOL

John Lilly
Data Tools
874 W. 1400 North
Orem, UT 84057-2916
801 225 3256
$14.95 + $1.50 s/h. Commercial

Utility for Personal Ancestral File. Has menu of 60 tags, 12 templates and a cut-and-paste feature. Tags can also be edited or new tags created; the "EDITED" tag adds the date you edited the note. Templates for census years, basic vitals, LDS events, etc., can be edited or can be used for complete references that you use repeatedly. Can cut any note or part of a note and copy to any number of other individuals' notes in the same or different database. Is a TSR (memory-resident) program.

On This Day (OTD)

The Software Construction Co.
P. O. Box 160
North Billerica, MA 01862
$25. Shareware

Event database. Operates from a command line. Enter a date and it will list what happened on that date. Includes astronomical events, birthdays of famous people, historical events, national observations, religious holidays and events. Registered users receive a database of more than 11,000 entries. You may also create your own personal database. List can be displayed on the screen or printed. In addition to Gregorian calendar, date can be specified in the Hebrew, Islamic or Julian calendar. Some command line requests quite complex such as adding days to an absolute date — 1/3+37 is the same as 2/9) or specific day — W(8/14) specifies the second Wednesday in August. Difficult to judge its value without the full database. Available on CompuServe as OTD.ZIP.

PAF NOTES

Commsoft, Inc.
7795 Bell Road, P. O. Box 310
Windsor CA 95492-0310
707 838 4300; 800 327 6687
$60. Commercial (Includes ROOTS WRITER & REVENT)

Utility for Personal Ancestral File. Written in 1990 by Ann Turner for COMMSOFT, developer of ROOTS III. Converts notes in the PAF note file (NOTES2.DAT) into external files which can be used with a text editor or word processor. Will put the RIN in the ID field of the individuals' records and replace any existing ID field data. No option to convert only notes of selected RINs. Can also be used to add external notes to a GEDCOM file. The GEDCOM file can be used to transfer external notes to the NOTES2.DAT file. This would be useful if you had many or long notes in your word processor that were longer than 78 character per line, which is the requirement for using IMPORT to move external text notes into PAF. This would also be useful if you receive a GEDCOM file from someone and the notes are all in external files.

PAF Replace

Jeffrey S. Morley
The Interconnect BBS
703 827 5762
Freeware

Utility for Personal Ancestral File. Written in 1988, this program will replace any one character in PAF notes with any other one character. Personal Ancestral File 2.0 allowed optional print characters, but 2.1 standardized this with the use of the ! only. However, those using the various programs which now generate a book report might find this useful if they use a single character to trigger the printing of biographical notes and then want to delete this for other purposes. Available on CompuServe as PAFREP.ARC and on GEnie as PAFREPL.

PAF Toolbox

Lewis T. Reinwald
2207 Richland St.
Silver Spring, MO 20910
301 585 8044
Freeware

Utility for Personal Ancestral File. Prints descendants list and also a worksheet version with a blank line for notes under each person. Prints a "relatives list" for any RIN to a specified number of generations, and gives their relationships. On all reports, there was no option to exclude existing notes, so all notes were included in each report. Has an interactive game of "family trivia" in which relatives of the selected RIN are shown with a list of their possible relationships. Prints a word search puzzle of selected generations. Prints to screen, disk or printer. Available on CompuServe as PAFTBX.ZIP.

PAF Viewer for Windows 1.2

George Lawrence
20326 Saticoy #8
Winnetka, CA 91306
Freeware.

Utility for Personal Ancestral File. Allows you to view different PAF data, even in several different databases, at the same time. Brings one or more charts on screen at one time or in a window when viewing data; you can stretch the windows to any size. Prints pedigree charts and family group charts as re-sized and with better fonts. Available on CompuServe as PAFVWI.ZIP.

PAF2PAF

Jack Chandler
812 Vermillion Dr.
Henderson, NV 89015
702 565 3158
Donation requested. Shareware

Utility for Personal Ancestral File. Will move one individual at a time to another PAF database. Will not preserve relationships, however. When viewing two databases at one time with the -d switch, you can shell out to DOS to get PAF2PAF and run it while examining the databases. Can also be run separately.

PAFability 2.06

Barbara Bennett
6426 Pound Apple Court
Columbia, MD 21045
410 381 1735
$10 + $2 s/h. Shareware

Utility for Personal Ancestral File. Prints a narrative book with index from Personal Ancestral File data files. Uses Record System, RIN or ID field numbering. Can select margins, number of generations. Can choose only a direct line or all ancestors. Parents of spouses are shown. Index in one or two columns, with option to include birth-death years and dot leaders. Has pull-down menus, on-line help and mouse support. Can handle full PAF database (65,535 individuals), and 60 children per individual. Prints at 10 cpi or 17 cpi to printer or disk. Earlier versions available on CompuServe as PAFABL.ZIP (ver. 1.2) and on GEnie as PAFABL12.ZIP.

PAFAIDE

Jeffrey Boston
No longer at the address listed on the disk
Freeware

Utility for Personal Ancestral File. Prints an ahnentafel with data in columns, lifeline chart showing lifespan of each individual, place sorted list, pedigree chart (similar to PAF's Ancestry Chart) with option to include all events including christening and burial with full places, and Tiny Tafel (but not in Tafel Matching System format). Can use <PgUp> and <PgDn> to browse on screen. There is no option to limit the data to be included. Prints to screen or disk. Written in 1988, this is still very useful. Available on CompuServe as PAFAID.ARC and on GEnie as PAFAIDE.ZIP.

PAFNAMES

Allen L. Wyatt
Discovery Computing, Inc.
P.O. Box 88
South Jordan, UT 84065
$20. Shareware

Utility for Personal Ancestral File. Prints alphabetical sort of all individuals in the database with option to list females by married names (in brackets) as well as by maiden names. Includes RIN, birth/christening year, death/burial year, own MRIN, spouse name and RIN, parent MRIN and father's name, or mother's name if no father entered. Prints to printer only, but can redirect output to a disk file with a utility like PRN2FILE. This is advisable if the database is large; in test with database of 3400 people, the report printed to disk was 680K and 98 pages. Available on CompuServe as PAFNAM.ZIP and on GEnie as PAFNAMES.ZIP.

PAFSPLIT

Ann Turner
418 Gilbert
Menlo Park, CA 94025
$15 + $2.50 (5.25") or $3 (3.5") shipping.
Commercial

Utility for Personal Ancestral File. This program is more efficient and accurate in splitting family groups from the database than is GEDCOM. Records to keep or remove are selected. Options include Ancestors (choose ancestors only, or include up to sibling, first cousin, second cousin, or third cousin level, or all connections), descendants (option to include parents of spouses, all descendants or only male line), blood relatives (all descendants of all ancestors of starting RIN), a list of RINs in a text file (could be a printout from PAF's Focus/Design Reports), an unconnected tree that was identified in the FOREST program, a range of RINs, and records based on the value of the UPDATE tag in PAF notes. Disk includes another program PAFSTAMP as well as three programs from Jack Chandler (RECLAIM 3.0, NOTECLEN, NAMECLEN) in a zipped file. See separate listings for these programs.

PAFSTAMP

Ann Turner
418 Gilbert
Menlo Park, CA 94025
Included on PAFSPLIT disk. Commercial

Utility for Personal Ancestral File. Automatically stamps an "UPDATE:" tag at the beginning of PAF notes with the current system date. A short memo can be also added. The PAFSPLIT program can select those records which were updated before, on or after a certain date and put them in a new database. This is a TSR (memory-resident) program which uses about 8K of memory.

PEDIGREE

John C. Barron
510 E. Braker Lane
Austin, TX 78753
$25. Shareware

Utility for Personal Ancestral File. Prints five generation pedigree charts by means of data entry or import from PAF via a menu option (not GEDCOM). Chart shows birth and death dates in fifth generation which PAF does not, but places in the other generations were shortened to two fields (showed county and state or state and country; no cities). A person on one chart can be transferred to a new chart, which avoids duplicate data entry.

PNames

Richard Cleaveland
2373 N. Fillmore St.
Arlington, VA 22207
$5.00 shareware

Utility for ROOTS III. Runs from a command line to produce a sorted or unsorted list of all the place names used in a ROOTS III database. It can be obtained from the producer or a bulletin board. It contains a manual on disk. Benefits of registration include free updates (if any) for one year. Producer provides support by mail, on Prodigy: PTGW13A or CompuServe 72077,357. Available on CompuServe as PNAME2.ZIP and GEnie as PNAMES2.ZIP. Named as a favorite utility in *Genealogical Computing*'s "Software to Beat" in 1992.

R-PLOT

Commsoft, Inc.
P. O. Box 310
Windsor, CA 95492-0310
707 838 4300; 800 327 6687
$60. Commercial

Utility for ROOTS III. Requires Windows (not included). Using a ROOTS III database, it will create box charts and pedigree charts. Drop charts up to 16 generations. (Does not include all descendants of one individual, but follows one line of descent with all siblings in each generation.) Can create large wall charts printed with a plotter. (If you do not have access to a plotter COMMSOFT has a service for printing your charts.) Supports dot matrix, laser, inkjet, color and plotter printers. Will produce charts in color on plotter or color printer. Includes manual. Works better on more powerful computers. Minimum of one megabyte of memory recommended. See sample chart on p. 166. Available from producer, who periodically has special sales, dealers who may have discount prices, and retail stores. Support: Phone: 707 838 4300 (9AM-4PM, Pacific); BBS: 707 838 6373; FAX: 707 838 6343; Prodigy: JJSR40A; GEnie: H.NURSE; CompuServe: 73710,773.

R3FixEtc

Brian Harney
111 Willowcrest Dr.
Frankfort, KY 40601
Freeware: No cost if copy obtained from BBS. If ordered, $5. donation (payable to Kentucky Genealogical Society)

Set of utilities for ROOTS III which generally condense ROOTS III reports by removing unnecessary blank lines. R3FixSum condenses the Summary report to 1/5 its usual size while arranging events in chronological order. R3FixSu2 adds spouses and text files to condensed Summary report. Produces a compact hardcopy record of your entire database. R3FixSu3 shows potential duplicate persons. R3FixGen shrinks a ROOTS III Genealogy report. R3FixIdx reformats an index into one column that can be edited in a word processor. Will reformat back to two or three columns (limited use since ROOTS updated version which formats for word processors). R3FixDes removes the page headings and blank lines between pages to produce one long continuous report. R3FixCal condenses the calendar report by removing blank lines. R3RenRef renames text files from ROOTS II to ROOTS III format. Producer provides support by mail.

R3MFNU 1.2

John Clement
6940 E. Girard #205
Denver, CO 80224
303 691 0613 (7AM to 8PM Mountain)
$5. Shareware; $7.50 + $2.50 s/h to order disk (Donation to Colorado Genealogical Society, Computer Interest Group. Make check to CGS-CIG.)

ROOTS III Utility. Menu-driven program that will take a ROOTS III major footnote list, add any external .SRC files and arrange in order by record number, title or author (last name or first name first). Allows you to create a bibliography from a ROOTS III major footnote list. Available on GEnie as R3MFNU22.ZIP.

R3PST

Richard Cleaveland
2373 N. Fillmore St.
Arlington, VA 22207-4953
$5. Shareware

Utility for ROOTS III. Runs from a command line or menu. Creates a timeline and pedigree chart. Dates in 10 year increments are listed across the top. Down the left side are ancestor surnames beginning with the surname of the key and other surnames below that in order that they joined the family. The given name of the individual is shown on the surname line with the first letter under the date the person was born. If there is a marriage date, a vertical line on the year of the marriage connects the spouses. The oldest date can either be on the left or the right. Manual on disk. Benefits of registration: free update for one year. Producer provides support by mail, on Prodigy: PTGW13A or CompuServe: 72077,357. See example of chart on p. 167.

RDF Convert

Blake A. Rosenvall
209 NE 176th Ave.
Vancouver, WA 98684
206 254 4770
$10. Shareware

Utility for Personal Ancestral File and Family Search. Will convert a data file from the Research Data Filer (RDF) program in PAF to a GEDCOM file, which can then be converted to PAF Family Records data files. Will also convert a GEDCOM file to an RDF data file. Can be used with GEDCOM downloads from any of the FamilySearch databases. It will not create RDF .doc files. Will only convert RDF records with the following in the event field: born, birth, blessed, blessing, christening, marriage, died, dead, death, buried or burial.

RDF2GED 1.3

John C. Barron
510 E. Braker Lane
Austin, TX 78753
$20. Shareware

Utility for Personal Ancestral File. Will convert a data file from the Research Data Filer (RDF) program in PAF to a GEDCOM file, an ASCII file or a comma delimited file. A GEDCOM file can then be converted to PAF Family Records data files. In the GEDCOM conversion, you are asked if you entered surnames first or last and if you entered places state-county-city or the reverse. All events in the RDF .dat file will be included in the GEDCOM file. You can name an RDF .doc file as well as the .dat file and the documentation will then be included in the individual's notes. Relationships given in RDF are linked in Family Records. Available on CompuServe as RDFGED.ZIP and on GEnie as RDF2GED.ZIP.

RECLAIM 3.0

Jack Chandler
812 Vermillion Dr.
Henderson, NV 89015
702 565 3158
$5. Shareware

Utility for Personal Ancestral File. Re-uses deleted RINs and MRINs by moving other RINs and MRINs from the end of the database to fill in the previously used but currently empty RINs and MRINs. Making a GEDCOM of the database and then gedcomming it back in to an empty directory will also fill in empty RINs but will result in many changed numbers. The benefit of RECLAIM is that it preserves most of the original RINs, changing only those which were moved from the end of the file; it is also easier and faster than gedcomming. A file can be printed listing the changes made. Has been tested to 42,000 RINs. Most useful after using Personal Ancestral File's Match/Merge or Ann Turner's PAFSPLIT which can result in a large number of deleted records. Available on CompuServe as RECLM.ZIP.

Revent

Commsoft, Inc.
P. O. Box 310
Windsor, CA 95492-0310
707 838 4300; 800 327 6687
$60. Commercial (Includes ROOTS WRITER & PAFNOTES)

Event database stand-alone program or utility to run within ROOTS III. Enter date in Anniversary routine in ROOTS or from command line and it will show what happened on that date in nine categories: History and Politics; Daily Life; Visual Arts; Religion, Philosophy & Learning; Literature and Theater; Science and Technology; Personal; Music; Birthdays. Any of these can be omitted by typing "N" next to the category. You can edit the database by adding to any of the categories. Includes manual. Available from producer, who periodically has special sales, dealers who may have discount prices, and retail stores. Support: Phone: 707 838 4300 (9AM-4 PM, Pacific); BBS: 707 838 6373; FAX: 707 838 6343; Prodigy: JJSR40A; GEnie: H.NURSE; CompuServe: 73710,773.

SDI Print 1.0

Patrick C. Deatherage
755 South Iowa
League City, TX 77573
713 332 3268
Freeware

Utility for FamilySearch. Menu-driven program to read a Social Security Death Index file downloaded from FamilySearch in GEDCOM format. Will display on the screen or print full information on name, social security number, birth and death, age at death, state where card was issued and state of residence at time of death with an option to print the localities associated with the zip code where individual resided at time of death. It will create the file in either Family History Center format or single line format (if more than one location, the locality part will take up more than one line). It will also simultaneously create an ASCII file or .DBF file for use with standard database programs from the information. Option to request an exact surname. Available on CompuServe as SDIPRT.ZIP and on GEnie as SDIPRT94.ZIP.

Soundex

James D. Waring Jr.
Waring Associates
Chicago, IL
312 631 5326
Freeware

Soundex utility: Runs from a command line but displays instructions for correct entry. Gives the Soundex code for a name. Available from CompuServe under the name SOUNDE.EXE. Rename to SOUNDEX.EXE to run. Type SOUNDEX plus up to 19 names separated by a space and press enter. List of names will appear on the screen and you can hard copy with the print screen command. It handles up to 10 letters to a name accurately. If more than 10, it prints the code with an asterisk and you should re-enter and eliminate some vowels or letters W, Y and H near the end for an accurate coding. If you limit entry to 10 letters, it will correctly code such names as Schmidt and Szul by ignoring the second consonant (c in Schmidt and z in Szul) which has the same code number as the initial s. Author can be reached on CompuServe: 72371,1711.

Soundex

Carl York
P. O. Box 3157
Knoxville, TN 37927
Freeware

Soundex utility. Available on CompuServe as SOUNDX.ARC. Type SOUNDEX and a screen will appear giving you the Soundex chart. Type in a name at the prompt and its Soundex code will appear on the screen. It will handle names of any length but does not correctly code such names as Schmidt and Szul as it codes the c and z. These letters should be ignored since they have the same code number as the initial s. Author can be reached on CompuServe: 72571,2445.

THE Jewish Calendar 1.12

Joseph Berry
Dataform Corporation
1498-M Reisterstown Rd.
Baltimore, MD 21208
301 764 5668
$7.50 Shareware

Very well written program. Menu driven, easy to use. Converts a civil calendar (years 1827 through 2205) to the Jewish calendar (years 5587 through 5965) and vice versa. Displays calendar on screen in color with both civil and Jewish dates, months and years. Press F6, then right or left arrows for earlier or later months. The F4 key will display all the Jewish holidays for the currently displayed year. It also displays statistics about the currently displayed year and the parshiot (weekly Torah readings) in the column along side of the Shabbat. You can also display the calendars in Hebrew with dates from right to left and the days of the week, Jewish months and holidays in Hebrew. Use print screen to make hard copy. Registration option for $14 will cover current version plus one free update when released. Future additions planned: Bar Mitzvah calculations; program will be made into a TSR (terminate and stay resident) so that the user can bring it up at any time from any application; a switch to display holidays and parshiot for Israel as opposed to just for outside Israel; print option for printing currently displayed month or an entire year; Yahrzeit data maintenance, display and retrieval and mouse support. Available on CompuServe as TJC.ARC. and on GEnie as TJC.ZIP.

Author can be reached on CompuServe: 73170,1341.

Tracer 2.2

Wayne R. Shepard
2339 45th Ave.
San Francisco, CA 94116
$35. Shareware

Written in 1986 for people who want to use Personal Ancestral File but have only one drive. This still appears on genealogy bulletin boards but is probably of little use today. Requires 256k. Includes a "Utility File Extract Module" for transferring data between the two programs but it requires two drives. Capacity of Tracer is not stated. It prints only a pedigree chart and a family group sheet. Available on CompuServe and GEnie as TRACER.ZIP.

Tree Charts

Quinsept, Inc.
P. O. Box 216
Lexington, MA 02173
800 637 7668
$60. Commercial; GEDCOM $35 additional

DOS, APPLE II, COMMODORE 64

Utility for Family Roots and Lineages. It uses a GEDCOM file to create pedigree and descendant box charts. Will accommodate up to 800 boxes in one wall size chart; charts can be combined. Box size and content can be specified. Grow chart in any direction from one person, or automatically connect any two selected people. Charts can be sent to the printer, viewed on the screen or printed to disk and edited before printing. Supports dot matrix, laser and inkjet printers. Printed manual included. Apple II requires 128K and Commodore 64 requires 64K. Support provided at above number 9AM-5PM (Eastern), off-hours by appointment, by mail, on Prodigy: CGMR62B,

CompuServe: 72470,3027 and GEnie S.VORENBERG. See sample chart on p. 168.

TTGEN 1.2

Tom P. Douglas
P.O. Box 10186
Colorado Springs, CO 80932-1186
719 635 2061
Freeware

Editor for tiny tafels that are compatible with the Tafel Matching System. Does not import data from other programs to create a tiny tafel, so new data must be entered manually. It is more useful, however, as an editor to work with an existing tiny tafel file. Since it generates the Soundex codes, it has an advantage over editing with a word processor. Uses Word Star commands for cursor control movement which is cumbersome for those not familiar with them. Written in 1988. Distributed with Brother's Keeper, which generates tiny tafels. Available on GEnie as TTGEN12.ARK.

Wall Chart

Ann Turner
418 Gilbert Ave.
Menlo Park, CA 94025
$10. Commercial; Demo free if obtained from bulletin board.

Creates an eight generation pedigree chart on two strips of four sheets hung side by side. It requires a dot matrix printer and is limited to 1000 people in a GEDCOM file. Author says it was the first program of its kind (1989) and may be outdated now (as more programs came along that now create similar charts). Chart can be sent to the printer, viewed on the screen or saved as an ASCII text file (where it can be retrieved and printed with other than dot matrix printers). Runs from a menu. If importing a GEDCOM file, it lists everyone in the file in alphabetical order and you select the subject. Charts include name, date and place of birth and death. Location limited to three characters and program will convert state and province names to two-letter code if they are written out in full. It will also print a 15 generation ahnentafel in two columns. Obtain from author. The demo version, available on CompuServe as WALLDE.ARC and on GEnie as WALLDEMO.ARC, will print a blank chart or one branch of the family tree. Support provided by mail, on CompuServe: 71336,1610 and GEnie A.TURNER1.

Weekday

No producer information

At the prompt, enter the present year and the date you are interested in (any year since 1752). It will tell you the day of the week. If it is a birthday, it will also tell you the age, year of retirement, number of years spent sleeping, eating and attending school or working. Available on CompuServe as WEEKDA.ZIP.

```
HUSBAND: Jacob GUTH                                              HUSB: Jacob GUTH              1848
                                                                 WIFE: Elisabetha (Elizabeth) MIC1857
BORN: 12 Dec 1848  PLACE: Oberlustadt, Pfalz, Bavaria, Germany
CHR:  17 Dec 1848  PLACE: Oberlustadt, Pfalz, Bavaria, Germany   PREPARED BY:
MARR: 22 Oct 1875  PLACE: Rockenhausen, Pfalz, Germany             Joan Neumann Lowrey
DIED: 12 Feb 1909  PLACE: Philadelphia, Philadelphia, PA           7371 Rue Michael
BUR:               PLACE: Philadelphia, Philadelphia, PA           La Jolla, CA 92037
FATHER: Philipp Heinrich GUTH       MOTHER: Eva Margaretha DEUBEL   619-454-7046
RECORD NUMBER: 141                  OTHER WIVES: 0
                                                                 PAGE: 69
WIFE:    Elisabetha (Elizabeth) MICHEL

BORN: 30 May 1857  PLACE: Rockenhausen, Pfalz, Bavaria, Germany
CHR:  21 Jun 1857  PLACE: Rockenhausen, Pfalz, Bavaria, Germany
DIED: 10 Apr 1940  PLACE: Philadelphia, Philadelphia, PA
BUR:               PLACE: Philadelphia, Philadelphia, PA
FATHER: Friedrich MICHEL            MOTHER: Anna Maria FUNK
RECORD NUMBER: 142                  OTHER HUSBS: 0
```

SEX	CHILDREN	BIRTH DATE CHRIS DATE	B)IRTH or C)HRIS PLACE	MARR DATE FIRST SPOUSE	DEATH DATE	DEATH PLACE	RECORD NUMBER
1 F	Carolina (Lena) GUTH	3 Apr 1876	B)Zweibruecken, Pfalz, Bavaria, German	Apr 1897 Louis GRESSEL	28 Apr 1929	Philadelphia, Philadelphia, PA	110
2 F	Elizabeth I. GUTH	26 Sep 1877	B)Metz, Alsace-Lorraine, Germa	Charles Frederick KLIPPEL	7 Nov 1951	Syracuse, Onondaga, NY	389
3 F	Anna (Annie) GUTH	1 Nov 1878	B)Germany	Fred HEBERGER	1977	Philadelphia, Philadelphia, PA	390
4 F	Maria (Mary) GUTH	1879	B)Germany	William KRAUS	1920		391
5 F	Martha GUTH	27 Jul 1883 19 Jan 1896	B)Pleasant Gap, Centre, PA		1900		397
6 F	Emma GUTH	9 Mar 1887	B)Lockhaven, Clinton, PA		1920		399
7 M	Friedrich Jacob GUTH	6 Mar 1891 19 Jan 1896	B)Scranton, Lackawanna, PA	27 Apr 1914 Isabelle (Belle) DANIELS	1957		394
8 F	(female) GUTH		B)PA		1920		392
9 F	(female) GUTH				1920		393
10 F	Clara Katherina GUTH	17 Feb 1893 19 Jan 1896	B)Scranton, Lackawanna, PA	Harry HOFFMAN	1957		395

Children continued on next page

Family Tree Print: Family group sheet.

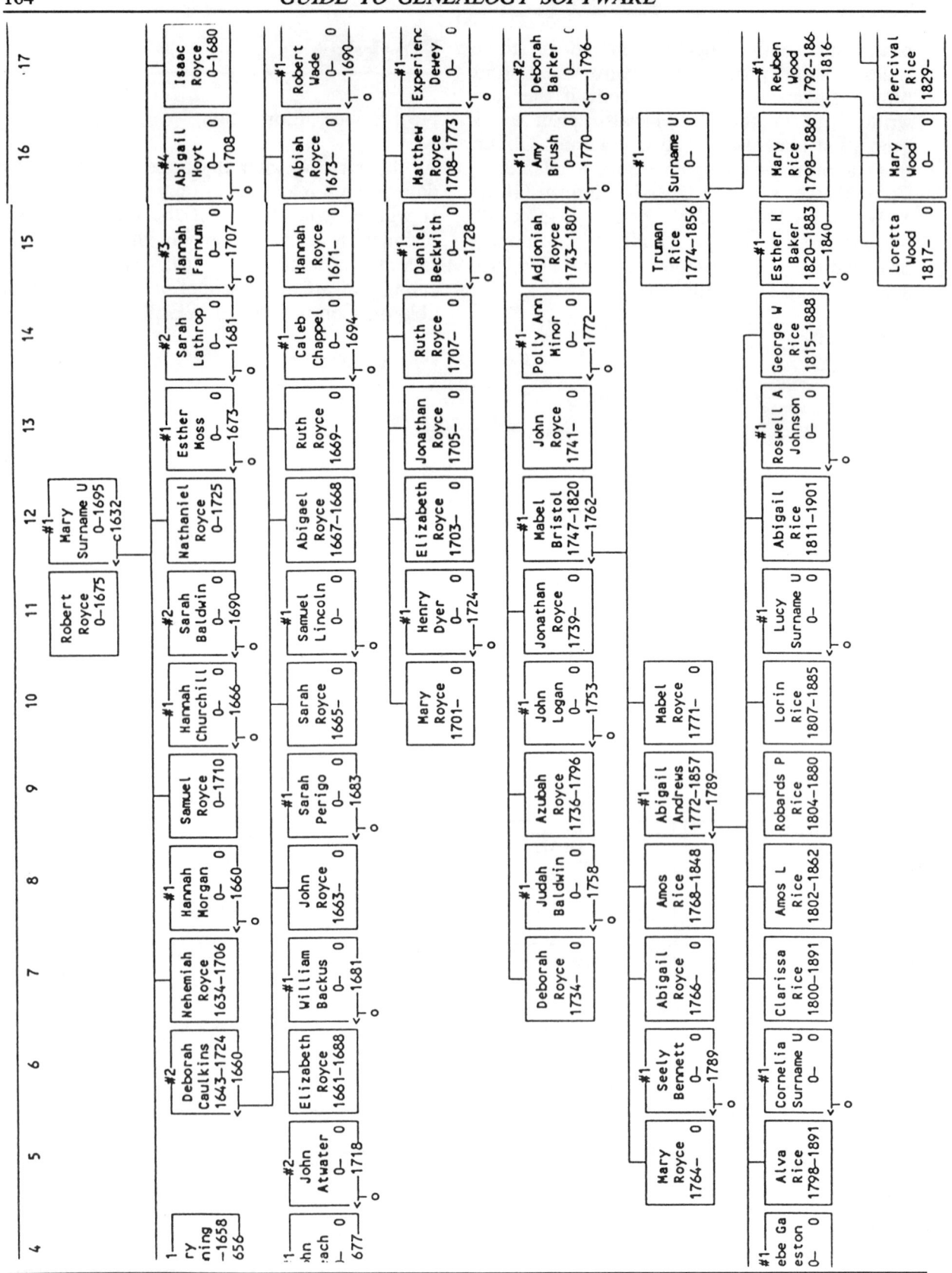

Dropline: Box chart.

UTILITIES

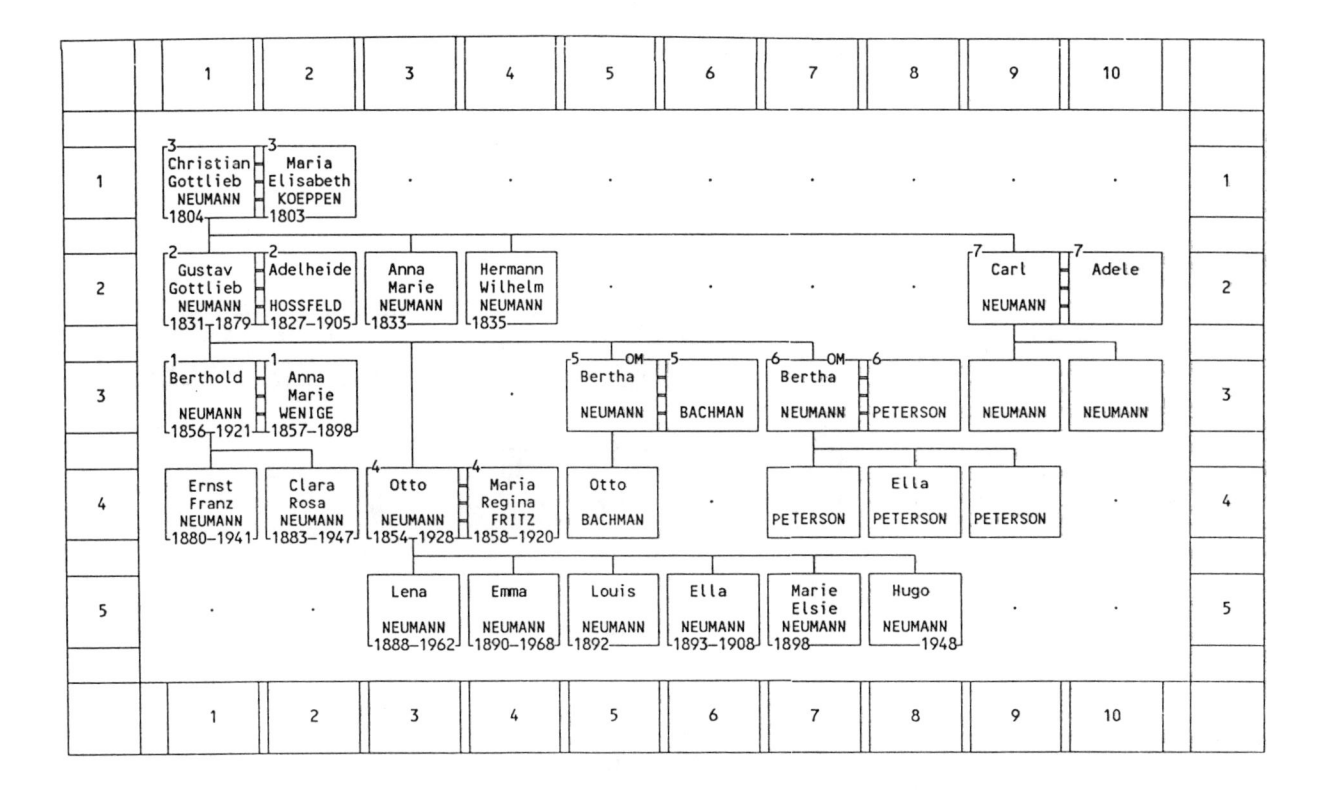

Family Tree Print: Box chart.

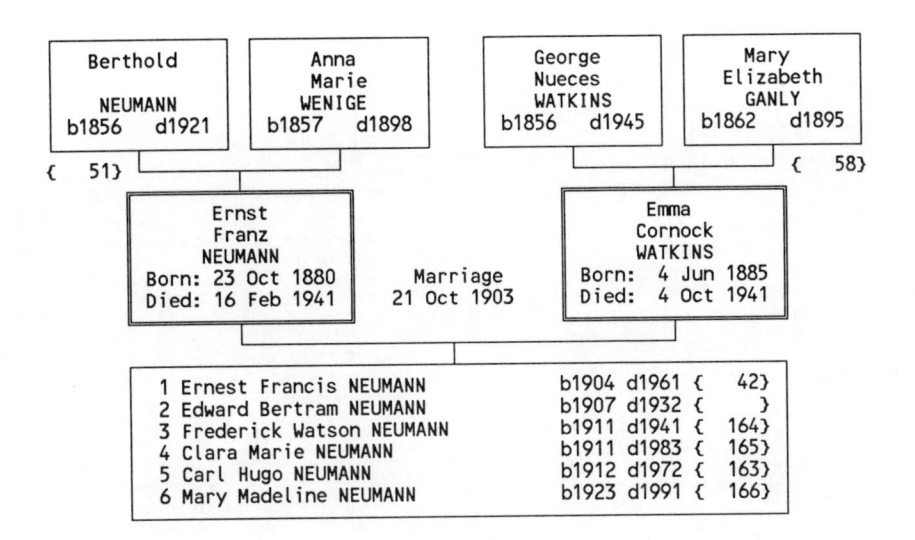

Family Tree Print: Just Ancestor box chart.

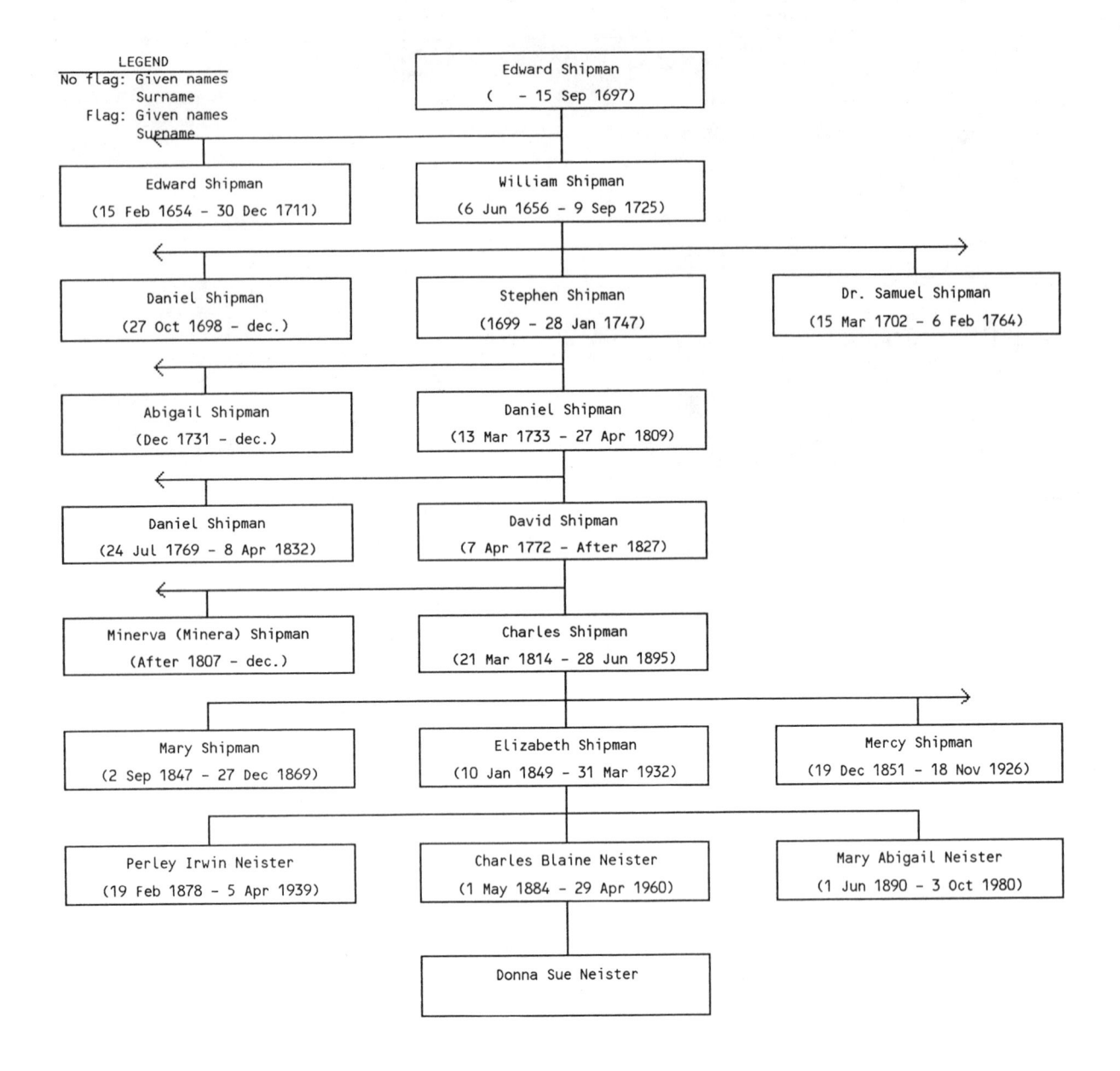

LEGEND
No flag: Given names
         Surname
Flag: Given names
      Su*rname*

```
                                    Edward Shipman
                                    (    - 15 Sep 1697)
                                           │
          ┌────────────────────────────────┤
    Edward Shipman                   William Shipman
    (15 Feb 1654 - 30 Dec 1711)      (6 Jun 1656 - 9 Sep 1725)
          │                                │
          ←────────────────────────────────┼────────────────────────────→
    Daniel Shipman                   Stephen Shipman                 Dr. Samuel Shipman
    (27 Oct 1698 - dec.)             (1699 - 28 Jan 1747)            (15 Mar 1702 - 6 Feb 1764)
          │                                │
          ←────────────────────────────────┤
    Abigail Shipman                  Daniel Shipman
    (Dec 1731 - dec.)                (13 Mar 1733 - 27 Apr 1809)
          │                                │
          ←────────────────────────────────┤
    Daniel Shipman                   David Shipman
    (24 Jul 1769 - 8 Apr 1832)       (7 Apr 1772 - After 1827)
          │                                │
          ←────────────────────────────────┤
    Minerva (Minera) Shipman         Charles Shipman
    (After 1807 - dec.)              (21 Mar 1814 - 28 Jun 1895)
                                           │
          ┌────────────────────────────────┼────────────────────────────→
    Mary Shipman                     Elizabeth Shipman               Mercy Shipman
    (2 Sep 1847 - 27 Dec 1869)       (10 Jan 1849 - 31 Mar 1932)     (19 Dec 1851 - 18 Nov 1926)
                                           │
          ┌────────────────────────────────┼────────────────────────────┐
    Perley Irwin Neister             Charles Blaine Neister          Mary Abigail Neister
    (19 Feb 1878 - 5 Apr 1939)       (1 May 1884 - 29 Apr 1960)      (1 Jun 1890 - 3 Oct 1980)
                                           │
                                    Donna Sue Neister
```

R-PLOT: Direct drop chart (partial).

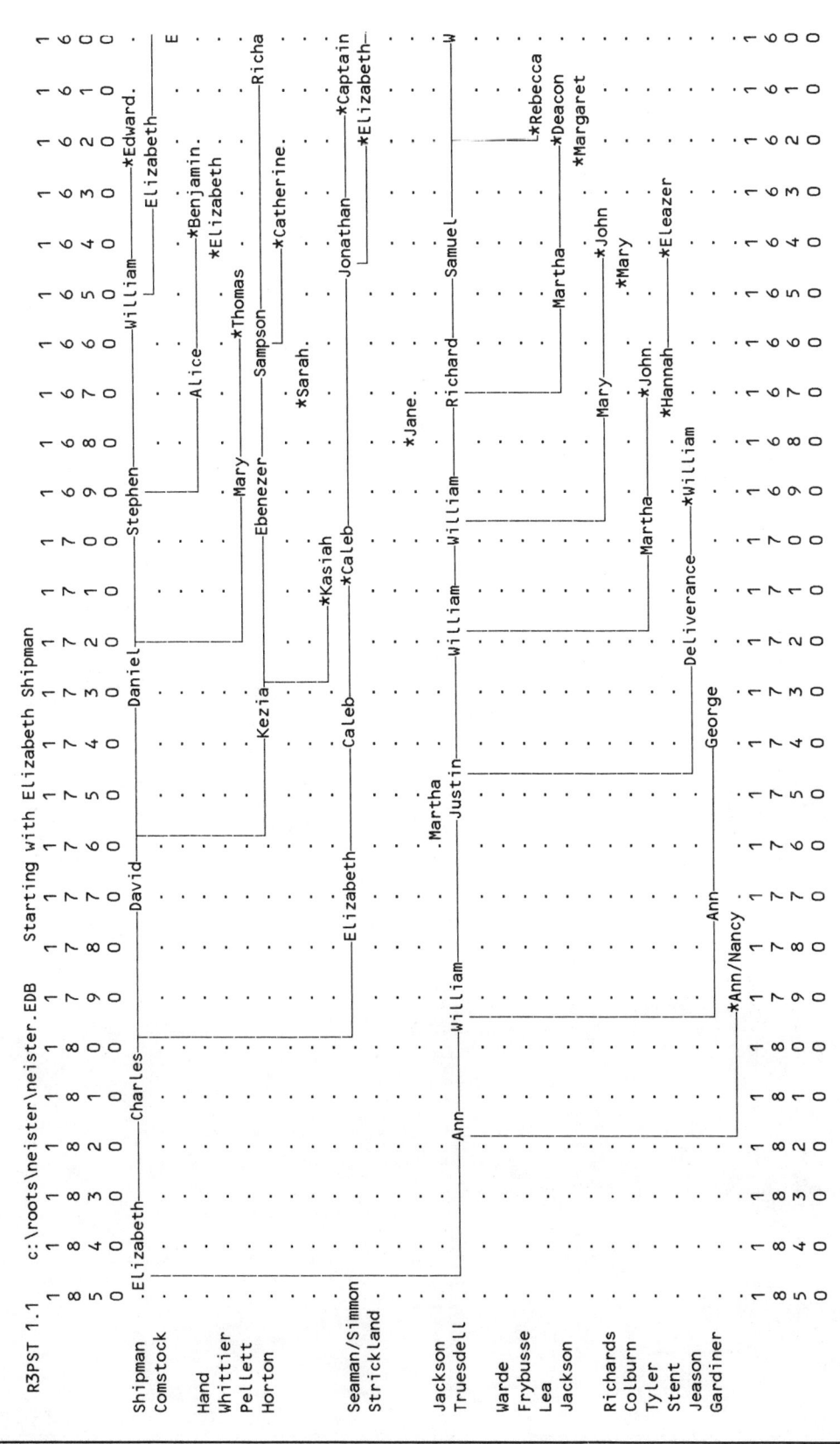

UTILITIES

```
R3PST 1.1    c:\roots\neister\neister.EDB    Starting with Elizabeth Shipman

                                                                           1 1 1 1 1 1 1 1 1 1 1 1
                                                                           6 6 6 6 6 6 6 6 6 6 6 6
                                                                           0 1 2 3 4 5 6 7 8 9 0 0
                                                                           0 0 0 0 0 0 0 0 0 0 0 0
                                                           ┌──────*Edward
                                                  ┌William─┤
                                                  │        └─Elizabeth─────E
                                        ┌──Alice──┤
                                        │         └──*Benjamin
                              ┌─Stephen─┤
                              │         │         ┌──*Thomas
                              │         └──Mary───┤
                              │                   └──*Elizabeth
                    ┌──David──┤
                    │         │         ┌─Sampson─────Richa
                    │         └─Ebenezer┤
                    │                   └──*Catherine
          ┌─Charles─┤
          │         │                   *Sarah
          │         │          ┌*Kasiah
          │         └──Daniel──┤
          │                    └*Caleb
Elizabeth─┤
          │                    *Jane
          │          ┌Elizabeth────Jonathan────*Captain
          │          │                         *Elizabeth
          │          │         ┌──Richard─────Samuel─────W
          │          │         │
          │          │         │                ┌─*Rebecca
          │    ┌─Ann─┤  William─┤  Martha──John──┤*Deacon
          │    │     │         │                └*Margaret
          │    │     │         │
          │    │     │William──┤         ┌──Mary
          │    │     └──Martha─┤  Mary───┤*John
          │    │               │         └*Hannah
          └Ann─┤   Deliverance─┤*William─────*Eleazer
               │               │
               │  ┌George──────┘
               └──┤                                                        1 1 1 1 1 1 1 1 1 1 1 1
                  *Ann/Nancy                                               8 8 8 8 8 8 8 8 8 8 8 8
                                                                           4 3 2 1 0 9 8 7 6 5 4 0
                                                                           0 0 0 0 0 0 0 0 0 0 0 0

Shipman
Comstock

Hand
Whittier
Pellett
Horton

Seaman/Simmon
Strickland

Jackson
Truesdell

Warde
Frybusse
Lea
Jackson

Richards
Colburn
Tyler
Stent
Jeason
Gardiner
```

R3PST.

Guide to Genealogy Software

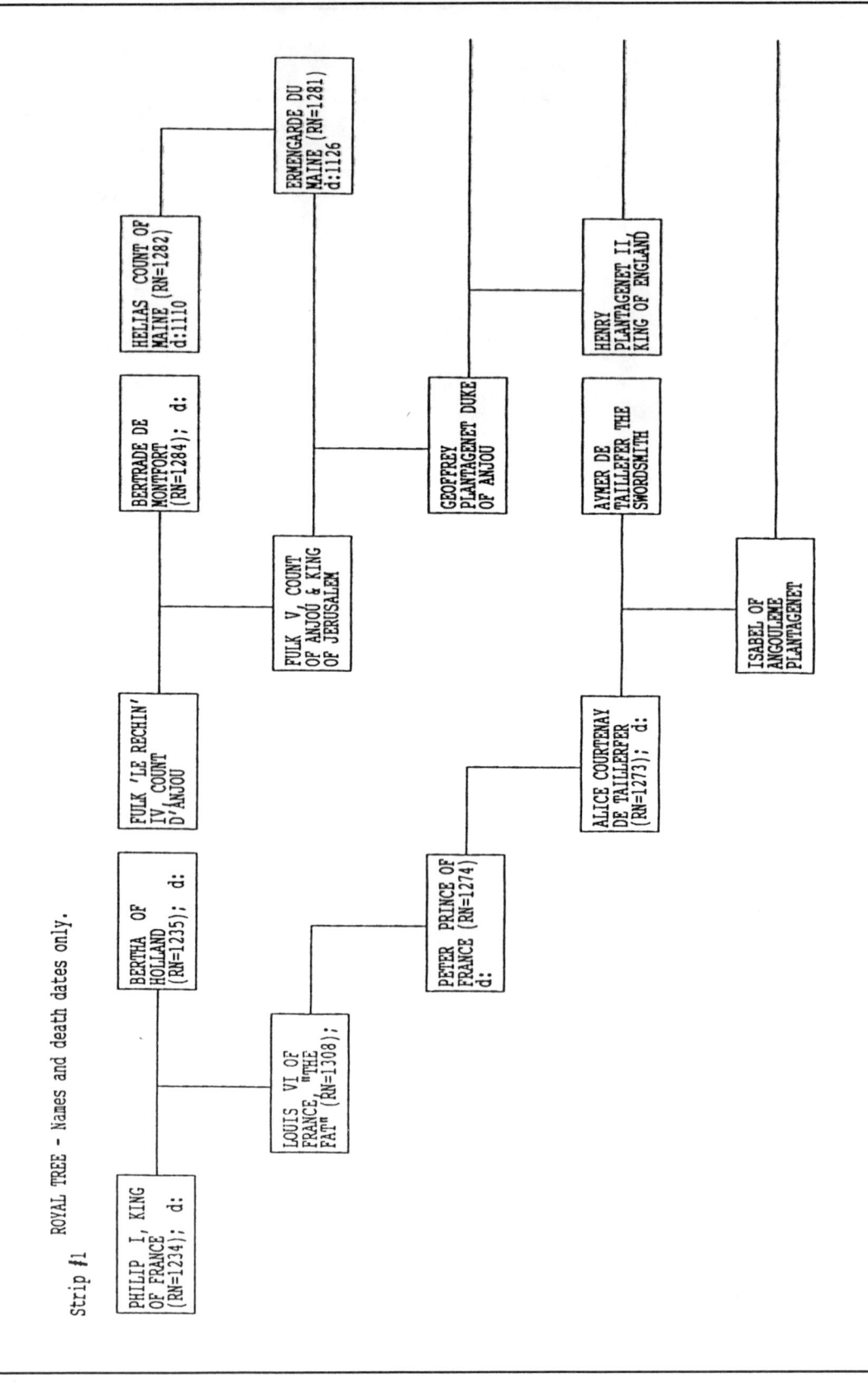

Strip #1 ROYAL TREE - Names and death dates only.

```
PHILIP I, KING
OF FRANCE
(RN=1234); d:
    |
    +---- BERTHA OF
    |     HOLLAND
    |     (RN=1235); d:
    |         |
    |         +---- FULK 'LE RECHIN'
    |         |     IV, COUNT
    |         |     D'ANJOU
    |         |         |
    |         |         +---- BERTRADE DE
    |         |               MONTFORT
    |         |               (RN=1284); d:
    |         |                   |
    |         |                   +---- HELIAS, COUNT OF
    |         |                   |     MAINE (RN=1282)
    |         |                   |     d:1110
    |         |                   |         |
    |         |                   |         +---- ERMENGARDE DU
    |         |                   |               MAINE (RN=1281)
    |         |                   |               d:1126
    |         |                   |
    |         |                   FULK V, COUNT
    |         |                   OF ANJOU & KING
    |         |                   OF JERUSALEM
    |         |                       |
    |         |                       GEOFFREY
    |         |                       PLANTAGENET, DUKE
    |         |                       OF ANJOU
    |         |                           |
    |         |                           HENRY
    |         |                           PLANTAGENET II,
    |         |                           KING OF ENGLAND
    |
    LOUIS VI OF
    FRANCE, "THE
    FAT" (RN=1308);
        |
        PETER, PRINCE OF
        FRANCE (RN=1274)
        d:
            |
            ALICE COURTENAY
            DE TAILLERFER
            (RN=1273); d:
                |
                AYMER DE
                TAILLEFER THE
                SWORDSMITH
                    |
                    ISABEL OF
                    ANGOULEME
                    PLANTAGENET
```

Tree Charts.

Other Programs

Other Programs

This is a miscellaneous assortment of programs that can be useful for genealogical researchers. These are generally programs where you input information as opposed to utilities which either take data from other programs or essentially give out information from a stored database such as soundex codes, calendar information, historical events, etc. Unless otherwise noted, programs are for DOS.

If you find a shareware program you like and use, please remember to send in your registration fee!

Autofone 1.1

Italy & Avalon, Inc.
3500 Gentry Rd.
Irving, TX 75062
214 650 9026 (8AM-5PM Central)
$15.95 Shareware

Utility to speed up searching the PhoneFile database on CompuServe. This contains addresses and phone numbers for over 92 million households in the US. It has been compiled from lists of credit card holders, utility company records and other sources. Search is by state on an exact spelling of a surname. In addition to the CompuServe charge, there is a surcharge for using PhoneFile. AutoFone allows you to set up your list of surnames to be searched before signing on. It will automatically go through all 50 states (plus the District of Columbia) and sign you off. By saving you the time of re-entering the data for each state, you save time and money (producer claims $3 savings per search). Available on CompuServe as AUTFN2.ZIP and on GEnie as AUTOFONE.ZIP. Support by mail, at above phone or on CompuServe: 76166,1345

Biography Maker 1.0

Banner Blue Software
P.O. Box 7865
Fremont, CA 94537
510 794 6850
To be announced - probably under $40; Free demo

New program under development which should be released by the time this book is published. It is designed to help in writing a biography or historical accounts of the lives of relatives. It will have a built-in word processor and database of over 2,000 writing ideas covering 80 topic categories. The topics will cover historical events from 1850 to the present as well as personal topics such as ancestry, education, occupation and many more. Once the birth and death date of the person are entered, it will prompt the user with historical events from the appropriate time period. It will take into consideration the occupation, age and education of the individual with the prompts. A blacksmith will have a different set of questions than an actress. It may also prompt with other questions such as, "Did the subject attend high school?" in order to eliminate ideas that would not apply. It automatically creates a table of contents based on your chapter titles. Can also be used to create a script for an oral interview. It can import and export information from/to other word processors in ASCII format. Registered users receive free technical support, notification of and substantial discounts on new versions of the product and on other programs by Banner Blue Software. Includes a printed manual and help screens. Supports dot matrix, laser and inkjet printers. Technical support available 8AM-5PM (Pacific) at the above number.

Cemetery Log Ver 1.0

Paul J. McGrath
64 Lorraine Dr.
North York, Ontario, Canada M2N 2E7
$15. Shareware

Cemetery data organizer. Supports database for nine cemeteries with each containing up to 32,768 graves. Data recorded includes cemetery name, plot identifier, site, grave, last name and maiden name, soundex (automatically calculated), first and middle name, sex, birth and death date and place, age at death and two lines of notes. You can display and/or print records sorted by grave location, name on the stone, date of death or birth. Benefits of registration: one free upgrade (enhanced sorting and printing routines being considered for future versions). Available on CompuServe as CMTYPG.ZIP.

Cemetery Research Database 5.0

Gale D. Wilkinson
GDW Software
5430 Meadow Dr.
Sumter, SC 29154
803 499 3533 (Evenings, Eastern time)
$19.95 + $3 s/h for regular version or laptop. Both programs for $34.95 plus $3. Shareware

Database program for organizing cemetery information. Supports multiple files so different areas can each have a database. Each cemetery is given a number, short name (six letters for DOS file name) and 25 character descriptive name. There are 10 lines for descriptive information. Cemetery name entered automatically when you give number and for each subsequent record until you change to different cemetery. On each record there is space for cemetery number and name, plot data, first, middle, last and maiden names, birthdate, death date, military service information. There are two lines for source data which you can print or leave out, and five lines of 70 characters each for remarks or legend information on each grave site. You can mark names in the legend information for indexing by using asterisks at the beginning and end of the name. After entering a name, the next record will display the same surname, cemetery name and source information by default. There are three different report format styles: 1) all names in database in order by cemetery, last name, first name, date of birth, date of death and five character military service data and legend data; 2) by cemetery as above except that within each cemetery the listings will be in the order you entered them (This shows which people are buried together; when adding names you can insert them in between other records) and 3) the same format, but for a selected cemetery. For all reports you can print an index which is in three columns, 17 characters per inch format. You can also print out the cemetery location data in ID number sequence. Contains a manual on disk and help screens. Requires a hard disk and Epson compatible printer. You can search by last name or maiden name (both searches can be actual spelling or Soundex), by cemetery ID number and search remarks for a last name. Author provides support by mail, phone or her BBS, Carolina Connections, at 803 499 4316. Benefits of registration: a copy of the utility CRDUTIL which will allow you to move cemeteries between data files to combine two cemeteries into one, to select records to move into a new file, rename cemeteries and print a master index of all listings in all databases. Reports can be printed to disk in ASCII format and further edited in a word processor. Available on CompuServe as CRD50S.ZIP and on GEnie as CRD50S.EXE.

A laptop version which will operate on a single floppy is available for the same price. The only difference is that it has no printing capability and it will not search for a name in the legend data area. Available on CompuServe as CRDLT3.EXE and on GEnie as CTDLT30S.EXE

Census Research Tool 7.0

Gale D. Wilkinson
GDW Software
5430 Meadow Dr.
Sumter, SC 29154
803 499 3533 (Evenings only, Eastern)
$29.95 + $3 s/h Shareware

Very helpful, easy to use program for organizing census research. The edit screen for each census year conforms with the information requested in the order it is listed. Each record ends with a remarks area that consists of five lines which show on the screen one line at a time. To save a record you continue to press enter until you have passed the five lines and the next edit screen will come up with certain information repeated. (The method of saving is not shown on the screen. You need to read the documentation to find this out.) Depending on the census year, it will repeat the reel number, page, district, household ID, family ID, state, county, town, last name, place of birth, father's and mother's place of birth. If you want to accept the repeat information, just press enter. If only a birth year or age are given, it will calculate the missing information. The following fields are required for all records: census year, state, county, town and last name. You can search for a record by last name, find a record by first name for a selected last name, soundex search (last name), record by county, find one record in one census or view records in the order entered. All reports are for one census year (as the information requested in different years is different). You can print a selected county summary, county detail, summary for one name, detail for one name, detail for one record, detail for one household, all records for one census. The "detail" reports print all the information as it appeared on the edit screen. Summary prints selected information in column form (1920, for example, shows household, family, last name, first name, age, color, sex, date of birth, town, county and state). You also have the choice of printing in alphabetical order or in order of entry. The summary report needs to print in condensed font which worked fine on an Epson dot matrix. On a laser it printed in courier and was incomplete. There are no options for selecting printers but you can print to a disk file and print through your own word processor. Contains document on disk and help screens. You can send reports to the printer or to a disk file. Benefits of registration: telephone support, future updates or revisions at a reduced price and a utility programs disk. The utility allows you to move data from one file to another, select specific records to move, change the position of records, pack the database and remove deleted records. Support provided by mail, phone or BBS (Carolina Connections) 803 499 4316. Available on CompuServe as CRT70A.ZIP and CRT70B.ZIP and on GEnie as CRT72S1. EXE and CRT72S2.EXE.

CHRONOS

Cascoly Software
4528 36th NE
Seattle, WA 98105
206 523 6135 (11AM-6PM Pacific Time)
800 242 4775, 713 524 6394 (ordering)
$30. Shareware

Historical timeline program charts your family members with historical events of your choosing. You must enter all people and all events; capacity of 300 each category per database. Recommended that the time span be less than 200 years. Can sort on group information entered, such as "Immigrant", "Irish," etc. for people, or "Wars", "Famine," etc., for events. Timeline showing people on top half and events on bottom half of screen can be displayed and printed; other printed reports include people by group (faction), events by group, age of everyone in the database when a particular event occurred. Support on CompuServe at CompuServe 76703,3046. Available on CompuServe as CHRNOS.ZIP.

Cumberland Diary 1.1

Ira J. Lund
Cumberland Software
385 Idaho Springs Road
Clarkesville, TN 37043
615 647 4012 (6-9PM weekdays, Central)
$20. Shareware

Computerized diary for maintaining a journal. Hard drive required as data is stored with program and would soon exceed disk size. Several diaries can be kept at once. Maximum 600 lines per entry. Each has a password (optional) for privacy. Data is encrypted whether you use a password or not. You add date (today's date is the default) so you don't have to make daily entries and there won't be blank pages for days without entries. Each day given a heading (32 characters). Search can be made by date or heading. You add the date you want, then search for it and press enter to display text screen to enter data. You can add dates at any time or delete. When browsing through entries, short cut keys take you to the next or previous keys. Will print selected entries by specifying beginning and ending dates or headings. Can also print entire diary with table of contents and title page. Spell checker with registered copies has cut and paste feature, text search ability. Can import and export an ASCII file. Can also export to Cumberland Story. Backup and restore utility. Benefits of registration include the spell checker, a printed manual and copies of Cumberland Tree and Cumberland Story. Available on CompuServe as CDIARY.ZIP. and on GEnie as CDIARY10.ZIP. Author can be reached on CompuServe: 70713,3476.

Cumberland Story 1.1

Ira J. Lund
Cumberland Software
385 Idaho Springs Road
Clarkesville, TN 37043
615 647 4012 (6-9PM weekdays, Central)
$25. Shareware

Guides you through writing a biography. Hard drive required as data is saved with program and it could soon exceed the size of a disk. Each book can contain a maximum of 240 chapters with 240 topics per chapter. Each topic can be up to 10 pages (approximately 6,600 words). Unlimited number of books. You can create an outline by selecting chapters and topics from a list. Chapters include Heritage (with topics such as My Maternal/Paternal Grandparents and My Brothers and Sisters), Childhood (topics: Family Traditions, Vacations, My Hometown, Childhood Friends and others), My Youth, College, Military Service, Vocations, Marriage and Family, Civic Activities, Hobbies and Talents, Church Activities, Retirement, Personal Traits, Retrospective Comments, To My Children and Favorite Stories and Poems. While almost every chapter has its own list of topics, you can display the list of all topics. The topic of one chapter may trigger a memory for an entirely different chapter. Some other topics are Vacations, My interests and Hobbies, Humorous Incidents, Reflections, Greatest Joys, Greatest Sorrows and What I Would Like You to Know. Once you have selected your topics, go to the topic menu to add the text. You can add, delete and move chapters and topics. They can be worked on in any order. The word processor contains a spell checker (registered versions only), cut and paste feature, text search ability. Foreign characters are supported. It will print a title page and table of contents. You can print the current topic, one or more chapters or the entire book. You enter beginning page numbers for each print job. Will import data from Cumberland Diary so you can constantly update your book without having to retype. You can also print to disk in ASCII format. Help screens provide aid, but manual on disk should also be printed as it is not always obvious how to get from one area to another. Program has no "save" option as it automatically saves when you exit a topic. This means you will not inadvertently lose any data, but you also cannot ignore anything you have written. Backup and restore utility. Benefits of registration include the spell checker, a printed manual and copies of Cumberland Tree and Cumberland Diary. Available on CompuServe as CSTORY.ZIP and on GEnie as CSTORY10.ZIP. Author can be reached on CompuServe: 70713,3476.

Family Census Research

Design Software
220 Stella
Burleson, TX 76028
817 295 8929 or 817 447 1445
$79.95 + $4. s/h (limited time special - $49.95)
  Commercial

Menu driven census organizer with templates for all available federal census years 1790 through 1920 with fill-in blanks. Information can be retrieved for viewing on the screen, printed or saved to a file in several different formats: individual or family grouping, chronological census history of an individual, all records for a given surname, all records for a given county or state, all records for heads of households, all records in alphabetical order, various indexes or files, optional long or condensed report versions, blanks forms for 1790-1920. Carry-over of data from one record to another. Generates soundex codes automatically. 1900 and 1920 census schedule indexes available for $14.95 for both years.

Family History Genealogy

Gold Trade Press, Inc.
P. O. Box 50346
Denton, TX 76206
817 898 1905 (6-10PM)
$59.95 Commercial; Demo $5.95 Shareware

Fill-in format for organizing your research. It is intended that you make a record for each event in a person's life — deeds, tax list, census, marriage, etc. It includes first and last name, date, event type, name of who was involved and relationship (family member or third party), brief description of the event, location, parents, 12 lines for associated names and nature or association, a line for comments and sources. You can name your own events, but manual contains suggestions for using various fields consistently which is necessary to produce useful lists as you can sort on any field and produce lists on the screen or send to printer or disk file. It will sort by names, time frame, type of event, place, etc. and will search for three different items (names, places, etc.) at once. By cross-referencing parents and children, it can also print a family tree listing up to 10 generations by accessing up to 3,000 "born" events in the database. Also prints family group sheets, descendant charts, chronological and user-defined lists. It is not a lineage-linked genealogy program. Available from the producer who will also provide support between 6 and 10PM local time. Printed manual and help screens.

Genealogical Cemetery Database

Design Software
220 Stella
Burleson, TX 76028
817 295 8929 or 817 447 1445
$49.95 + $3. s/h (limited time special $29.95)
Commercial

Menu driven cemetery information organizer. Data carry-over, blank research forms for use in the field. Maximum of 10,000 cemeteries with one million burial records per database. Room for inscriptions, military markers, etc. Generates soundex codes automatically. Some of the report/print options: all records in a given cemetery or county (short or long version), all records in a given state, all records for a given surname, alphabetical listing of entire database. Supports dot matrix and laser printers.

Genealogical Event Database (GED)

The Dollarhide Systems
203 W. Holly St., Suite M4
Bellingham, WA 98225
206 671 3808
$15. Shareware

Program for organizing your research material. Enter one line of information for each document or event. Preset columns for Book/page, Identification number, Soundex code, name, type of event (one letter code), year, location and record type. Block command to delete, move or recall a group of records; find and replace feature. Sorts can be done on any field. Can be transferred to Research Log in Everyone's Family Tree. Available on CompuServe as GED.ARC and on GEnie as GEDDB.EXE.

Gensource

William C. Busby
5744 Manzanillo Loop NE
Albuquerque, NM 87111
505 299 6450
$49. Commercial

System for filing source information, research notes, etc. on disk. Includes manual on disk. Supports dot matrix printers. Support by mail. Order from producer.

Indexx

John J. Armstrong
5009 Utah Dr.
Greenville, TX 75402-6239
903 454 8209
$75. Commercial; Demo $7.50

Indexing program for books already in print, census and other data on paper that needs an index. A hard drive is required. Printed manual and help screens. Type in information to be indexed. Program will sort on names, places and soundex. Groups of records can be isolated for printing or other editing. Supports dot matrix, laser and inkjet printers. Printing can be done to disk for printing through a word processor or in comma delimited format. Proof-reading features to verify accuracy. Varied output formats (see examples) including surname with given names on separate indented lines or run-in format where given names are run together. Choice of landscape or regular format, number of columns and large and small font sizes. Order from producer who provides support by mail and at above phone number.

IXM and IX3

Brian Harney
111 Willowcrest Dr.
Frankfort, KY 40601
502 857 4452 (5PM-10PM Eastern)
$15. Commercial

DOS, TRS80 Model 3 & 4

Creates "back of the book" indexes. Type in information to be indexed (32 characters per entry) with three to five digit page numbers in ASCII format. Handles over one million entries. Keystroke savers to speed data entry on repeat information. Quality check on data and report of errors. Can edit within the program or in a word processor. Can be used on a floppy (10,000-20,000 entries per 360K disk) but will run faster on hard drive. Three different print formats. Output can be sent to disk and printed through a word processor. Configuration screen with test print feature. Support by phone at above number and by mail.

Life History Disk

Star-Com Microsystems
25 West 1480 North
Orem, UT 84057
801 225 1480
$19.95 + $2. s/h; Free demo. Commercial

DOS, MACINTOSH, APPLE II.

Biography writing program used in conjunction with any word processor. Includes printed manual and manual on disk. Supports dot matrix, laser and inkjet printers. User support provided by mail or at above number (9AM-6PM Mountain).

Mapper 4.6

Russell Holsclaw
7472 Mt. Sherman Rd.
Longmont, CO 80503
Public domain

This program will print a plat map based on a surveyor's description of a tract of land. First use your word processor to create survey description file giving the course and distance for the boundaries giving measurements in rods, poles, feed and chains. An unknown boundary can be entered if it cannot be read or isn't in measured terms ("follow the meander of the creek") but the program may not be able to create a map in some cases if there are two unknowns. Then create your caption in the word processor and begin the program. It will ask the scale you want and print a plat map. Available on CompuServe as MAPR46.ZIP and on GEnie as MAPPER.ZIP.

MEMORIES?

Senior Software Systems
8804 Wildridge Dr.
Austin, TX 78759-7329
800 637 9949 (orders only)
$79.95 + 3 shipping. Commercial

Biography writing program which "interviews" you (or you can use it to interview someone else) with 1,200 questions in eight categories such as "It All Started When", "Early Life Memories", "Adolescence", as well as "Looking Back", and "Bits of Wisdom for Future Generations". Topics include "16 Tons" (work, choices, bosses and losses), "My Closest Friend", "Mischief" (pranks, getting caught), "Bark & Purr" (dogs, cats, special times, sad times), "Understanding Men/Women" (love, wants, words & needs, reading between the lines). Each topic has 240 lines, but you can add chapters and topics, including a "continued" one to add more. You can arrange the chapters and topics in the order you want, jump around when writing and put ideas on other topics on a notepad to come back to later. Automatically saves your material when you exit the topic. Creates title page and table of contents and book can be saved to a file in ASCII format and further edited and printed through your word processor if you want. You can work on more than one book at a time. Includes a printed manual and help screens. Support provided by phone at 512 345 8137.

Resource Links

Data Tools
874 W. 1400 North
Orem, UT 84057-2916
801 225 3256
Commercial; in beta test

Program to organize family history materials. Keeps track of all resources, artifacts, certificates, photos, letters, histories, videotapes, etc. that you have for each person. Can produce cross-referenced lists, such as everyone for whom you have a birth certificate or a photo. Entry screen for each person; select resource from a list to create a new entry. Individuals and dates must be entered, but GEDCOM import is planned.

ROOTS WRITER

Commsoft, Inc.
P. O. Box 310
Windsor, CA 95492-0310
707 838 4300; 800 327 6687
$60. Commercial (Includes REVENT & PAF-NOTES)

Usually used as a ROOTS III utility, it is actually a stand-alone text editor (a basic "word processor"). When installed in the ROOTS program, a function key automatically puts you into the text editor and gives the file the correct name. Many function keys (save, erase, main menu) have the same use in ROOTS and ROOTS WRITER. Has cut and paste, search and replace, macros. Does not support foreign characters. When used as a stand-alone program it also has tab and margin settings, page length and other features which are not used within ROOTS as these are set by the type of ROOTS report selected. ROOTS WRITER has the advantage of being a small program that doesn't use much memory and is supported by Commsoft. Printed manual and help screen of commands. Available from producer, who periodically has special sales, dealers who may have discount prices, and retail stores. Support: Phone: 707 838 4300 (9AM-4PM, Pacific); BBS: 707 838 6373; FAX: 707 838 6343; Prodigy: JJSR40A; GEnie: H.NURSE; CompuServe: 73710,773.

SCRAPS 1.7

Raymond Lowe
Scraps
P.O. Box 2
Cheung Chau, Hong Kong
$25; $35 with disk.   Shareware

A Freeform Personal Information Manager that can be used to store, manage, index and retrieve pieces, or "scraps," of information. Full text of research notes can be entered, stored and sorted. Every word is indexed for retrieval. The length of each piece of text is limited only by memory, but short pieces (about 2000 words maximum) are recommended. Can import and export word processor files. Finds and groups by specific word, phrase, or by creation, last-modified or reminder dates. Has on-line help. Includes a perpetual calendar. Is menu driven and easy to use. Includes setup files and alarm modules for using with Windows or DesQview. Not written specifically for genealogy, this program also has a "ToDo List", phone dialer, calculator, and appointment calendar with reminder alarm.

Sesame

Commsoft, Inc.
P. O. Box 310
Windsor, CA 95492-0310
707 838 4300; 800 327 6687
$195. Commercial

DOS/WINDOWS and MACINTOSH

IBM requirements: one megabyte RAM, Windows 2.1 or later, 20 megabyte hard drive, 80286 processor or later, graphics adaptor and monitor, mouse, graphics printer; Macintosh requirements: one megabyte RAM, Macintosh Plus or higher, color or monochrome, graphics printer.

An all-purpose genealogy database program which is GEDCOM compatible for import and export. Designed to help you organize and analyze all your genealogy research with the capability of transferring it to other genealogy or database programs. Files can be transferred between IBM and Macintosh; imports data from Personal Ancestral File Research Data Filer. Fields can be any length so information does not have to be shortened. Each item of information can be 65,000 characters long. Supports foreign characters, macros for entering repeat information. Fill-in templates for many categories: census (1790-1910), deeds, wills, address list, research, register, telephone list or design your own form. It can sort and select on any field, cut and paste between files. Individuals can be linked. Design your own printed reports which are printed through Windows. This is intended as a supplement to a lineage-linked genealogy program, not a replacement. It does not print family group sheets, pedigree charts, etc. Supports dot matrix, laser and inkjet printers. Includes manual and help screens. Available from producer, who periodically has special sales, dealers who may have discount prices, and retail stores. Support: Phone: 707 838 4300 (9AM-4PM, Pacific); BBS: 707 838 6373; FAX: 707 838 6343; Prodigy: JJSR40A; GEnie: H.NURSE; CompuServe: 73710,773.

ShareSpell

Robert Bequette
Acropolis Software
P. O. Box 5037
Fair Oaks, CA 95628
$20. Shareware

Spell checker for text files. Has a dictionary of over 112,000 words to which you can add your own words. Stops at questionable words and gives you the option of selecting a word from the list, manually changing, marking and ignoring the word or continuing with no change. If you make changes you have the option to keep or ignore change. If you keep them it saves the changed file under the original name and the old one with a .BAK extension. Can be installed to operate within ROOTS III to spell check text files created with Roots Writer or other text editor. Producer can be contacted by mail or on CompuServe: 75146,3471.

SKY Index

SKY Software
P.O. Box 394
Maine, NY 13802-0394
607 786 0769 (10AM-6PM Eastern)
$74.95 + $4. shipping (U.S. & Canada)

Indexing program. Supports most popular printers with pica, elite and compressed type and six or eight lines per inch. Can add a string of characters to the front of any field in your database (for creating cumulative indexes for periodicals), choice of indents or run-in styles and choice of number of spaces to indent subtopics. Prime topic and subtopic fields can be up to 999 characters long and can be adjusted. Can print even pages and then odd for printing on both sides. Displays previous, current and next records on screen. Help screens. All data fields are alphanumeric and keyboard macros are available for repeat information. Search and replace, including wild cards.

The Indexer 2.7

Words on Disk
P. O. Box 4881
Troy, MI 48099-4881
$44.95 + $2. s/h; Free demo ($2. s/h)

Back of the book indexing program. Menu driven, 20 minute demo which serves as tutorial. On-line documentation to explain every phase of the program. Data entry screen which allows you to store up to three commonly used names which can be inserted with a function key, select a constant volume/page number or choose to be prompted for them after each name is entered. Supports different font sizes, one to 13 columns, column width 15-195, print surnames in all upper case or initial capital. Can send report to the printer or print to disk. Multiple files can be merged and sorted.

Tiny Tafel Editor 1.04

Christopher E. Long
632 Camelia St.
Atlantic Beach, FL 32233
904 246 4706 (9AM-10PM Eastern);
BBS 904 249 9515
$10. Shareware

Aid for creating or editing a Tiny Tafel report. For each family line you fill in a menu which asks for family name, date and place of earliest and latest in line. The program automatically inserts correct format. No printed instructions, but many help screens which are actually helpful and relevant. Author can be reach on CompuServe: 76500,2073.

Video Display Editor (VDE) 1.52

Eric Meyer
401 - 12th Ave. SE, #139
Norman, OK 73071
Freeware

Text editor that can be used to create text files by itself or with genealogy programs that do not have their own text editor built in. Includes multiple files, cut and paste, block copy, move, delete, find/replace, undo deletions, automatic save, macros, utilities to split or compare files, count words, word wrap, reformat, left and right margins, variable tabs, center, flush right, proportional spacing, multiple file formats including ASCII, WordStar, WordPerfect, XyWrite. Can be used with ROOTS III and PAF. Available on CompuServe as VDE162.ZIP.

Virtual BookMaker

Randall Kopchak
It's All Relative
2233 Keeven Lane
Florissant, MO 63031
$25. Commercial

DOS or ATARI ST

Creates a slide show that will run on your computer integrating photographs, maps and text. The file that is created can be run from the floppy without a CD-ROM drive. If you want to create your own presentations, you need an XA CD-ROM drive, Photo CD disc, 386 PC or better running Windows 3.1 or higher, VGA and 640K of memory. A sound card is optional. If you do not have a CD-ROM, but would like a virtual book of your own, the company will create one for you for $20. Send up to six black and white photographs or copies of old documents (no originals, please) and an outline of your text. Voice files should be on cassette, but should not be used if you plan to run your story from a floppy disk due to size constraints. Producer can be contacted on CompuServe (70357,2312) or GEnie (GREG).

Omitted Programs

The following programs were not included for various reasons, the primary one being there was no answer to our questionnaire and we had no first-hand information on the program. Quite a few addresses are no longer current although the programs may still be available.

Below is a list of the addresses we used. Some programs are no longer on the market and some of the older utilities have been made obsolete by later versions of the program they were designed to supplement.

Name	Producer	System	Reason not included
AGP: A Genealogy Program	Rasche 5205 Brandonway Ct. Dublin, OH 43017-8598	Atari	No answer.
Ahnentafel	Ann Turner 418 Gilbert Ave. Menlo Park, CA 94025	DOS	Prints an Ahnentafel with dates and places, to 23 generations. PAF's Ahnentafel now includes dates and places and will go up to 32 generations. (Written in 1989)
Ancestral Line	B & J Research P. O. Box 457 Sapulpa, OK 74067	DOS	No answer
Arbor-Aide	Software Solutions 7378 Zurawski Court Custer, WI 54423	DOS	No answer
Census db	Geneware P. O. Box 55249 Riverside, CA 92517	DOS	Returned by the Post Office
dGENE	Fairway Systems 9143 - 122 Place S.E. Renton, WA 98056	DOS, CP/M	No answer
F-Tree	G & M Systems P. O. Box 850331 Yukon, OK 73085	DOS	No answer
Family	Barry E. Kelly 117 Peach Rd. Atco, NJ 08004	DOS	No answer

Name	Producer	System	Reason not included
Family	PFA, Inc. 8600 E. Old Spanish Trail #79 Tucson, AZ 85710	DOS?, Commodore, Apple, TRS 80	No answer
Family Tree Etc. Ver. 5.03	Pine Cone Software P. O. Box 1163 Columbus, IN 47202	DOS	No answer
Family Tree	Genealogy Software P. O. Box 611170 Port Huron, MI 48061		No answer
First Family	Computerology, Inc. P. O. Box 30113 San Antonio, TX 78285	DOS	Returned by the Post Office
FT-More Ver 2.3	Robert L. Mosher 106 Nawiliwili St. Honolulu, HI 96825	DOS	Returned by the Post Office
gen'Logical PATHFINDER	Eileen Polakoff Research 240 West End Ave., Suite 15A New York, NY 10023		Not marketed.
Genafile	Traces P. O. Box 168 Center, MO 63436	Apple II Commodore	No answer
Genassist	Prometheus Software Systems 4310 S. Semoran Blvd., #587 Orlando, FL 32822	DOS	No answer. Apparently still available. Reviewed in *Genealogical Computing* Oct. 1992.
Genea	Richard G. Vincens 4710-3 Lakeside Club Blvd. East Ft. Meyers, FL 33905	DOS	Returned by the Post Office
Genea-Link	Family Tree Computer Center P. O. Box 338 Orem, UT 84056	DOS	Returned by the Post Office
Genea-Logical Records System Ver 1	R. F. Hatch & Assoc. Inc. RR #1 Wallacetown, ON N0L 2M0 Canada	DOS	No answer

Name	Producer	System	Reason not included
Genealogical Explorer Ver 2.0.2	Joel Finkle 9235 Fern Lane Des Plaines, IL 60016	Macintosh	No answer
Genealogy Assistant	L & H Enterprises 9723A Folsom Blvd., #223 Sacramento, CA 95827	DOS	No answer
Genealogy Data Base Ver 1.1	Kevin Mennitt 208 Baker Ave. Westfield, NJ 07090	Macintosh	No answer
Genealogy db	Geneware P. O. Box 55249 Riverside, CA 92517	DOS	Returned by the Post Office
Genealogy on Display	Melvin O. Duke P. O. Box 20836 San Jose, CA 95160	DOS	No longer supported by author. Runs in Basic, not QBasic
Genealogy Research III	USD Inc. 251 Round Lake Rd. Vermontville, MI 49096	DOS	No answer
Generation Gap Plus	Flying Pigs Software P. O. Box 688 St. George, UT 84770	Atari	No answer
Generations	Micro-80 Inc. 2665 Busby Grove Rd. Oak Harbor, WA 98277	DOS	No answer
Griot Alternative Ver 2.0	Thierry Pertuy 28 Ave. France-Lanord 54600 Villers-les-Nancy, France	DOS	In French only, did not contact
Horizons	Lifestyle Software Group 63 Orange St. St. Augustine, FL 32084	DOS	No answer
Hyper-Genealogy	The Harbinger Group 6253 BenMore Dr. Fridley, MN 55432	Macintosh	No answer
Hyper-Tree Ver 1.1	Joe Cornich 29331 Sunspot Circle Anchorage, AK 99507	Macintosh	Returned by the Post Office
Hypergene Ver 1.0	Compsevco 1921 Corporate Square Slidell, LA 70458	Macintosh	Returned by the Post Office

Name	Producer	System	Reason not included
Index Master Ver 1.11	Michael Cooley P. O. Box 593 Santa Cruz, CA 95061-0593	DOS	No answer
Journal Writer Ver 1.0	Eagle Systems P. O. Box 5600 Provo, UT 84603	DOS	No answer
Lineage Master	GeneaLogic Systems 140 w. 900 So. Orem, UT 84058	DOS	No answer
MacAncestors	Bill Blue, Seattle Gen. Soc. P. O. Box 549 Seattle, WA 98111	Macintosh	Discontinued
MacGene	Applied Ideas, Inc. P. O. Box 3225 Manhattan Beach, CA 90266	Macintosh	No answer
MacGenie	Te Corporation P. O. Box 140 Campton, NH 03223	Macintosh	Discontinued
My Family Record Ver 3.0	Everton 3223 S. Main St. Nibley, UT 84321	DOS	No answer
My Roots	Mark Peters 1513 Towhee Lane Naperville, IL 60565	DOS, Apple II	No answer
My Story	Kidd and Kidd, Inc. P. O. Box 778 Oneida, TN 37841	DOS	Returned by the Post Office
Norgen	Norris Software, Ltd. 3208 West Lake St., #65 Minneapolis, MN 55416	Amiga	No answer
Our Family	James G. Vaughan P. O Box 843 University, MS 38677	DOS	No answer
Pedigree Ver 3.0	EROSystems 1642 Noreen Dr. San Jose, CA 95124	Commodore 64	Returned by the Post Office

Name	Producer	System	Reason not included
Phoenix	Gentech P. O. Box 3303 Eugene, OR 97403	Macintosh	No answer
Prism	Gary R. Austin 1458 - 10th St. Grand Rapids, MI 49504	DOS	No answer
Roots and Branches Ver 1.2	Douglass A. White P. O. Box 1113 Fairfield, IA 52556	Macintosh	No answer
Roots Master	RKS Software 3820 N. Dittmar Rd. Arlington, VA 22207	DOS	No answer
SunriseGEN	Sunrise Development Sweden	Macintosh	No address for info. Available in US through Computerware at 800 326 0092.
The Family Tree	Valley Software 1028 Tuscany Pl. Cupertino, CA 95014	DOS	No answer
The Genealogy Assistant Programs	L & H Enterprises 9723 A Folsom Blvd., #223 Sacramento, CA 95827	DOS	No answer
The Register Program	Applied Computing Services 14410 SE Petrovitsky Rd., #203 Renton, WA 98058	DOS	Returned by the Post Office
Your Family Tree	Hurdware P. O. Box 241746 Memphis, TN 38124	DOS	No answer

Glossary

Ancestral File: A database of more than 10 million names in linked genealogies. It is available on CD-ROM as part of Family-Search. These names have been submitted by many researchers and may contain several generations of a family. It also contains the names and addresses of people who have submitted the information and you can contact them for further information.

ASCII: An acronym for American Standard Code for Information Interchange, it is an information coding system for letters, numbers and symbols. In an ASCII file, text has been saved without special word processing formatting codes and so can be exchanged between different programs.

BBS: Bulletin Board System. See p. 8 for more information.

Cascading pedigree chart: A series of pedigree charts showing all ancestors in the database for a specified number of generations from the first person. There are three to six generations on one page and the pages are linked by means of continuation chart numbers. If a parent of the person in the right hand column is known, this person will be continued on another pedigree chart. The page numbers or identification numbers will be referenced on both charts. In this way a large pedigree can be followed but the printout will still be small enough to keep in a book.

Case sensitive: Case refers to upper and lower case letters. If a search is "case sensitive" it means that an upper case letter is considered different from a lower case letter. If you are searching for "Charles" and you enter "charles" in the search criteria, the program will not find it.

CompuServe: An electronic computer network. See p. 8 for more information.

Download: Copy to disk from a BBS or other computer system, such as FamilySearch. See p. 9 for more information.

Event: A happening in a person's life, usually something that has a date. An event can be birth, death, marriage, burial, immigration, etc. Event field names, or labels, might also include topics such as religion, occupation and medical history.

FamilySearch: A system of computerized databases on CD-ROM available at the Family History Library in Salt Lake City and most Family History Centers operated by the Church of Jesus Christ of Latter-day Saints. It contains millions of names in several databases, including the International Genealogical Index (IGI), Ancestral File, Social Security Death Index (SSDI) and Military Death Index. At present this information may only be accessed at these facilities and some public libraries, but the information can be printed to paper or copied to a disk and brought home where you can add it to your own genealogy database or use your word processor or some of the utility programs to search and sort it in many ways.

Field: An area in an edit screen where data is entered. A name field may consist of one field in which all names (first, middle and last) are entered or there may be a separate field for each name.

GEnie: An electronic computer network. See p. 8 for more information..

Hot key: A key which has been designated to take the place of several keystrokes. Function keys (F1-F12 at the top or F1-F10 at the side of a keyboard) are used as hot keys. By pressing a function key you may be able to immediately bring up a pedigree screen or jump to a print menu. Combining the control or alternate key with other keys can also create a hot key. To bring up an edit screen for a person on a list, you might press Alt-E.

IGI: International Genealogical Index. A database of more than 147 million names of deceased persons. It is available on fiche and on CD-ROM as part of FamilySearch. Most names have been extracted from various original records from all over the world; many other have been submitted by LDS Church members. The records are predominately baptisms, listing the child's and parents' names, and marriages, listing the spouse's names; these people are not linked to anyone else. The date and place of the event are also given. The source of the data in each record is found in the batch number in the right column.

Label: Name for an event.

Military Death Index, or Military Index: A database of 100,000 men and women who died in the Korean or Viet Nam Wars. It is available on CD-ROM as part of Family-Search. It lists the birth and death dates, residence, place of death, rank and service number. Viet Nam deaths also list religion, marital status and race.

MRIN: Marriage Record Identification Number. Number, usually assigned by the computer, for a marriage record.

Prodigy: An electronic computer network. See p. 8 for more information.

RIN: Record Identification Number. Number, usually assigned by the program, for an individual's record.

Social Security Death Index: An index of deaths of people who had Social Security numbers, received Social Security benefits during their lifetimes and whose deaths were reported to Social Security. Most deaths are from the 1962-88 period. The record gives information on birth date, death date, last place of residence, place where death benefit was sent, the social security number and the state where it was issued. You can write to the Social Security Administration Freedom of Information Office and obtain a copy of the original application.

Soundex: System for indexing names which gives the same code to names that sound alike but may be spelled differently. A Soundex code starts with the letter of the name followed by three numerals for the consonants in the name.

Support (help): Assistance provided by the producer of a program when you have a problem, or perhaps by a user group.

Supports (mouse, foreign characters): If a program "supports" a feature, it means this item will function with the program. For example, if foreign characters are supported, then you can use characters such as ü or ñ.

Tiny Tafel: An abbreviated ahnentafel. See p. 20 for more information.

User-defined: Custom selection made by the user. A user-defined field is one for which the user can supply the field name, or label. A user-defined chart means the user can select the data to be included, the sorting order, the arrangement on the page, etc.

Wall chart: A multi-page chart that is taped together to form one large chart. This type of chart cannot be kept in a book on separate pages.

Wild cards: Symbols that stand for one or more letters. The term usually is used in DOS commands but can also be used within some programs. An asterisk (*) represents any character or characters on either side and immediately adjacent to the dot. If you ask for files *.EXE, it means all files that end in .EXE no matter what the first part of the filename may be; DE*.DAT means all files beginning with DE and ending with .DAT. A question mark (?) stands for one character in a position in the file name. If you ask for ??NAME.DAT it means the first two letters could be anything, then the next four would be NAME and the extension DAT.

Index to Programs

All programs are indexed by name and producer. In addition, programs in the Utilities and Other Programs section are also indexed by type. All non-DOS programs are also indexed by type of computer or system. Programs whose names begin with "The" are indexed under "T" as most of the authors emphasize this word in their program name. Some of the programs are known by their initials which includes the "T".

Acropolis Software   181
AGP: A Genealogy Program   183
AHNDES   141
Ahnentafel   183
Amiga   127, 133, 151, 186
Ancestral Line   183
Apple   184
Apple II   66, 92, 98, 135, 162, 178, 184, 186
Applied Computing Services   187
Applied Ideas, Inc.   186
Arbor-Aide   183
Armstrong, John J.   178
Atari   97, 182, 183, 185
Austin, Gary R.   187
Autofone   173
B & J Research   183
Banner Blue Software   85, 173
Barron, John C.   143, 154, 158, 160
Bdate   141
Beinert, Bill   151
Bennett, Barbara   156
Bequette, Robert   181
Berry, Joseph   161
Billard, Robert Lott   146
Biography Maker   173
Biography writing program   173, 176, 178, 179
Blue, Bill   186
Boston, Jeffrey   157
Brother's Keeper   37
Brown, Phillip E.   54
Busby, William C.   178
Cain, Philip   148
Cal.exe   142
Calendar   141, 142, 150
    Jewish   154, 161
Cannon, Steven M.   145, 146, 153
Cascade   142
Cascoly Software   175
Cemetery Log   173

Cemetery recording program   173, 174, 177
Cemetery Research Database   174
Census db   183
Census recording program   174, 176
Census Research Tool   174
Chandler, Jack   141, 153-156, 160
Charts, Box   143, 145, 146, 151
Cherry Tree Software   80
Cherry, Rick   80
CHRONOS   175
Church of Jesus Christ of Latter-day Saints   106
Cleaveland, Richard   143, 149, 158, 159
Clement Custom Programming   149
Clement, John   159
Clement, Rex   149
COLA   142
Commodore   184
Commodore 128   66
Commodore 64   66, 98, 162, 186
Common Sense Software   145, 150
Commsoft, Inc.   115, 141, 152, 158, 160, 179, 180
Compsevco   185
Computerology, Inc   184
Cooley, Michael   186
Cornich, Joe   185
Cost of living adjustment   142
CP/M   183
Cumberland Diary   175
Cumberland Software   44, 175, 176
Cumberland Story   176
Cumberland Tree   44
Data Base Systems   92, 150
Data Tools   155, 179
Database files   144, 148, 151
Dataform Corporation   161
Date calculator   141, 143, 144, 147, 150, 163
Dateline   143

Deatherage, Patrick C. 143, 153, 160
DESCEND 143
Design Software 176, 177
Devoe, Dan and Leonard 141
DFoot 143
DGENE 183
Diary program 175
Dollarhide Systems 47, 177
Douglas, Tom P. 162
Dropline 143, 164
Duke, Melvin O. 185
Eagle Systems 186
Easter 143
EDITPAF 144
EROSystems 186
EstiDate 144
Event database 144, 152, 155
EVENTS 144
Everton 186
Everyone's Family Tree 47
EZ-Tree 133
F-Tree 183
Fairway Systems 183
Family 183, 184
Family Attic 144
Family Census Research 176
Family Connections 51
Family Heritage File 133
Family History Genealogy 177
Family History Program (for Windows) 53
Family History System 54
Family History System utility
    GEDCOM 148
Family Origins 59
Family Records Utility (FRU) 145
Family Reunion 65
Family Roots 66
Family Roots utility
    Tree Charts 162
Family Technologies 77
Family Ties 75
Family Ties utility
    Family Tree Print (FTP) 145
Family Treasures 77
Family Tree 184
Family Tree Computer Center 184
Family Tree Etc. 184
Family Tree Journal 80
Family Tree Maker 85
Family Tree Maker utility
    FTMgedFX 147
Family Tree Print (FTP) 145, 165, 166
Family Viewer 146
FamilyPerfect 145

FamilySearch 151
FAMSORT 146
FAMware 65, 126
Fan Chart Generator 146
Feast 147
Finkle, Joel 185
First Family 184
Flying Pigs Software 185
Forest 147
FR PRINT 147
FT-More 184
FTMgedFX 147
G & M Systems 183
Gafford, Durwood 142
GCFiler 148
GDW Software 174
GED2TT 148
GEDBROWS 152
GEDCOM for
    Family History System 148
    Family Ties 145
    Genealogy on Display 148
    Linkages 149
GEDCOM utility 146
    Family Attic 144
    Family Tree Print (FTP) 145
    GCFiler 148
    GED2TT 148
    GEDCompanion 149
    GEDPST 149
    GENCHECK 150
    Graftree 151
    Wall Chart 162
GEDCompanion 149
GEDPST 149
Gen'Logical PATHFINDER 184
GEN-BOOK 149
Genafile 184
Genassist 184
GENCHECK 150
GENE-GENEX-GEDCOMG 91
GENE-PAF 150
Genea 184
Genea-Link 184
Genea-Logical Records System 184
GeneaLogic Systems 186
Genealogical Cemetery Database 177
Genealogical Data Base Systems 92
Genealogical Data Base Systems Book
    150
Genealogical Event Database (GED) 177
Genealogical Explorer 185
Genealogical Information Manager (GIM)
    93

INDEX

Genealogy Assistant 185
Genealogy Data Base 185
Genealogy db 185
Genealogy on Display 185
Genealogy on Display utility
    GEDCOM 148
Genealogy Research III 185
Genealogy Software 134, 184
GENENUM 150
Generation Gap Plus 185
Generations 185
Geneware 183, 185
GENKIT 150
GENP 133, 151
GENP MultiMedia 151
GENP utility
    GENP MultiMedia 151
Gensource 178
Gentech 187
GIPSI 151
Gold Trade Press, Inc. 177
Graftree 151
Griot Alternative 185
Guardian Data Systems 110
Haberer, Brent 53
Harbinger Group, The 185
Harney, Brian 147, 158, 178
Hass, Jim 133
Hatch, R. F. & Assoc. Inc. 184
HeartWood 95
HeartWood Software, Inc. 95
Henry 152
Historiograph 152
Holsclaw, Russell 179
Horizons 185
HOTNOTES 153
HQ Pedigree Print 153
Hurdware 187
Hyper-Genealogy 185
Hyper-Tree 185
Hypergene 185
IGI 153
Import 153
Index Master 186
Indexing program 178, 181
Indexx 178
Interconnect BBS 156
International Genealogical Index (IGI) 151, 153
It's All Relative 97
Italy & Avalon, Inc. 173
Itasca Softwords 99
IX3 178
IXM 178

Jarnberg, Carl 143
JCAL - The Jewish Calendar 154
Journal Writer 186
Kelly, Barry E. 183
Kidd and Kidd, Inc 186
KinQuest 134
KinWrite 154
Kleiman, David 144
Kobb, Alan 144
Kopchak, Greg & Randall 97
Kopchak, Randall 182
Koppenhaver, Andrew 91, 150
L & H Enterprises 185, 187
Land measurement 150
Landen, Wes 105
Language translation 144
Lawrence, George 156
LDB Associates. 154
Leister Productions 114
Life History Disk 178
Lifestyle Software Group 185
Lilly, John 155
Lineage Master 186
Lineages 98
Lineages utility
    Tree Charts 162
Linkages utility
    GEDCOM 149
Long, Christopher E. 68, 146, 181
Lowcase 154
Lowe, Raymond 180
Lund, Ira J. 44, 175, 176
MacAncestors 186
MacGene 186
MacGenie 186
Macintosh 66, 75, 95, 99, 114, 133, 149, 178, 180, 185-187
MacRoots II 99
Madsen, Brian C. 93
Map drawing program 179
Mapper 179
Marriage Search 154
Maynard, Dave 141
McClendon, Judson D. 142
McGrath, Paul J. 173
MEMORIES? 179
Mendosa, Rick 142
Mennitt, Kevin 185
Meyer, Eric 182
Micro-80 Inc. 185
Military Death Index 151
Miller, Craig 150
Millier, Marc 147
Morley, Jeffrey 156

Morris, Andrew J. 144
Mosher, Robert L. 184
Multi-media presentation 182
MVP Software 127
My Family 134
My Family Rerord 186
My Roots 186
My Story 186
NAMECLEN 154
NickelWare 134
Norgen 186
Norris Software, Ltd. 186
NOTECLEN 155
NOTETOOL 155
On This Day (OTD) 155
Orelle Corporation 134, 148
Origin 101
Our Family 186
PAF NOTES 155
PAF Replace 156
PAF Toolbox 156
PAF utility 149
    AHNDES 141
    Cascade 142
    DESCEND 143
    EDITPAF 144
    Family Records Utility (FRU) 146
    Family Tree Print (FTP) 145
    FamilyPerfect 145
    FAMSORT 146
    Forest 147
    FR PRINT 148
    GEN-BOOK 149
    GENE-PAF 150
    GENENUM 150
    Henry 152
    HOTNOTES 153
    HQ Pedigree Print 153
    Import 153
    KinWrite 154
    Lowcase 154
    Marriage Search 154
    NAMECLEN 154
    NOTECLEN 155
    NOTETOOL 155
    PAF NOTES 155
    PAF Replace 156
    PAF Toolbox 156
    PAF Viewer for Windows 156
    PAF2PAF 156
    PAFability 156
    PAFAIDE 157
    PAFNAMES 157
    PAFSPLIT 157

    PAFSTAMP 158
    PEDIGREE 158
    RDF Convert 159
    RDF2GED 160
    RECLAIM 160
    Tracer 162
PAF Viewer for Windows 156
PAF2PAF 156
PAFability 156
PAFAIDE 157
PAFNAMES 157
PAFSPLIT 157
PAFSTAMP 158
Parents 134
Parsons Technology 59
Pedigree 103, 158, 186
Pedigree Pursuit 105
Pedigree Software 103
Penner, Lester 154
Personal Ancestral File 106
    See also PAF
Pertuy, Thierry 185
Peters, Mark 186
PFA, Inc. 184
Phoenix 187
PhoneFile utility 173
Photo Family Genealogy 134
Pine Cone Software 184
PNames 158
Polakoff, Eileen Research 184
PractiComp 134
Prism 187
Prometheus Software Systems 184
Quinsept, Inc. 51, 66, 98, 162
R-PLOT 158
R3FixEtc 158
R3MFNU 159
R3PST 159, 167
Rasche 183
Rayburn, Larry M. 146
RDF Convert 159
RDF2GED 160
RECLAIM 160
Reinwald, Lewis T. 156
Relativity 110
Research organizer 177-180
Research Services 151
Resource Links 179
Reunion 114
Revent 160
RKS Software 187
Roots and Branches 187
Roots and Relatives 135
ROOTS III 115

utility 179
ROOTS III utility
   Dateline 143
   DFoot 143
   PNames 158
   R-PLOT 158
   R3FixEtc 158
   R3MFNU 159
   R3PST 159
   Revent 160
Roots Master 187
ROOTS WRITER 179
Rosenvall, Blake A. 159
Scott, Robert J. 144, 147
SCRAPS 180
SDI Print 160
Seattle Gen. Soc. 186
Senior Software Systems 179
Sesame 180
ShareSpell 181
Shepard, Wayne R. 162
Silicon Roots! Associates 153
SKY Index 181
SKY Software 181
Social Security Death Index (SSDI) 151, 160
Software Construction Co. 155
Software Solutions 183
Soundex 144, 150, 161
   Daitch/Mokotoff 144
   HIAS (Hebrew Immigrant Aid Society) 144
   New York Health Department 144
Spell checker 181
Star-Com Microsystems 133, 178
Steed, John 37, 148, 149
Sturgeon, Craig L. 144
Sunrise Development 187
SunriseGEN 187
Taylor, Mark 149
Te Corporation 186
Terrett Systems 101
The Family Edge 120
The Family Tree 187
The Genealogy Assistant Programs 187
The Indexer 181
THE Jewish Calendar 161
The Master Genealogist 124
The Register Program 187
Tiny tafel 148, 162
Tiny Tafel Editor 181
Tiny Tafel program 181
Tracer 162
Traces 184

Tree Charts 162, 168
Tree Easy 126
TRS 184
TRS80 178
TTGEN 162
Turner, Ann 147, 152, 157, 158, 162, 183
Unter, Jan 153
USD Inc. 185
Valley Software 187
Vaughan, James G. 186
Velke, Bob 124
Video Display Editor (VDE) 182
Vincens, Richard G. 184
Virtual BookMaker 182
Wagstaff, E. Neil 75
Waldron, Patrick J. 142
Wall Chart 162
Waring, James D. Jr. 161
Wasden, D. Blain 93
Webber, Keith 154
Weekday 163
Wehmeyer, Keith R. 145, 150
White, Douglass A. 187
Wilkinson, Gale D. 174
Windows 53, 134, 156
WL Futures Associates 105
Word processor 179, 182
Words on Disk 181
Wyatt, Allen L. 157
York, Carl 120, 161
Your Family Tree 127, 187